CHILDREN'S PLAY
AND
PLAYGROUNDS

CHILDREN'S PLAY AND PLAYGROUNDS

JOE L. FROST
University of Texas at Austin

BARRY L. KLEIN
Georgia State University

ALLYN AND BACON, INC.

Boston   London   Sydney

Library of Congress Cataloging in Publication Data

Frost, Joe L
    Children's play and playgrounds.

    Bibliography: p.
    Includes index.
    1. Playgrounds—Design and construction.   2.
Play—Philosophy.   I. Klein, Barry L., 1946–
joint author.   II. Title.
√ GV425.F76   790'.068   79–4175
    ISBN 0–205–06588–0
    ISBN 0–205–06586–4 pbk.

Printed in United States of America

A little known fact is that families, not authors, bear the greatest burden in producing a book. They share the frustrations yet are denied the gratifications. We can't change that, but we can let them know—we know.

To Betty, Nita and Terry.

Joe Frost

To Joshua and Jeri
Who taught me to play.
To Barbara
Who taught me to love.

Barry Klein

CONTENTS

PREFACE

This book is the outgrowth of the authors' direct involvement with appraising existing playgrounds, conducting research on children's play, teaching graduate courses on play and playgrounds, and designing and building play environments in a variety of contexts. Our purpose is clear and simple—to help improve the dismal, sterile outdoor areas that adults call playgrounds.

We believe that much of the present effort toward this end is misdirected for these reasons:

1. It is aimed at isolated goals such as improving motor development, without due regard for cognition, socialization, affect, language, and creativity.

2. Playgrounds are developed without consideration for the range of natural play forms of children.

3. Playgrounds are typically developed to be "maintenance free" and for appeal to the adult eye rather than for play function and child appeal.

4. Playgrounds are unduly hazardous for two main reasons: a. they are typically enclaves of steel structures and concrete-like surfaces, designed with no identifiable developmental guidelines, and b. children are too restricted in play time and equipment choices to develop skills necessary for safe functioning on playgrounds.

In Chapters 1 and 2 we explore the nature of play, its importance, and how it is nurtured. Chapter 1 is historical and theoretical, tracing the emergence of play theory and illustrating how play develops naturally in children. The content of this chapter leads us to perhaps the single most important guiding principle for playgrounds—they must be appropriate to the *natural* play tendencies of children. All of our experiences, direct observations, and research, have led to this conclusion; no less for outdoor learning environments than for indoor ones. Development cannot be short-circuited. The simple conclusion is that playground developers must first of all be students of child development.

In Chapter 2 we pursue the development theme, summarizing research on the interrelationships between play and culture, imagination, sex differences, perceptual-motor development, and play objects. Finally, we tie this content to the design of the total outdoor play environment. The playground is an extension of the indoor learning environment, a living laboratory for learning, doing, and developing, not just for perceptual-motor refinement but for the full interrelated array of skills.

The remainder of the book draws from theory and research on development but is devoted primarily to the actual design and development of playgrounds. We devote a chapter to each of the four major types of playgrounds* currently existing in the United States; (1) the traditional or conventional, (2) the creative, (3) the contemporary, and (4) the adventure playground.

Chapter 3 serves two main purposes. It reveals the existing state of playgrounds in America, and it describes the traditional or conventional playground—an arena of concrete and steel typically including a jungle gym, merry-go-round, seesaw, swings and slide—all designed for gross-motor or exercise play and limited involvement. The entire book can be considered as an appeal to redevelop such environments.

The reader is introduced to fundamentals of playground development and supervision in

Chapter 4. Chapter 5 is a key section describing tested methods for organized parents, children, and community groups to design and build their own playgrounds. The value of such involvement extends far beyond the tangible product (playground) in psychological and social benefits. The content of Chapter 5 contrasts sharply with the description of conventional playgrounds in Chapter 2 by spelling out criteria for child-oriented creative playgrounds.

The most illustrated section of the book, Chapter 6, offers dozens of photographs and narrative descriptions of hand-built equipment for inclusion on playgrounds. This chapter highlights the creative playground, a semiformal environment constructed creatively from existing commercial equipment, purchased or gift equipment, and an infinite range of scrounged materials (e.g., tires, lumber, utility poles, railroad ties, cable spools, pipe). Such a playground is frequently planned and constructed by parents, teachers, and children with the help of a playground specialist. The playground includes permanent equipment, sand and water, and an array of movable materials to accommodate all forms of play. Areas for special activities such as art, gardening, and caring for animals are frequently included.

Chapter 7, describing contemporary or designer's playgrounds, is included to show a contrast between this growing type of playground and other types, to show recent developments in commercial equipment and architectural design, and to highlight strengths and weaknesses.

The contemporary playground is a formal environment usually professionally designed, frequently of high esthetic quality, with variable function equipment and linked play zones. The equipment is usually a mix of commercial wood and/or metal structures. Natural stone, timbers (e.g., railroad ties, utility poles), dirt mounds, and concrete are used for terracing and challenge.

---

*The basic definitions of these types are adapted from Joe L. Frost, The American Playground Movement, *Childhood Education, 1978, 54*(4), 176–182.

The major shortcomings of such environments are the failure to adequately provide for dramatic and construction play. Some of the same restrictions applicable to conventional playgrounds are found here; the absence of movable materials caused by a lack of storage and play leaders, the relatively small return in play function for money invested, and the hazardous conditions presented by rock and concrete walls, walks, and pyramids.

The final two chapters (8 and 9) focus on adventure playgrounds for both normal and handicapped children. Most of the content on adventure playgrounds resulted from personal visits to Scandinavian and English playgrounds. American playground developers presently give more lip service than actual effort to such environments.

The adventure playground is a highly informal environment utilizing a fenced area, storage facility with tools, a wide range of scrap building materials, and one or more play leaders. Children are free to express themselves (with adult assistance as needed) in a wide range of creative forms of play. Tools and building materials are frequently supplemented with opportunities for cooking, gardening, and caring for animals.

One of the most startling revelations to the authors during the planning and development of this book was the realization that the play needs of handicapped children are largely overlooked and unfulfilled, that handicapped children have untapped reservoirs of ability to play constructively, and that they can gain higher levels of independence and skill in challenging play environments.

We are indebted to many people who helped form the ideas in this book. Risking the possible omission of some who made substantial contributions we wish to express our thanks to the following friends and professional associates.

Sheila Campbell, Betty Wagner, Eric Strickland, Michael Henniger, Libby Vernon, Alita Zaepfel, Norman Stuemke, Debbie Johnson, Kathy McCord, Pam Pearce, Joel Hodges, Faye Inglis, Daniel Garcia, Jim West, Rick Strot, Hettie Worley, Jackie Myers, Mavis Williams, Laura Williams, Glen French, Bud Weiner, Norm Barrett, Charlie Gibson, Isamu Nouguchi, Naud Burnett, Howard Garrett, Richard Dattner, Ron Hartley, Nan Simpson, Eva Insulander, Bill Mc-Culloch, Helga Pederson, Thomas Foersom, Jens Sigsgaard, Bill Vance, Paul Hogan, D. R. Bearman, Jerry Fergeson, Jack Mahan, Barbara Klein, Betty Frost, Howard Minsk, Donna Ulrici, Olga Jarrett, Gary Weld, Ruth Hough, John Trevino, Wayne Schade, Sister Ramona Bezner, Kathleen McDonald, Paul Rode, Keith Turner, Andrew Cohen, Mary Ann Fowkes.

We also express our appreciation to the principals and staffs of the following schools:

Redeemer Lutheran School, Austin, Texas

Ortega Elementary School, Austin, Texas

Allison Elementary School, Austin, Texas

Briar Patch School, Austin, Texas

University of Texas Nursery School, Austin, Texas

Govalle Elementary School, Austin, Texas

Spicewood Springs Elementary School, Austin, Texas

Lockhart Elementary School, Lockhart, Texas

Casis Elementary School, Austin, Texas

Gullett Elementary School, Austin, Texas

St. Martin Hall Children's School; Our Lady of the Lake University, San Antonio, Texas

Cambridge Elementary School, San Antonio, Texas

Memorial Elementary School, Del Rio, Texas

Faubion Elementary School, Cedar Park, Texas

High Meadows School, Roswell, Georgia

Central Presbyterian Child Development Center, Atlanta, Georgia

Bethesda Elementary School, Gwinette County, Georgia

Mount Zion Elementary School, Clayton County, Georgia

George Walton Academy, Atlanta, Georgia

Willo Way School, Stone Mountain, Georgia

Joe L. Frost
Barry L. Klein

1
THE NATURE OF PLAY

"Play is the highest expression of human development in childhood for it alone is the free expression of what is in a child's soul."

Friedrich Froebel

Play is universal and essential to humanity. Since the dawn of civilization, people have left artifacts and records depicting the importance of play to physical, intellectual, emotional, social, and spiritual well being of the individual. The Greek philosophers Plato (427–347 B.C.) and Aristotle (384–322 B.C.) recognized the value of play for promoting healthy development. Early educators such as John Amos Comenius (1592–1670), Jean-Jacques Rousseau (1712–1778), Johann Pestalozzi (1746–1827), and Friedrich Froebel (1782–1852) rebelled against the harsh discipline and rote memorization that characterized the education of children during their life-times and stressed the importance of play as both a natural occupation of childhood and as a vehicle for learning.

Froebel, the originator of the kindergarten, best articulated the contribution of play to the development of the child. Writing in 1826 he made the following statement about play:

Play is the purest, most spiritual activity of man at this stage, and at the same time, typical of human life as a whole—of the inner hidden natural life in man and all things. It gives, therefore, joy, freedom, contentment, inner and outer rest, peace with the world. (Harris, 1906, p. 55)

1

Although the importance of play has long been appreciated, theorists have presented contrasting definitions of play and have disagreed about the biological and psychological motivation and utility of play. At first it would seem that play would readily lend itself to definition. Unlike abstract constructs such as intelligence, self-concept and motivation, play can readily be observed and measured. However, after examining various definitions of play it appears that there is little general agreement. Mitchell and Mason (1948, pp. 103–104) illustrate this point by presenting the following collection of definitions:

Schiller (1875): The aimless expenditure of exuberant energy.

Froebel (1887): The natural unfolding of the germinal leaves of childhood.

Spencer (1873): Superfluous actions taking place instinctively in the absence of real actions ... Activity performed for the immediate gratification derived, without regard for ulterior benefits.

Groos (1898): Instinctive practice, without serious intent, of activities that will later be essential to life.

Dewey (1922): Activities not consciously performed for the sake of any result beyond themselves.

Gulick (1920): What we do because we want to do it.

These definitions represent a variety of theoretical positions ranging from Schiller's and Spencer's view of play as expenditure of excess energy, to Groos's theory of play as instinctive practice for later life, to Gulick's theory of play as recapitulation to earlier stages of man. It is important to study the classical theories because they serve as the foundation for contemporary theories. In this chapter we will examine both classical and contemporary theories of play. The most comprehensive contemporary theory, that of Jean Piaget, will be the basis for conclusions and recommendations about play environments and equipment, thus laying the groundwork for chapters on playgrounds that follow.

CLASSICAL THEORIES OF PLAY

The Surplus Energy Theory

When asked to explain the motivating factor behind children's play, a common response among educators is "Children need to run off excess energy. . . ." Without realizing the origin of their view, many people promote the surplus energy theory of Karl Groos. The evolution of this idea can be traced from Aristotle, to the poet Schiller in 1800, to its formal appearance in Herbert Spencer's writings in 1875.

The main idea behind this particular explanation of play is that the organism (both animal and human) expends energy either in goal-directed activity, which becomes work, or goalless activity, which becomes play. Play occurs when the organism has more energy available than it needs to expend for work. Spencer theorized that "the animal works when some want is the motive for his activity, and plays when the superabundance of energy forms this motive—when overflowing life itself urges him to action" (Groos, 1898, p. 2).

Tolman (1932) maintained that a sensory-motor-hunger accounts for behavior left over after satisfaction of the food-, sex-, contact-, and rest-hungers. He argued that the satisfaction of hunger leaves the organism in a condition of unspent energy that must be discharged through play.

The Relaxation Theory

In contrast to the surplus energy theory of play, Patrick (1916) argued that play serves a person's need for relaxation as a relief from mental fatigue. Patrick maintained that work in a modern society calls for abstract reasoning, high concentration, and fine-motor activity. These work demands are comparatively recent in human history and are more likely to cause nervous disorders than the work demands of older or less advanced societies. In these societies, according to Patrick, people made greater use of their large muscles in activities such as running, jumping, and throwing; the same activities that modern humans use for recreation and relaxation.

Patrick's theory certainly has both appeal and application to today's high-stress society; however, it does not adequately explain the play of children. If play is motivated by the need to recuperate from work, then why do children play? Patrick argued that "He plays because he is a child and to the child's natural and active life we give the name 'play' to distinguish it from the life of conscious self-direction, of strain, and effort and inhibition which evolution has imposed on the adult human being" (Patrick, 1916, pp. 79–80).

The Recapitulation Theory

The recapitulation theory of play has its origins in Darwin's conception of the evolution of humans from lower species of animals. This theory maintains that play is a result of human biological inheritance; through play the evolutionary history of the species is recapitulated or repeated. Luther Gulick (1898) and G. Stanley Hall (1906) formalized this view of play. From this point of view, water play might be interpreted as recapitulation to primeval origins in the sea; crawling and digging in sand as reflections of early land animals; climbing trees as a throwback to their monkeylike ancestors; and the gang play of young boys as echoes of primitive tribal life. This theory, which was popular at the turn of the century, does not take into consideration the social learning aspects of play or play with modern toys and games. However, Hall was very influential in stimulating an interest in research with children.

The Instinct-Practice Theory of Play

Karl Groos in *The Play of Animals* (1898) maintained that play in young animals is preparation for adult life. Although animals inherit instinctive behaviors, practice is needed to perfect them. Lower forms of animal life are able to be independent of their parents from the moment of birth. However, Groos states that higher "animals cannot be said to play because they are young and frolicsome, but rather they have a period of youth in order to play" (1898, p. 76). The higher up the animal scale, the more necessary it is for the young ones to have a period of pre-exercise in which they can practice the skills they will need to use in adult life.

There presently exists a wealth of experimental and descriptive data that clearly demonstrates the importance of early experiences on later life. Certainly the opportunity or lack of opportunity for a child to engage in play experiences would have consequences for later life. However, in Groos' terms the human infant would play in order to train for precise skills in adult life. A modern view of the function of child play for later life would be that play leads to mastery of self and environment from a general developmental aspect, that is, personality and intelligence, as opposed to specific skills.

CONTEMPORARY THEORIES OF PLAY

Contemporary psychology is dominated by three main theories, psychoanalytical, Piagetian, and behaviorism. The psychoanalytic theories of

Freud and Erikson are primarily concerned with the dynamics of personality development. From this theoretical base, play may be viewed as a class of affective behavior. The cognitive-developmental theory of Jean Piaget is concerned with the process and content of intellectual development. Therefore, from a Piagetian position, play may be viewed as cognitive behavior. The section to follow will treat these two main theories. Views on social play will be abstracted from a number of sources. The stimulus-response (S-R) theories of Hull, Thorndike, and Skinner address the contingency relationships between the organism and environment. From an S-R position, play is not viewed as a special class of behavior, but simply part of the response repertoire of the organism and will not be treated in this discussion.

The Psychoanalytical Theory

The interest of psychoanalysts with the nature of children's play stems from the observations of Freud. Freud's ideas were later formalized by Robert Wälder (1933) and expanded by Erik Erikson (1950). In his classic article, Wälder (1933, p. 209) discussed the limitations of the theory. He maintained that play has multiple functions and cannot be explained by a single interpretation.

Freud maintained that play is motivated chiefly by what he called the pleasure principle (1955). Pleasure is achieved, according to Freud, through wish fulfillment in play. For example, the child who plays at being an astronaut, race car driver, nurse, or mother is expressing a desire to be one. In playing, the child is able to bend reality in order to gain gratification. Freud also felt that play has a therapeutic value in that it helps children to master unpleasant experiences.

Wälder argued that Freud's original concept of cathartic play, that is, play that reduces

anxiety, does not explain the repetition of the play activity associated with an unpleasant experience. In explaining this phenomenon Wälder refers to the concept of "repetition compulsion." When a child has an unpleasant experience, it may be too difficult for him to assimilate it all at once. The child recreates the experience over and over again in play, thus gradually diminishing the intensity of the experience.

Brown, Curry, and Titlnich (1971) give a graphic example of repetition compulsion in their description of how a group of preschoolers dealt with a traumatic experience. A group of children in an early childhood center were playing outside while a workman climbed up a ladder to make some repairs on the building. Unfortunately, the workman fell from the ladder and was seriously injured. The children watched as the teachers administered emergency first aid and saw an ambulance take him to the hospital. The teachers observed that for several weeks after this incident the children enacted through play the events that they had observed. One child playing the part of the workman would climb up on a stack of large building blocks and pretend to fall to the ground. Other children playing the part of the teachers would administer first aid while other children would pretend to be ambulance attendants. Immediately after the incident, the role play took place frequently during the day. After several days had passed the frequency diminished; after several weeks had passed the role play rarely occurred and then only in a very abbreviated manner. Thus, the children were able to play out and eventually master the anxiety associated with the experience.

Freud also dealt with the question of reality in children's play and adult fantasy which he saw as similar processes. He compared the child at play to the creative writer in that the child creates his or her own imaginary world. Although the child engages in fantasy, he or she

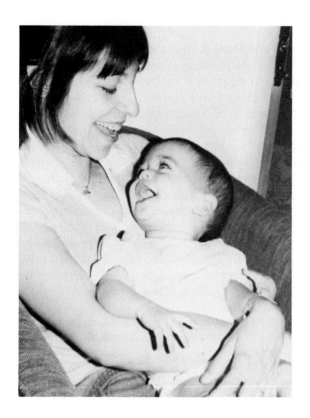

In autocosmic play the play of the child centers on her own body and the body of her mother.

the understanding of children's play. In *Childhood and Society* (1950) Erikson describes play as developmental progression in which the child adds new, more complex understandings about the world at each stage. The first stage begins at birth and is called autocosmic play. At first this play is centered on the infant's own body and consists "in the exploration by repetition of sensual perceptions, of kinesthetic sensations, of vocalizations, etc." (Erikson, 1950, p. 220). In the later part of this stage the object of the infant's play turns toward other people and things. Erikson cites as examples the infant crying out to the mother in different pitches to see what response each pitch will bring, or he or she may explore the mother's face and body with his or her hands. Erikson views autocosmic play as the child's first orientation to the geography of the world.

The next stage of play is called the microsphere which is the small world of manageable toys and objects. Erikson describes the microsphere as a harbor that the child establishes to return to when his or her ego needs an overhaul. Erikson states that the world of things has its own laws and it may "resist reconstruction, or it may simply break to pieces; it may prove to belong to somebody else and be subject to confiscation by superiors" (p. 221). If the child is unable to master the microsphere, he or she may regress into the autosphere and self-involvement.

The third stage of play occurs when the child reaches nursery school age and enters into the macrosphere and shares play with others. Although this is the final stage of play, each of the earlier stages becomes integrated into and subordinated to the developmental stage above it. Therefore, macrosphere play will contain elements of the earlier two stages. A major task at this stage is to learn when to engage in solitary play and when to participate in social play. Solitary play then "retains an indispensable

takes the play very seriously and expends large amounts of energy on it. Freud maintained that "The opposite of play is not what is serious but what is real" (1959, p. 143). He viewed a child's fantasy as being centered around real objects while adult fantasy is covert and separate from reality. In summing up this distinction Wälder stated that "Fantasy woven about a real object is however nothing other than play" (Wälder, 1933, p. 223).

Erik Erikson built upon the work of Freud and Wälder and has added a new dimension to harbor for the overhauling of shattered emotions after periods of rough going in the social seas" (Erikson, p. 22). Erikson concludes that play has a unique and personal meaning for each child, and that the meaning can only be determined by careful observation of its form and content and of the verbalizations and feelings that are associated with it.

Piaget's Cognitive-Developmental Theory

The Swiss psychologist Jean Piaget offers the most comprehensive theoretical framework available for understanding the intellectual development of the child. His theory of development is based primarily on a biological model of environment-organism interchange. Play has a dual role in Piaget's theory. It serves both as a vehicle for knowing about the world and as a by-product or indicator of the child's level of cognitive development. To fully comprehend Piaget's theory of play, it is important to understand the relationship between play and the larger theory. While the scope of this text does not allow for a detailed description of the theory, a few comments on the basic components of Piagetian theory are in order.[1]

Piaget's rich description of intellectual development may be divided into two components: stage-independent theory and stage-dependent theory. Stage-independent theory is concerned with the process by which the child comes to know the world, and the general principles by which the individual changes his or her intellectual state during the course of development. The stage-dependent portion of Piagetian theory

_____

1. For a comprehensive description and analysis of Piaget's work see Flavell, J. H., The Developmental Psychology of Jean Piaget, Princeton, N.J.: Van Nostrand-Reinhold, 1963.

is concerned with the progression of intelligent behavior from birth through adolescence. Piaget divides this time span into three major epochs called periods with various subperiods, stages, and substages within these. Table 1 provides an outline of progression of cognitive development.

Piaget views intelligence as the organization of adaptive behavior. Adaptation is said to occur whenever a given organism-environment interchange has the effect of modifying the organism in such a way that further interchanges, favorable to its preservation, are enhanced (Flavell, p. 45). The process of adaptation occurs through the mutually reciprocal processes of assimilation and accommodation. Flavell draws analogies between assimilation and accommodation and the ingestion and digestion of food.

First the organism must and will transform the substance it takes in order to incorporate their food values into its system. An initial transformation occurs when the substance is ingested by chewing. Thus, hard and sharply contoured objects become pulpy and formless. Still more drastic changes occur as the substance is slowly digested, and eventually it will lose its original identity entirely by becoming part of the structure of the organism. (p. 45)

Cognitive assimilation is then "the action of the organism on surrounding objects, insofar as the action depends on previous behavior involving the same of similar objects" (Piaget, 1966, p. 7). However, quite often a new piece of information cannot be accommodated by the already existing mental structure. The organism then faces the alternative of either rejecting this new material or modifying its own structure to accommodate the material. In this way the environment acts upon the organism. For example, suppose a young child has learned the word "dog" and to identify a certain class of animals as dogs. Now suppose that on a visit to a farm she sees a large, four-legged animal with a tail and says "Look Mommy a dog!" Her mother

Table 1 Periods of Intellectual Development

	Approximate Age Range
Sensorimotor period—six stages	
1. Exercising the readymade sensorimotor schemata	0– 1 month
2. Primary circular reaction	1– 4 months
3. Secondary circular reactions	4– 8 months
4. Coordination of secondary schemata	8–12 months
5. Tertiary circular reactions	12–18 months
6. Invention of new means through mental combinations	18–24 months
Concrete operations period	
Preoperational subperiod	2– 7 years
Concrete operations subperiod	7–11 years
Formal operations period	11–15 years

then explains that the animal is not a dog but a horse, a separate class of animal with distinct characteristics. At this point the child either rejects the new information and continues to call it a dog or creates a new schema for horse; in other words her mental structure has changed in order to accommodate the new information.

Along with the processes of assimilation and accommodation, Piaget assigns four general factors to mental development: maturation, experience, social transmission, and equilibration. Piaget calls equilibration the fundamental factor of development because it balances and regulates the other three. The continuous process of assimilation creates a state of disequilibrium. It is this state of imbalance that provides the primary motivation for learning.

Piaget (1962) devoted a separate book to the development and nature of play titled *Play, Dreams, and Imitation in Childhood.* Given Piaget's notion of adaptation in which the equilibrium of assimilation and accommodation is part of every act of intelligent behavior, there are two important kinds of behaviors that do not manifest this delicate balance. The first is behavior that includes all the various forms of play, dreams, and make-believe. The second is imitation that includes all copying or imitative behavior.

Play may be viewed as the assimilation of environmental stimuli with little regard to the limitations imposed by accommodations.

In play the primary object is to mold reality to the whim of the cognizer, in other words, to assimilate reality to various schemas with little concern for precise accommodation to that reality. Thus, as Piaget puts it, in play there is the "primacy of assimilation over accommodation." In imitation, on the other hand, it is accommodation which reigns supreme. All energy is focused on taking exact account of the structural niceties of the reality one is imitating and in precisely dovetailing one's schematic repertoire to these details. In other words, as in play the primary concern is to adapt reality to the self (assimilation), in imitation the paramount object is to adapt the self to reality (accommodation). (Flavell, pp. 65–66)

Like Freud, Piaget attributes the initial appearance of play to the pleasure derived from the infant's mastery of his own behavior. As Piaget states, "Play . . . proceeds by relaxation of the effort at adaptation and by maintenance or exercise of activities for the mere pleasure of mastering them and acquiring thereby a feeling of virtuosity of power" (1952, p. 89).

The Emergence of Play. Piaget describes the emergence of play during the first months of life and traces its further development through the six stages of the sensorimotor period that span the first two years of life.

In stage 1 of the sensorimotor period (0–1 month), infants exercise their "wired-in" responses. These include orienting toward light and sound, sucking, grasping, and so on. At this stage it might be said that infants are playing when they continue to suck after their hunger has been satisfied. However, Piaget maintains that this playlike behavior serves an adaptive purpose in that it develops infants' proficiency at sucking and cannot be classified as true play.

Stage 2 (1–4 months) is marked by repetitious actions on the part of infants for no apparent motivation other than the pleasure derived from them. Piaget states that children look for the sake of looking and grasp for the sake of grasping. When these actions no longer serve the development of cognitive schemata and when they become play is not often clear; however, it is at this point that play emerges.

Play begins, then, with the first dissociation between assimilation and accommodation. After learning to grasp, swing, throw, etc. which involve both an effort of accommodation to new situations, and an effort of repetition, reproduction, and generalization, the child sooner or later grasps for the pleasure of grasping, swings for the sake of swinging, etc. In a word, he repeats his behavior not in any further effort to learn or to investigate, but for the mere joy of mastering it and of showing off to himself his own power of subduing reality. Assimilation is dissociated by subordinating it and tending to function by itself, and from then on practice play occurs. (Piaget, 1962, p. 162)

In stage 3 of the sensorimotor period (4–8 months) "real" play is fully developed. It is at this stage that children learn that their actions can affect objects in their environment. Piaget cites as an example the change in the behavior of his daughter Lucienne who discovered that she could make objects hanging from the top of her cot swing. At three and one-half months she studied the phenomenon seriously without smiling "with an appearance of intense interest." At four months, however, "she never indulged in this activity . . . without a show of great pride and power." As Piaget explained "there was merely assimilation to the activity itself, i.e. use of the phenomenon for the pleasure of the activity, and that is play" (Piaget, 1962, p. 92).

In stage 4 (8–12 months) children begin to apply already learned actions to new situations. The distinction between play and adaptive behavior also becomes more apparent with the differentiation of means from ends. Piaget described the behavior of Laurent who, at seven and one-half months, clearly demonstrated the attainment of object permanence by removing an obstacle such as a hand or piece of cardboard placed between him and a toy he desires. After practicing this behavior several times "he reached the stage of momentarily forgetting the toy and pushed aside the obstacle, bursting into laughter. What had been intelligent adaptation has thus become play, through transfer of interest to the action itself, regardless of its aim" (Piaget, 1962, p. 92).

Stage 5 (12–18 months) is characterized by "experiments in order to see the results" and ritualized play. For example, when Jacqueline's hand slipped from her hair and splashed into the bath water, she immediately repeated the action, varying the heights, as she would if it were a tertiary circular reaction, but always grasping her hair first. On another occasion Jacqueline "amused herself by making an orange skin on a table sway from side to side. But as she had looked under the skin just before setting it in motion, she did it again as a ritual at least twenty times" (Piaget, 1962, p. 95).

Many children in this stage develop the annoying behavior of dropping objects, usually food from the tray of their high chair. Prior to stage 4 children are primarily concerned with the act of letting go. After the attainment of this stage, children are primarily concerned with the end results of their actions, such as watching the food splat on the floor. In this way children make a distinction between the means, letting go, and the end, the splat.

Stage 6 (18–24 months) marks the emergence of symbolic play and make-believe. What had previously been simple motor games now become representations of earlier experiences. Piaget cites as an example the behavior of Jacqueline who saw a cloth that reminded her of a pillow. She grabbed the cloth, held a fold of it in her right hand, sucked her thumb, and lay down on her side, laughing and pretending to go to sleep. In another observation Lucienne accidentally fell backward while sitting on her cot. Seeing a pillow, she seized it and pressed it against her face as though sleeping on it while smiling broadly. Then after a moment she "sat up delightedly." This procedure was repeated many times during the day, even in places other than the cot and using her hands in the place of a pillow (Piaget, 1962, pp. 96–97). Piaget explains that two new elements have now been added to the exercise of previous schemata. First, the child no longer exercised the schema with the familiar object (the pillow). Instead, she applies the schema to new objects that do not necessarily serve the functions of adaptation, i.e., she does not ordinarily sleep with her head on a piece of cloth. Second, the inclusion of these different objects in the schema does not expand the schema in any way other than allowing the child to exercise the schema in a pleasurable, playful way. As Piaget states, "It is the union of these two conditions—application of the schema to inadequate objects and evocation for pleasure—which in our opinion characterized the beginning of pretense" (Piaget, 1962, p. 97).

Having examined Piaget's description of the development of play during the first two years of life, let us now turn to a broader view of Piaget's stages of cognitive play, revisiting symbolic play and progressing to games with

Table 2 Categories of Cognitive Play

Piaget's Periods of Cognitive Development	K. Buhler (1937)	Piaget (1962)		Smilansky (1968)
Sensorimotor period (0–24 months)	Functional games	Practice games		Functional play
Concrete operations period				
Preoperational subperiod (2–7 years)	Construction games	Symbolic games	Construction Play	Construction play
	Make-believe games			Dramatic play
Concrete operations (7–11 years) subperiod	Collective games	Games with rules		Games with rules
Formal operations period (11–15 years)				

rules. Piaget built upon the work of Charlotte Buhler (1935) who developed an inventory of children's play during the first year of life and of Karl Buhler (1937) who first described the developmental progression of games (Table 2). Piaget describes three stages of games that roughly approximate the stages of intellectual development. These stages are practice games or functional play which predominate during the sensorimotor period (0–2 years) just described, symbolic games which emerge during the pre-operational subperiod (2–7 years), and games with rules which emerge during the concrete operations subperiod and continue through the formal operations period (11–15 years).

Functional Play. The first play of children consists of simple, repetitive actions. This play, which is called functional or exercise play, occurs during the early sensorimotor period of development in which infants exercise their readymade or "wired-in" repertoire of behavior. These behaviors soon give way to newly acquired motor responses. For example, children discover that they can strike a suspended toy and cause it to move back and forth. At first children stare intently at the toy and strike it again and again until this new action is mastered. Play begins when children engage in the activity for functional pleasure (Buhler, 1937). Children no longer stare intently, but now laugh and smile at the results of their actions. Functional play may also include vocalizations. Valentine (1942) observed that, at four months, infants practice "singing" or babbling for pleasure, "starting on a high note and running down a kind of scale." Functional play does not involve symbolism or any specific play technique, but consists in repeating an action for the pleasure of it (Piaget, 1962). As children repeat their actions, they eventually try new combinations that are in some ways similar to previously

In functional play the child repeats an action already learned for sheer pleasure. This is the only type of play taking place during the sensorimotor period (infancy and toddlerhood). The infant shakes a rattle, the older child tries out a swing or a balance beam.

learned ones. For example, children first learn that they can make a sound by shaking a rattle. They next learn that they can make a different sound by striking the rattle against the side of the crib or playpen. Thus, through functional play children learn their physical capabilities and cause and effect relationships by acting on their environment. Functional play is not limited to the first two years of life but is to be found throughout childhood whenever a new skill is acquired. Functional play is accompanied by the pleasure of being the cause of an event and a feeling of power that comes with the mastery of a new action.

For practical purposes we reemphasize that functional or exercise play does not disappear with the onset of other forms of play. Rather, exercise play becomes more complex, involves new play materials or equipment and is frequently integrated with dramatic and construction play. In the outdoor play environment, exercise play for children in the early childhood age range (about 2–8) or Piaget's preoperational period is typically accommodated by seesaws, merry-go-rounds, slides, and teeter-totters. In fact public school playgrounds are traditionally equipped as though this were the only form of play. Understanding the nature of play helps the adults responsible for children's play to supplement this traditional equipment and promote construction and dramatic play as well as exercise play.

Construction Play. Piaget, in contrast to Buhler and Smilansky does not view construction play as a distinct stage of play as he does with functional and symbolic play and games with rules. He maintains that construction play transcends the other three categories of play and occupies a position between play and work. While the three stages of games (practice, symbolic, and games with rules) correspond to the three forms of intelligence (sensorimotor, representational, and reflective), construction games are not a distinct stage like the others but rather "occupy at the second and particularly at the third level, a position half-way between play and intelligent work or between play and imitation" (Piaget, 1962, p. 113).

On the other hand Smilansky views construction play as a distinct stage that emerges around 22–24 months of age. At this stage children begin to use various play materials and functional or goalless play gives way to purposeful play that results in a "creation." Children are now able to sustain their play and to attend for longer periods of time. "Development from functional play to constructive play is progression from manipulations of form to formation" (Smilansky, 1968, p. 6).

Two- and three-year-olds build upon functional play, replacing random movements with purposeful movements, language, imitation, and dramatics. Later, they will include others in their activity, giving rise to sociodramatic play. Play equipment should adjust to more than one child and more than one developmental level. Equipment such as building blocks, paints, play, carpentry tools and wood, materials for collage and construction, scissors and paste, sand and water allow for multiple usage, and satisfy children's urge to create and to have an impact on their environment.

That Piaget does not assign construction activity the status of play stage in no way diminishes the need to provide an environment for its enhancement. Perhaps nowhere is this done as well as on the adventure playgrounds of certain European countries such as England and those in Scandinavia. Construction areas form a major area of these environments. Scrap lumber, tools and full-time play leaders are available. Purposeful activities such as building housing for farm animals and play structures for exercise and dramatic play are regular "construction play" activities for children. Americans

Constructive or construction play begins at about age two. Play solely for pleasure gives way to purposeful play that results in a "creation." This form of activity transcends play and work, having some characteristics of both. The child constructs ships, cars, bridges and sand houses. Almost any raw material will do.

and people of many other countries are now redeveloping many of their playgrounds to promote such valuable activities.

Symbolic Play. By the end of the second year children begin to make use of words and images in guiding their behavior, and it is at this point that functional or practice games develop into symbolic behavior or games of make-believe. However, some of the elements of symbolic play are present at an earlier age. Valentine (1942) reported that "real play with an imaginary object" appears at about one year, and that direct imitation becomes increasingly apparent in the play of children at the beginning of their second year. In describing the behavior of his daughter, Piaget (1962) reported the following:

At 1;6 she pretended to eat and drink without having anything in her hand. At 1;7 she pretended to drink out of a box and then held it to the mouths of all who were present. These last symbols had been prepared for during the preceding month or two by a progressive ritualization, the principal stages of which consisted in playing at drinking out of empty glasses and then repeating the action making noises with lips and throat. (1962, p. 97)

Symbolic play, frequently called dramatic play, involves representation of an absent object. In the example cited, drinking from an empty box and imagining it as a cup filled with liquid is symbolically representing the cup by the box. The child is satisfied with the pretense because the link between the signifier and signified is entirely subjective.

Piaget asks the question, why does play

In symbolic or dramatic play, the child pretends, makes believe, or assumes a role.
A stick is a gun, a doll is a sister, or the child is the grown-up driver of a race car.

become symbolic instead of continuing merely as a sensorimotor exercise of mental development? The answer to this question lies in the fact that two-year-olds live in a world dominated by elders whose interests and rules remain external to them, and in a physical world that they understand only slightly and which does not satisfy their intellectual and affective needs. They are unable to accommodate themselves to the environment that is reality; they must assimilate reality or, in other words, create their own reality. They construct a system of symbols for self-expression including both language and actions from information transmitted to them by adults and peers. Through language and their actions children resolve, through symbolic play, the conflicts they meet. They also explore and resolve role conflicts and unsatisfied needs, leading to increased mastery of their environment and extension of self. For example, a two-year-old asks his mother for a cookie. His mother replies, "I'm sorry but you can't have a cookie now. We are going to eat supper in a few minutes." The child then brings his hands to his mouth and chews and smacks his lips as if he were eating a cookie. Thus, through imagination, he has resolved a conflict.

Sociodramatic Play. The most highly developed form of symbolic play is sociodramatic play. In dramatic play children pretend or take on the role of someone else, imitating actions and speech they have encountered in some situation. When the imitation is carried out with another role-player, the play becomes sociodramatic. Sociodramatic play contains two elements. The first and central element is the imitative one in which children imitate real-life people and situations that they have experienced firsthand. This is the reality element. However, because of children's inability to imitate exactly that which they observe, the element of nonreality or make-believe enters into their play. Make-believe aids in imitation and gives children satisfaction by enabling them to enter the world of adults (Smilansky, 1968, p. 7).

In her classic study, the *Effects of Socio-dramatic Play on Disadvantaged Preschool Children*, Smilansky (1968) spelled out the following six criteria for well-developed sociodramatic play:

1. *Imitative role play.* The child undertakes a make-believe role and expresses it in imitative action and/or verbalization. Example: "I am the daddy, you will be the mommy, and the doll is our baby."

2. *Make-believe in regard to objects.* Movements or verbal descriptions are substituted for real objects. Example: "I am drinking from the bottle," when the child is drinking from his fist.

3. *Make-believe in regard to actions and situations.* Verbal descriptions are substituted for actions and situations. Example: "Let's pretend I already returned from work, I cooked the food, and now I am setting the table," when only the last activity is actually imitated.

4. *Persistence.* The child persists in a play episode for at least ten minutes.

5. *Interaction.* There are at least two players interacting in the framework of the play episode.

6. *Verbal communication.* There is some verbal interaction related to the play episode.

The first four criteria apply to dramatic play in general, the last two to the sociodramatic play only. If a child playing by herself makes a declaration such as, "I am Jamie Sommers the Bionic Woman," only dramatic play has occurred. On the other hand, if she makes the same declaration to another child who takes on or is assigned an imaginary role, then a sociodramatic play episode has begun.

Smilansky (1968) maintains that sociodramatic play contributes to the development of creativity, intellectual growth, and social skills. Through participation in sociodramatic play the child learns to synthesize scattered experiences and create new ones; learns to identify and enact central characteristics of a given role and to concentrate around a given theme; learns to control herself and to discipline her own actions in relation to a context; learns flexibility in responding to other role players; facilitates the transition from an egocentric being to a social being; facilitates more abstract thought and the ability to generalize behavior to different situations (pp. 12–15).

It would be difficult to overemphasize the role of symbolic or dramatic play in social and intellectual development. It is a major avenue for integrating cultural and social mores of the adult world while developing language and concepts of time, space, number, and so on. Many preschool indoor environments contain dramatic play spaces and rich arrays of supporting materials and equipment, for example, the house play center is a common fixture. But outdoor play environments, particularly public school and city park playgrounds, are frequently barren of needed props for dramatic play—play houses, water and sand areas, wheeled vehicle areas, dress-up clothes, containers, tools, and so forth. The consumer of play theory is likely to be a proponent of dramatic play for children.

Games with Rules. As children move from the preoperational subperiod of development (2–7 years) to the concrete operations subperiod (7–11 years), through the vehicle of sociodramatic play they become more and more social beings. Prior to this time, children's perceptions of their environment were limited to "before the eye reality" and from their egocentric perspective

At about school age or during the latter part of the preoperational period, games with rules emerge. Rules are a regulation imposed by the group and their violation carries a sanction. From ball games and hopscotch to follow-the-leader, games with rules are serious business.

only. Now children are able to learn and imitate the roles of others. At about six years of age, children's play takes on a new dimension in that it is bound by rules. The following example illustrates this transition: Given a handful of marbles, the 15-month-old would play with them by himself by rolling them on the floor or putting them in a cup and shaking them (functional play); the three-year-old might line them up in various patterns or use them to decorate a mud pie (construction play); the four-year-old might declare "Let's pretend that these marbles are diamonds and that we have to protect them from robbers!" (sociodramatic play). The six-year-old, however, would play a game of marbles. His actions and the actions of his play-

mates would be regulated by a commonly agreed upon set of rules: the marbles must all be placed in a ring; each player must attempt to knock his opponent's marbles out of the ring; the players will lag to see who goes first; no substitutions may be made and so on. Any change in the rules must be agreed upon by the other players. Any violation of the rules will be met with protests and perhaps aggression on the part of the other players.

In sociodramatic play, rules are also present, but they are imposed by standards of life. Dentists examine teeth, mechanics fix cars. Games with rules tend to emphasize one skill at a time; they are competitive rather than co-operative; and they demand a minimum of verbalization. Smilansky (1968) believes that games with rules are valuable in teaching specific skills or content, but that sociodramatic play is more relevant for overall social and intellectual development.

In explaining the relatively late appearance of games with rules and their persistence through adolescence and into adulthood, Piaget states that the explanation is simple, "they are the ludic activity of the socialized being. Just as the symbol replaces mere practice as soon as thought makes its appearance, so the rule replaces the symbol and integrates practice as soon as certain social relationships are formed, and the question is to discover these relationships" (1962, p. 142).

Games with rules represent a high form of play development. Hence children have to accept prearranged rules and adjust to them. More important, they learn to control their behavior within limits. This appears to be assisted by the American emphasis on competitive sports, beginning at an early age. Little league baseball and football, coupled with college and professional sports on television stimulate children to participate in highly organized competitive games with rules at an early age. This stringent, probably unhealthy, emphasis can be tempered by the provision of age-appropriate games areas and equipment on playgrounds, supervised by adults who value spontaneous games with minimal adult or peer pressure.

Although there are disagreements (see Smilansky, 1968; Eifermann, 1971) about details of Piagetian play theory, the general principles have yet to be seriously threatened by researchers. For the practitioner concerned with designing and using play environments that enhance all types of play, Piaget offers the most comprehensive and perhaps best body of theory yet available. In general terms the following principles seem to be accurate:

- Play is a critically important avenue for social, cultural, affective, physical and mental development (Chapter 2 is an elaboration of this principle.)
- Healthy children in all cultures play.
- There are universal types of play engaged in by children everywhere.
- The content of children's play differs markedly across cultures.
- Play generally develops in a cumulative hierarchy fashion, with each successive stage integrating the preceding stage(s).
- There are marked individual differences among children in rate and timing of play development.
- Children need props (materials and equipment) for their play.
- Elders and television are important models for the content of children's play.

Views of Social Play

Many years ago Bailey (1933) and Isaacs (1933) noted that the three-year-old hunts out live contact with other children in order to play with them, and during the three- to four-year-old period the child reaches the height of concentration with other children. This sociability appeared to result from and depend on the child's experience in kindergarten.

Categories of Social Play. In her classic study, Parten (1932) discovered that social participation among preschoolers increased with the child's age. Parten defined six social play categories: unoccupied behavior, solitary play, onlooker behavior, parallel play, associative play, and cooperative play. Her category system is still being used and refined by researchers and students of play.

Play is an important vehicle for social development. Initially children play alone and make no effort to include children near them (solitary play). In the next stage, parallel play, they play independently but the activity chosen brings them among other children. In associative play they play with other children but the interest is in the association rather than the common activity or product. With increased maturity children engage in cooperative play, interacting with others to make a product (constructive play), dramatize situations of adult and group life (symbolic play), or striving to attain some competitive goal (games with rules).

Unoccupied behavior The child is not playing but occupies him- or herself with watching anything that happens to be of momentary interest. When there is nothing exciting taking place, he plays with his own body, gets on and off chairs, just stands around, follows the teacher or sits in one spot glancing around the room (Playground).

Onlooker behavior The child spends most of his time watching the other children play. He often talks to the children being observed, asks questions or gives suggestions, but does not overtly enter into the play. This type differs from unoccupied in that the onlooker is definitely observing particular groups of children rather than anything that

In unoccupied behavior the child is not playing but stands around or sits in one place.

In onlooker behavior children spend most of their time watching other children play. They sit close enough to hear and see what is going on in the group.

happens to be exciting. The child stands or sits within speaking distance from other children.

Solitary play The child plays alone and independently with toys that are different from those used by the children within speaking distance and makes no effort to get close to other children. He pursues his own activity without reference to what others are doing.

Parallel play The child plays independently, but the activity chosen naturally brings him among other children. He plays with toys that are like those the children around him are using but he plays with the toys as he sees fit, and does not try to influence or modify the activity of the children near him. He plays beside rather than with the other children.

Associative play The child plays with other children. The communication concerns the common activity; there is a borrowing and loaning of play materials; following one another with trains or wagons; mild attempts to control which children may or may not play in the group. All the members engage in similar activity, there is no division of labor, and no organization of the activity around materials, goal or product. The children do not subordinate their individual interests to that of the group.

Cooperative play The child plays in a group that is organized for the purpose of making some material product or of striving to attain some competitive goal, or of dramatizing situations of adult and group life, or of playing formal games.

Parten (1932) reported that from two to two and one-half years of age preschoolers engaged primarily in solitary play, from two and one-half to three and one-half parallel play, and from three and one-half to four and one-half associative play, and from four and one-half on, cooperative play. In a replication of Parten's study, Barnes (1971) found that three- and four-year-olds displayed significantly more unoccupied, solitary and onlooker activity and significantly less associative and cooperative play than Parten found in her original sample. Barnes suggested that caution should be exercised in using Parten's data for the purpose of establishing play norms. Barnes concluded that today's preschoolers are less skilled in associative and cooperative activities than were their contemporaries of the late 1920s. In a study comparing the free play behaviors of middle- and lower-class preschoolers,

Rubin, Maioni, and Hornung (1976) reported that middle-class children engaged in significantly less parallel and functional play, and significantly more associative, cooperative, and constructive play than did their lower-class age mates. The middle-class preschoolers engaged in associative and cooperative play approximately 40 percent of the time, a figure directly corroborating Parten's study. On the other hand, the lower-class preschoolers engaged in the two highest levels of social play 27 percent of the time, thereby supporting Barnes's study (Rubin, Maioni, and Hornung, 1976, p. 418). ·

In light of recent research, the role of solitary play in development should be reconsidered. Beginning with Parten (1932), psychologists and early educators have maintained that solitary behavior is the least mature of all play forms. Moore, Evertson, and Brophy (1974) studied the solitary play behavior of 116 white, middle-class kindergarten children. Their findings did not support the traditional image of solitary play as indicative of poor or immature social adjustment. To the contrary, solitary involved active, goal-directed activities such as blocks, arts and crafts, large muscle play, puzzles, workbooks, and reading (most of these activities are not usually defined as play). They concluded that solitary play appears to be independent, task-oriented behavior that is functional to school situations and indicative of maturity rather than immaturity (p. 834).

Seagoe (1970) developed an instrument called the Play Report to analyze children's play as an index of degree of socialization. The Play Report, based upon Sullivan's (1953) concept of emotional-social development, is a structured interview in which the child responds to a set of five questions with two responses required for each item: "What do you spend most of your time playing at school?", "What do you spend most of your time playing at home?", "What do

you spend most of your time playing at other places?", "What do you like to play most?", "What do you like to play least?"

A scoring guide was developed paralleling the theoretical framework. It requires categorizing each response and giving it a numerical weight in terms of the social context indicated. The categories are:

1. *Informal-Individual* play that is self-directed and not imitative of adults nor formally patterned.

2. *Adult-Oriented* play that is adult-directed and formally patterned though not imitative of adult life.

3. *Informal-Social* play that is self-directed, imitative of adult life but not formally patterned.

4. *Individual-Competitive* play that is formally patterned toward individual victory.

5. *Cooperative-Competitive* play that is formally patterned toward team victory. ·

The Play Report was standardized on a population of 1,245 suburban, middle-class children aged five to eleven years. Seagoe analyzed the data in terms of sex and age differences. She found that boys engage in play requiring more complex interpersonal interaction earlier and emphasize it more at all ages. Girls play with friends as much as boys do, but their play is more often of an informal-individual or a competitive nature. Boys also appear to anticipate and welcome more socially complex forms of play. The school leads the home in encouraging play socialization. It achieves less socialization with girls, however, than boys. This may be due to the impact of team sports on boys.

Iwanaga (1973) developed a scheme for classifying the structure of play from a cognitive role-taking perspective. Play structure refers to the way in which children structure their interactions with peers while playing together. She maintains that, while the content of play behavior may vary from one setting to another, the interpersonal play structure tends to remain constant.

Independent structure Play activity that involves only a single child, no peer interaction.

Parallel structure Involves undifferentiated roles assigned to self and others; two or more children structure a situation in which they are engaged in the same activity; they play independently but maintain awareness of and contact with each other by pointing out to each other what they are doing. An example would be several children building independent block structures and one another's attention to their constructions, "Look what I built!"

Complementary structure Two or more children are engaged in the same activity, but take different roles. For example, children playing hospital where one child is the doctor, another a nurse, and a third the patient.

Integrative structure Here the child's awareness of the presence of companions, seen in parallel and complementary structures, grows more intense in that there is an increased checking out of how the play companion is behaving through visual, verbal and physical contacts; the child seems more aware of the shifts in peers' behaviors. This increased awareness is accompanied by greater adjustment of the child's own behavior in response to shifts and adjustments made by companions.

Iwanaga (1973) conducted a study in which she used her taxonomy of interpersonal play

Table 3 Categories of Social Play

Parten (1932) Developmental stages	Erikson (1950) Categories refer to broad stages of development	Seagoe (1970) Play Report: based on structured interviews with child	Iwanaga (1973) Categories pertain to how an individual child structures the play situation in regard to other children
Solitary Play plays alone and independently; different activity; no reference to others	*Autocosmic* world of self; explores own body and body of mother; repetition of activity	*Informal-Individual* self-directed; not imitative of adults; not formally patterned	*Independent* no involvement of peers in play
Parallel Play plays independently but near or among others; similar toys or activities; beside but not with	*Microcosmic* world of small, manageable toys and objects; solitary play; pleasure derived from mastery of toys	*Adult-Oriented* adult-directed; formally patterned; not imitative of adult life	*Parallel* play with peers; undifferentiated roles; roles enacted independently; close physical proximity; awareness of activity of others
Associative Play plays with others; conversation is about common activity, but does not subordinate own interests to group	*Macrocosmic* world shared with others	*Informal-Social* self-directed; imitative of adult life; not formally patterned	*Complementary* differentiated roles, enacted independently; some cooperation but each child engages in a different activity; little adjustment to others' behavior
Cooperative activity-organized; differentiation of roles; complementary actions		*Individual-Competitive* formally patterned; directed toward individual victory	*Integrative* roles enacted interactively; intense awareness of others; adjustment of behavior to shifts in others; complementary roles
		Cooperative-Competitive formally patterned toward team victory	

structure to observe the play of 30 three-, four-, and five-year-old children from an all Chinese nursery school in Chicago. She found that the number of the types of interpersonal play structure engaged in increased with age. The three-year-olds engaged in two types: independent and parallel; the four-year-olds in three types: independent, parallel and complementary; and the five-year-olds engaged in the first three types plus integrative play structure.

As the reader has seen, social play can be categorized in a number of ways. Table 3 compares the categories of Parten, Erikson, Seagoe, and Iwanaga. There is general agreement that children develop from playing alone, or egocentrically, to playing cooperatively with others. However, as children develop social awareness they do not outgrow their need for solitary activity. Rather, they appear to engage in increasingly reflective activity or merely seek private places for quiet and relaxation.

In the chapters to follow the authors will explore ways to construct equipment and arrange play environments that take into account the social play needs of young children. For example, cooperative play is stimulated by substituting a horizontal tire swing that seats three people for the traditional one-seat swing. Complex climbing/sliding structures that accommodate several children at once replace the narrow ladder/slides that force one-at-a-time play.

Loose parts are provided in abundance to support cooperative constructions. Open, grassy spaces and appropriate props are available for games with rules that involve many children. Cooperative/dramatic play is enhanced by indoor/outdoor integration of play equipment and themes. In addition, out of the way, cozy places are provided for quiet, reflective activity.

CONCLUSION: WHAT IS PLAY?

The work of theorists and/or philosophers dating back to Plato, of professional educators of the past two hundred years, and of researchers during this century have yet to yield a universally acceptable scientific definition of play. Undoubtedly, the conclusions of Piaget come closest to this goal. Such a generic term as play, like intelligence, subordinates a wide range of behaviors and an enormous array of developmental factors. Despite the difficulty of definition, play is an accepted phenomenon in human development and in fact has historically been given a central role by leading thinkers.

At the present time it seems useful to isolate commonly accepted characteristics of play in the absence of an exact definition. The characteristics are: (1) play is active, (2) play is spontaneous, (3) play is fun, (4) play is purposeless, (5) play is self-initiated, (6) play is serious, and

Table 4 The Play-work Continuum

Play Is; Work May Be	Work/Play	Work May Be; Play Is Not
Active ←	→	Passive
Spontaneous ←	→	Forced
Fun ←	→	Drudgery
Purposeless ←	→	Bound to exterior goals
Self-initiated ←	→	Other-initiated
Serious ←	→	Unconcerned

(7) play is linked to exploratory work/play behaviors and to learning. These characteristics are useful in distinguishing between play and non-play behaviors such as work. Play and work lie on a continuum. Behaviors are classified as more or less playful depending on the point at which they lie on that continuum. At some point play becomes work/play and eventually work (see Table 4).

PHOTO ESSAY: WHAT IS PLAY?

Play is fun. Unlike work and other activities, play is always pleasing. When drudgery or boredom set in, play has ceased to exist and something else is taking place.

Play is active. Children move in their life spaces, soaking up sensations of texture, weight, form, and space.

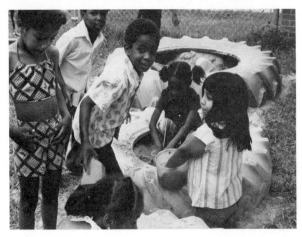

Play is spontaneous. It is stimulated by a sight, a sound, an aroma or an event that somehow appeals to the adventuresome spirit. Child's play is free, unconstrained, and impetuous, yet natural.

Play is purposeless. That is, play has no goals outside itself. Children play for the sake of the activity. There is no external (to play) intent, design, resolution, ambition, or ulterior motive.

Play is serious. Children do not take their play lightly. The seriousness of child's play is paralleled by the intensity of adults' work, yet the two are not the same. The seriousness of play is allied with intensity rather than solemnity.

◀ *Play is self-initiated.* No one makes the choice for the child whether he or she will play. Children can follow adults' directions but the activity that ensues is not play. In play the child is not obliged, extorted, compelled, required, subjected, or coerced.

Play is learning and development. That is, play is the chief avenue of learning during early childhood. Cognitive, physical, social, affective, and emotional development spring from a rich range of play activities.

Caring for animals

Painting play equipment

Cleaning up the play area

Caring for baby sister

Following directions of the teacher

◀ Taking equipment in and out of storage

Play is closely linked to exploratory and work/play behaviors. These behaviors may have many of the characteristics of play but are lacking in one or more.

SUMMARY

While theorists have long recognized the importance of play in contributing to the development of the child, they have also presented contrasting definitions of play and have disagreed about why children play. The motivation to play has been attributed to the need to "run off" excess energy, the need to relax and seek relief from tension, recapitulation to earlier stages of evolution, and the necessity of practicing skills that will be used in adulthood. While there may be some common-sense wisdom contained in these theories, they are for the most part archaic and insufficient in explaining play.

The psychoanalytic theories of Freud and Erikson have contributed significantly to the understanding of play. From their perspective, play contributes to the development of a healthy personality. Through play children gain pleasure by fulfilling their wishes; play has a therapeutic value in that it helps children to overcome and eventually master fears and unpleasant experiences. Through play children develop mastery of their physical and social environment.

Piaget has linked the development of play to cognitive development. Like Freud, Piaget attributes the initial appearance of play to the pleasure derived from the infants' mastery of their own behavior. Play is both a vehicle and a by-product of cognitive development in that through play children produce interesting effects in the environment and discover cause and effect relationships resulting from their own behavior. Children then use play to perfect the behavior and to cause the interesting effect to reoccur at will.

A review of the work of Piaget (1962), Valentine (1942), Smilansky (1968), Buhler (1937), and Isaacs (1933) gives the substance for a series of stages in the child's cognitive play development: functional or exercise play, beginning shortly after birth; construction play, beginning around age two; symbolic or dramatic play, emerging about two and one-half; and games with rules emerging around age six or seven. Smilansky defined in detail sociodramatic play which is the most highly developed form of symbolic play. Parten (1933) described the progression of social play: solitary play from two to two and one-half years, parallel play from two and one-half to three and one-half years; from three and one-half to four and one-half associative play; and from four and one-half years on cooperative play.

Eifermann (1971), contrary to Piaget's belief that games with rules increase with age, found a sharp decline in participation in games with rules among children who were functioning in the late concrete and early formal operational periods. She also disputed Piaget's notion that rule-governed games must necessarily be competitive. In direct contradiction to Smilansky's (1968) study, Eifermann found that low SES children engaged in symbolic play at a significantly greater rate than did their high SES peers.

After having reviewed major theories of play spanning the last 3,000 years, from Plato to Piaget, it is still not possible to arrive at a simple, clear, scientific definition of play. There are, however, some commonly agreed upon characteristics of play that serve to distinguish it from other behaviors. Erikson advises that play has a very personal meaning for each individual. Perhaps the best thing that we as adults can do to discover this meaning is to go out and play.

REFERENCES

Bailey, N. Mental growth during the first three years. A developmental study of sixty-one children by repeated tests. *Genetic Psychology Monographs, 14,* 1933.

Barnes, K. Preschool play norms: A replication. *Developmental Psychology,* 1971, *51,* 99–103.

Beach, F. A. Current concepts of play in animals. *American Naturalist*, 1945, 79, 523–541.

Brown, N., Curry, N. E., and Titlnich, E. T. How groups of children deal with stress through play. In Curry, N. E., and Arnaud, S. (eds.). *Play: The Child's Drive Toward Self-realization*. Washington, D.C.: National Association for the Education of Young Children, 1971.

Buhler, C. *From Birth to Maturity*. London: Routledge and Kegan Paul, 1935.

Buhler, K. *The Mental Development of the Child*. London: Routledge and Kegan Paul, 1937.

Dewey, John. *Human Nature and Conduct*. New York: Henry Holt, 1922.

Eifermann, E. Social play in childhood. In Herron, R. and Sutton-Smith, B. *Child's Play*. New York: John Wiley, 1971. (A more detailed description appears in Rivka R. Eifermann, School Children's Games, U.S. Office of Education, Bureau of Research. June, 1968, Mimeographed Report.)

Erikson, E. H. *Childhood and Society*. New York: Norton, 1950.

Flavell, J. H. *The Developmental Psychology of Jean Piaget*. Princeton, N.J.: Van Nostrand-Reinhold, 1963.

Freud, S. Beyond the pleasure principle. In J. Strachey (ed. and trans.), *The Standard Edition of the Complete Psychological Works of S. Freud, 1920–22*. Vol. 18. London: Hogarth, 1955.

Froebel, F. *The Education of Man*. W. N. Hailmann (trans.). New York: D. Appleton, 1887.

Groos, Karl. *The Play of Animals*. New York: D. Appleton, 1898.

———. *The Play of Man*. New York: D. Appleton, 1901.

Gilmore, J. B. Play: A special behavior. In *Current Research in Motivation*, edited by R. N. Haber, 343–355. New York: Holt, Rinehart & Winston, 1966.

Gulick, Luther H. *A Philosophy of Play*. Washington, D.C.: McGrath, 1920.

Hall, Stanley G. *Youth*. New York: D. Appleton, 1906.

Harris, W. T. (ed.). The Mottoes and Commentaries of Friedrich Froebel's *Mother Play*. New York: D. Appleton, 1906.

Huizinga, J. *Homo Ludens: A Study of the Play Element in Culture*. Boston: Beacon, 1950.

Isaacs, S. *Social Development in Young Children: A Study of Beginnings*. London: Routledge and Kegan Paul, 1933.

Iwanaga, M. Development of interpersonal play structure in three, four, and five year-old children. *Journal of Research and Development in Education*, 1973, 6(3), 71–82.

Millar, Susanna. *The Psychology of Play*. Baltimore: Penguin Books, 1968.

Mitchell, Elmer D., and Mason, Bernard S. *The Theory of Play*. New York: A. S. Barnes, 1948.

Moore, N., Evertson, C. M., and Brophy, J. E. Solitary play: Some functional reconsiderations. *Developmental Psychology*, 1974, 10, 830–834.

Parten, M. Social participation among preschool children. *Journal of Abnormal and Social Psychology*, 1932, 27, 243–369.

Patrick, G. T. W. *The Psychology of Relations*. New York: Houghton-Mifflin, 1916.

Piaget, J. *The Origins of Intelligence in Children*. New York: International University Press, 1952.

———. *Play, Dreams and Imitation in Childhood*. New York: W. W. Norton, 1962.

———. Response to Brian Sutton-Smith. In Herron, R., and Sutton-Smith, B. *Child's Play*. New York: John Wiley, 1971, 337–339. (originally published in *Psychological Review*, 1966, 73(1), 111–112.

Piers, Maria (ed.). *Play and Development*. New York: W. W. Norton, 1972.

Rubin, K., Maioni, T., and Hornung, M. Free play behaviors in middle- and lower-class preschoolers: Parten and Piaget revisited, *Child Development*, 1976, 47, 414–419.

Schiller, Friedrich. *Essays Esthetical and Philosophical*. London: Bell and Sons, 1875.

Seagoe, M. Y. An instrument for the analysis of children's play in an index of degree of socialization. *Journal of School Psychology*, 1970, 8(2), 139–144.

Smilansky, S. *The Effects of Socio-dramatic Play on Disadvantaged Preschool Children*. New York: John Wiley, 1968.

Spencer, Herbert. *Principles of Psychology*. New York: D. Appleton, 1873.

Stern, W. *Psychology of Early Childhood*. New York: Henry Holt, 1924.

Sullivan, H. S. *The Interpersonal Theory of Psychiatry*. New York: W. W. Norton, 1953.

Sutton-Smith, B. Piaget on play: A critique. In Herron, R., and Sutton-Smith, B. *Child's Play*. New York: John Wiley, 1971, 326–336 (originally published in *Psychological Review*, 1966, 73(1), 104–110.

————. A reply to Piaget: A play theory of copy. In Herron, R., and Sutton-Smith, B. *Child's Play*. New York: John Wiley, 1971, 340–342.

Tolman, E. C. *Purposive Behavior in Animals and Man*. New York: Century, 1932. (Republished: New York: Meredith, 1967.)

Valentine, C. W. *The Psychology of Early Childhood*. Cleveland: Sherwood, 1942.

Wälder, R. The psychoanalytical theory of play. *Psychoanalytic Quarterly*, 1933, 2, 208–224.

2

THE IMPORTANCE AND NURTURE OF PLAY

"A human is most human . . . when at play."

M. J. Ellis*

Traditionally, there has been little appreciation in American culture for the importance of play and its contribution to child development. This has been due in part to the puritan work ethic which views anything that is fun or not related to work with suspicion. In addition, assembly-line technology has dominated the American educational system and play has been relegated the role of the ten-minute coffee break, whereby little "workers" are allowed a few minutes to run off excess energy so that they can better concentrate and produce more work (see the excess energy theory of play in Chapter 1).

Against this backdrop of historical disregard for play, Sara Arnaud (1974) declares, "Nourishers of curious minds, take heed. The case for play has gained new respectability." She points to the fact that play is now deemed worthy of serious scientific study. Just as the 1960s saw the "rediscovery" of early childhood education (Frost, 1968) in which there was a proliferation of studies and experiments concerned with providing optimal learning conditions for young children, so in the 1970s we have seen a rediscovery of children's play in which there have been a large number of investigations into the nature and function of play. Arnaud (1974, p. 73) attributes this shift in attitude toward play to several independent factors:

*Why People Play. Englewood Cliffs, N.J.: Prentice-Hall, 1973, p. 1.

1. The work of ethologists such as Goodall-van Lawick's study of chimpanzees, DeVore's study of baboons, Harlow's work with rhesus monkeys, and other studies with a variety of mammals have shown that many species engage in playful activities. In general, it has been found that the more intelligent the animal, the greater the quantity and variety of play behavior. Through play, animals develop skills needed for survival and become socialized into the group.

2. Piaget's rich description of the scope and sequence of intellectual development and his study of play have shown that intellectual competence is achieved through intense interaction (play) with the environment.

3. Dissatisfaction with traditional early childhood programs and a movement toward programs that emphasize problem-solving skills and learner autonomy.

4. Movement away from a work ethic to a leisure ethic in which individuals devote increasingly greater time, energy, and money to leisure activities in the form of recreation, sports, travel, and the arts.

With the rediscovery of play has come a wealth of investigations into the relationship between play and other areas of human development as well as the relationship between play, toys, and play environments. The central purpose of this chapter then is to describe these relationships and to draw implications about the role of adults in children's play.

CULTURE AND PLAY

As with cognitive development, the development of play follows a universal, invariant sequence. The content of a child's play and the rate with which she moves through the developmental sequence of play is in part a function of the specific culture in which she lives. One method of making cross-cultural and intracultural comparisons is to study the games children play. Roberts, Arth, and Bush (1959) distinguished between games and amusements. A game is characterized by organization, competition, two or more sides, criteria for determining a winner, and agreed upon rules, whereas noncompetitive activities are described as amusements. Games may be grouped into three classes on the basis of outcome attributes: (1) games of physical skill, in which the outcome is determined by the player's motor activities; (2) games of strategy, in which the outcome is determined by rational choices among possible courses of action; and (3) games of chance, in which the outcome is determined by guesses or by some uncontrolled artifact such as dice or a wheel. In addition games are also models of various cultural activities and therefore exercises in cultural mastery. For example, games of skill are related to mastery of the environment, games of strategy are related to mastery of the social system, and games of chance are related to mastery of the supernatural. There is a relationship between the complexity of cultures and the complexity of games: "simple" societies do not have a need for games of strategy, but in complex societies all types of games are present. Thus, while games are universal there is a great deal of variation in the type and number of games from one culture to another.

Stress Reduction Through Games

Roberts and Sutton-Smith (1962) developed and tested what they called the conflict-enculturation theory of games. They hypothesized that the child-rearing practices of various cultures would reflect the essential characteristics of a culture, and that these patterns in themselves would create stresses. Children would then compensate for this stress by playing games that relieve it (stress-reduction model). In addition, the playing of these games would aid in the enculturation of the child.

The results of this study showed a definite association between style of child rearing and the predominance of a particular type of game found in a given society. Tribes possessing games of strategy were found to be more likely to have high ratings on child-training procedures that involved rewarding children for being obedient, punished for being disobedient, anxiety about nonperformance of obedience, and high frequency of obedient behaviors. Roberts and Sutton-Smith argue that conflicts over obedience are manifested in games that provide the players opportunity to control others. Games of strategy provide opportunities to force obedience on others and thereby allow the players to reduce their aggressive and hostile feelings induced by strict child-rearing practices.

Games of chance predominated in societies in which children were reared for responsibility or stressed strict routines that allowed little scope for individuality or creative problem solving. Life in general was marked by drudgery and children were required not to reason but to do as they were told. As a result, children saw their lives as being dominated by fate or luck.

Games of physical skill were found in societies stressing achievement and performance. These games are often used by tribal societies as training procedures for hunting. In societies that consistently pressure children to perform better, anxiety concerning performance and failure develop. Anxiety over achievement may then be lessened through play where the sanctions for failure are not as great. In summary,

Each type of game in unique fashion contributes information as to the relative values and nature of different types of chance, skill, and strategy in assuaging conflict and in learning how to handle social competition. Between the ages of seven and twelve the child learns, in simple direct form, how to take a chance, how to show skill, and how to deceive. Increasingly, in complex games, he learns the reversibility of these styles—when to rely on one type of success gambit rather than another, how to combine them, etc. What he learns from the games are the cognitive operations involved in competitive success (p. 183).

The stress-reduction model of play has also been seen in psychoanalytic theories of play. When children are disturbed by a particular incident they recreate the experience over and over again in play, gradually diminishing the intensity of the experience (a common play theme in Northern Ireland is sniper and bomber). When this stress-reduction model is applied to American culture some very disturbing trends arise. In observing the play of young children, it is obvious that many of the themes enacted in their play are taken from the popular media (television, movies, comic books). One set of play themes involves violent acts with weapons. Here the dichotomy between fantasy and reality is not clear. A child may watch a television fantasy depicting violent acts and death followed by a news story involving the same elements. Fact and fantasy become blurred and the child may come to believe (and rightly so) that he lives in a dangerous world (recently the legal defense of a 15-year-old accused of murdering an elderly woman was based on the fact that he was addicted to violent television dramas). A visit to any toy store will also reflect these same themes. The shelves are lined with a variety of realistic-looking weapons and artifacts of war.

Another commonly observed play theme involves taking the role of one of a variety of super heroes (Superman, Batman, Wonder Woman). The play theme involves the acquisition of god-like qualities and conflict between good and evil. Typically, this play is stereotyped and nonelaborated (jumping, running, wrestling). DeMille (1967) speaks to play themes derived from the popular media:

Television and comic book fantasy can hardly be expected to cultivate the imagination, because it is already completely formed, on the screen or on the page. Nothing is left for the child to do but absorb it. The experience of the child is passive. It is not his imagination that is being exercised but that of some middle-aged writer. (p. 18)

Play as Preparation for Adult Life

While the stress-reduction approach presents a plausible explanation concerning the functional relationship between culture and games, play may also have different adaptive roles in different cultures. One of the classical theories of play examined earlier was the instinct-practice theory of Karl Groos (1898) in which play was viewed as a vehicle for perfecting instincts and skills needed in later life. In Western societies little direct correspondence can be seen between the play behavior of young children and skills needed in adulthood. This is due in part to the advanced technological nature of Western civilization and a dichotomy between work and play. In nontechnological societies, however, there seems to be a greater correspondence between children's play and adult role behavior. Leacock (1971) points out in her description of play in African villages that "playing house" is a rehearsal for adult roles by children around the world. In Western societies this activity plays primarily a socialization function; however, in African societies it entails technical as well as social practice. In playing house children learn and perfect skills that will be needed in adult life. Boys and girls build small

Play carries cultural genes. Through play the activities of elders are passed on to children. Patterns of rearing children, preparation for adult living, and simply learning to enjoy life are all inherent in the play of the child.

thatch houses and make and use a variety of tools, utensils, and weapons. Unlike in Western culture there is a smooth natural transition from play to work. She presents the following description of tribal life in Uganda.

A boy tagging after his father watches him milk the cows or thatch the house, whittle a hoe handle or roast a bit of meat on a stick. Playing with a small gourd, a child learns to balance it on his head, and is applauded when he goes to the watering-place with other children and brings back a little water in it. As he learns, he carries an increasing load, and gradually the play activity turns into a general contribution to the household water supply.

Turnbull (1961) also points to this phenomenon in his description of the play of Pygmy children.

Like children everywhere, Pygmy children love to imitate their adult idols ... at an early age boys and girls are "playing house" or "playing hunting" and one day they find the games they have been playing are not games any longer, but the real thing for they have become adults. (p. 129)

IMAGINATION AND PLAY

A number of terms are used for the flights of imagination that take place in children's play: make-believe play, imaginative play, fantasy play, pretend play, and symbolic or dramatic play. The nature of dramatic play was discussed in Chapter 1. In this section we will elaborate further on this important form of play, giving special attention to its nurture by adults.

In Chapter 1 Piaget's work revealed a developmental progression across the various stages of play. There also appears to be a developmental progression within stages. Learning to play with objects progresses from simple, single transformations to multiple, more complex ones (Fein, 1975). Fein's two-year-old children could pretend

to feed a realistic, plush toy horse from a plastic egg cup, and they could substitute either a flat metal horse or a clam shell but they could not make both substitutions at once. The greater the abstractness or number of substitutions required, the more difficult the task. This suggests that realistic supports (toys) are needed for the early development of make-believe play (around 18 to 28 months).

Young children also need stage-specific materials in learning to represent or imitate people and objects. They initially imitate through gestures the action of other persons and movement of inanimate, mobile objects and develop to gestural representations of static objects (Werner and Kaplan, 1963). Such progression was demonstrated by Overton and Jackson (1973), as follows: (a) object present (toothbrush) and action sequence (brushing the teeth) modeled; (b) object present but sequence not modeled; (c) object absent and the child directed to pretend. In pretending, children used a body part as an object (finger as toothbrush) before using symbolic gestures (hand as if holding toothbrush). Further, children directed actions toward or pretended about themselves (brush teeth, drink) earlier than they employed actions or materials of the external world (hammer, nail). This appeared to result simply from the lack of familiarity with the relation between action and object. It seems important, then, that children have access to a wide array of materials as they explore and develop through play.

There is also evidence that adults can modify or improve make-believe play. Freyberg (1973) improved the imaginative play of disadvantaged children through role playing. She believes that this can best be accomplished during sensitive periods when children have the potential for imaginative play and should not be forced. Saltz and Johnson (1974) increased the dramatic play of disadvantaged preschoolers by giving them opportunities to act out fairy tales such as *The Three Pigs* and *Hansel and Gretel*.

The Role of Adults in Make-Believe Play

What then is the role of adults in fostering children's make-believe play? Smilansky (1968) urges adults to look for the presence or absence of the six criteria for sociodramatic play of which make-believe play is an important element (imitative role play, make-believe in regard to objects, make-believe in regard to actions and situations, persistence, interaction, verbal communication). If one or more of the elements is missing from a child's play, then the parent or teacher can intervene and remediate the deficient areas. Adults may intervene from inside the play as a coplayer or from outside the play as an adult. Intervening from outside the play, one can make suggestions to the child: "Nurse, maybe you could check the heart"; establish contact between players, "Mr. Grocer, I wonder if that person wants to buy something?"; or give directions to facilitate play, "Call the doctor and ask what to do." Interventions from outside the play should be made in accordance with the make-believe theme, and the teacher should address the child in his role, not as himself, "Pilot, do you need to put more gas in the airplane?" Through play intervention the adult assists the child in elaborating roles, extending receptive and expressive language, and learning new functional relationships among individuals and things.

Parents and teachers need to be more sensitive to the quality of children's play, spend more time in make-believe related activities with children. The content of the make-believe play may be derived from a variety of sources including folk tales, story books, television, and real life (Singer, 1973). Parents should closely monitor their children's viewing especially with regard to violence-oriented programs. Television viewing

Both parents and teachers strive to create an atmosphere conducive to dramatic play.

should be selective, that is, the set should not be left running all day and used primarily as an electronic babysitter. A recent evaluation of the impact of *Sesame Street* clearly showed that those children who benefited most from the program had parents who watch with them and related to the program during other times of the day.

The vast majority of toys purchased for children are of little or no value. Toys should be simple in design so that the quality of imaginativeness comes from the child, not the toy. Toys should be selected that will help establish an atmosphere conducive to dramatic play both in the school and at home. Many of these can be leftover items such as cooking utensils, empty containers, and articles of clothing. Toys that have multiple function, such as building blocks, are generally superior to those with more limited function, such as puzzles. Once the child can solve a puzzle it loses much of its value.

LANGUAGE AND PLAY

As we have seen, language has an important role during play but, conversely, play has an important role in the development of language. As the child explores or plays with objects, discovering meanings and relationships, language is attached and intelligent behavior is enhanced.

Language serves several functions during play (Smilansky, 1968): it appears as an imitation of adult speech, it is used for make-believe (let's pretend), and it serves for the management of play in the form of explanations, commands, and discussion. In addition, speech allows children to amplify the meaning of what they visualize; it sustains their imaginative role; it enables them to hear themselves from the "outside"; it allows them to sense the inner conversation taking place between themselves and the person (within them) who is taking the role; and it adds new words to their vocabulary.

Play with Language

A little recognized but valuable activity is children's play with language itself. Garvey (1977) documented the progression of this activity beginning in infancy. During the babbling stage of six to ten months, the infant produces a great variety of random sounds. By one year of age the child engages in long episodes of melodic vocal modulation of single vowels. As the child begins to talk, episodes of verbal play can be identified. The adult models early vocal play by tongue clicking, tummy tickling, and mock threats previewed by oooh sounds, all accompanied by signs of pleasure.

During the toddler period (two to three) children learn sounds that allow them to identify events and actions of self, others, and objects such as the telephone, dog, and automobile horn. Through speech children can now use these sounds to accompany their physical movements. Playing with sounds appears to be private activity or at least requires considerable familiarity with the play partner. This type of playful language exploration, repetitive and predictably structured, is a form of practice play.

Anthony experimented with nonsense syllables and words:

Let Bobo bink.
Bink ben bink.
Blue rink.

He substituted words:

What color mop.
What color glass.

He built up and broke down sentences:

Stop it.
Stop the ball,
    and Anthony jump out again.
Anthony jump (Garvey, p. 65).

From about age three and a half virtually all types of language structures are used in social play. The analytical language, usually private, is replaced by language more like normal conversation in play with peers. This social play with language takes three forms: spontaneous rhyming and word play, fantasy and nonsense, and play with conversation.

Speech enters into all aspects of play as a vehicle for mere pleasure and as a means of managing complex activities of make-believe. For the most part early language play is spontaneously generated rather than quoted, having little apparent relationship with home or nursery school experiences. But as children enter the stage of dramatic or make-believe play, familiar props and adult-type language enter play activities with increasing frequency. This seems to result from opportunities to interact with others rather than from explicit adult instructions. Piaget appeared to understand this principle for when asked to state the educational implications of his theory of cognitive development, he replied that there were only two: first, provide the child with a wealth of unstructured materials and ample opportunity to play with them; and, second, ask a lot of good questions.

Does Adult Intervention Make a Difference?

Given these important relationships between language and play, the natural inclination is to explore ways to enhance them. Does direct intervention by adults make a difference?

The answer to this question appears to be, Yes. Smilansky (1968) divided disadvantaged children into three treatment groups. In group A the children were provided with a rich variety of experiences and field trips followed by discussions. In group B the children were systematically "taught" how to engage in and sustain sociodramatic play. Group C received a combination of treatment A and B.

Improvement in verbal communication although slight was noted in groups B and C. After the nine-week period of intervention, the children in group B engaged in lively, verbal negotiations,

Adult interaction with children during play results in increased language use and influences their subsequent play behaviors.

although the quality of discussion was far from adequate to satisfy the demands of the play situation. The children in group C showed even more marked improvement.

In a study by Lovinger (1974), a speech specialist interacted with four- and five-year-old children during free play one hour per day for twenty-five weeks. The specialist used three levels of interaction: (a) following, adding to, and enriching the natural play of the children; (b) using experiences the children had to play out, such as a visit to the zoo; (c) creating a play situation and encouraging the children to become involved. This daily hour of intervention was not a training program per se, and the children were not required or encouraged to imitate, but rather were encouraged to respond to the speech specialist's play and verbalizations in any way they desired.

The play intervention was effective in increasing the verbal expression and play complexity for the experimental group while no changes were found for the control group. The development of sociodramatic play in preschool, disadvantaged children resulted in increased language use and increased their ability to deal with a psycholinguistic task (the verbal expression scale of the Illinois Test of Psycholinguistic Abilities). Thus, a functional relationship was established between play and language.

The wise adult is aware of the language activities of children, understands the nature and stage of their verbalizations, and realizes that language development is essentially a spontaneous process of trial and error as opposed to a process of imposed rules. The adult role is to provide a wide range of unstructured play materials and to serve mediating, motivating roles. There is time for individual privacy, time for social play, and time for interacting with adults. Some adult verbalizations help to extend play while others have a negative influence. Some motivate play not yet thought of by the child. A steady stream of adult talk is usually less helpful than a well-placed question or remark modulated in stress and rhythm to the circumstance of the moment. The facilitative, not the directive, adult is needed in children's play environments.

SEX DIFFERENCES IN PLAY

Sex differences in children's play appear early in life and may be attributed in large part to culturally determined adult expectations. Typically, sex differences in play are studied from a perspective of toy and game preferences.

Sex differences in toy preference appear as early as 13–14 months (Jacklin, Maccoby, and Dick, 1975). Goldberg and Lewis (1969) found striking sex differences in 13-month-old infants toward their mothers and in their play. Girls were found to be more dependent, showed less exploratory behavior, and their play reflected a quieter style. Boys were independent, showed more exploratory behavior, played with toys requiring gross motor activity, were more vigorous and tended to run and bang in their play. Fein et al. (1975) found that the toy preferences of 20-month-old children during free play and toy ownership match adult stereotypes. In relation to toy ownership, girls had boy toys and boys were less likely to have girl toys. Rosenberg and Sutton-Smith (1960) conducted a large-scale survey of the play activities of boys and girls. The results showed that, while the play activities conformed to sex role stereotypes, girls now evidenced greater interest in male activities than in the past.

Sex Differences on Playgrounds

Only a limited number of studies of sex differences have been conducted on outdoor play environments. In a study prepared for *Ms.* magazine, Lever (1977) observed 181 10- and 11-year-old boys and girls for nearly a year. The girls tended to play indoors, limiting their body movement, their vocal expression, and their play areas. Boys on the other hand preferred outdoor play, especially team sports and fantasy games such as "War." They played in larger, more mixed age groups and learned to resolve disputes more quickly. Lever believes that play for the fifth-grade boy provides a direct rehearsal for competitive work situations and survival in the adult world.

Significant sex differences are also found among younger children on playgrounds. In a study by Frost and Campbell (1977) second-grade boys engaged in richer forms of play—dramatic and games with rules—more frequently than girls. The girls played at the lower levels—parallel and functional—more frequently than the boys. Similarly, Henniger's (1977) study of nursery school children revealed differences between boy and girl play. In the indoor environment there were significantly greater amounts of dramatic play for girls and constructive play for boys. The outdoor environment was observed to be an important stimulus for the dramatic play of boys.

Sex Differences: Cultural or Biological?

Conclusions drawn from studies by Erikson (1951) and Honzik (1951) and Lewis (1972) question whether sex-stereotyped play behavior is determined exclusively by social learning.

When preadolescents were asked to create an exciting motion picture scene using blocks, dolls, animals, and other toys, Erikson reported significant sex-related differences in the scenes produced. Girls tended to create indoor scenes, with significantly greater use of family dolls, furniture, and domestic animals, while boys characteristically created outdoor scenes, with significantly greater use of blocks, vehicles, and uniformed male dolls. In addition to these differences in choice of play materials, boys and girls

could also be distinguished by the spatial configurations they constructed and by the themes related to these configurations. For example, girls showed an interest in open, inner space, as portrayed by scenes representing interiors of homes without walls and in the entrance into that space such as ornamental gateways. Boys, on the other hand, were concerned with construction activity as represented by tall towers, turrets, and buildings. Girls also showed some anxiety about having the inner space intruded upon by animals, men, or boys, while boys indicated some anxiety about the collapse of erected structures or of falling from heights.

While some of these differences may reflect learned, sex-stereotyped behaviors, other aspects of the findings are less easily explained by social-learning theory. For example, it is not clear why the concern for gateways and entrances should more likely be part of a girl's learning history than a boy's. Nor is it evident from the child's learning history why girls should be more concerned about intruders, or boys about buildings collapsing, especially since the likelihood of either event having actually occurred in the child's life was exceedingly low.

Erikson rejected the notion that sex-related differences in fantasy play are entirely a function of cultural conditioning. He concluded that the results of his dramatic production procedure reflected basic psychological differences that, in turn, reflect the differences in the anatomy and functioning of the two sexes.

While Erikson's study was primarily concerned with sex differences in spatial arrangements of the blocks and boys, Honzik (1951) was concerned with sex differences in the occurrence of various play materials used in the children's constructions. Using the same procedure and materials as Erikson as well as a similar population, Honzik reported that boys used more blocks, vehicles, and persons in uniform at all ages, while girls used more play furniture and persons in preferred animal toys more than boys, while boys played more with nontoy objects than did girls. The style of play also differed. Boys used more gross motor activity and girls used more fine motor activity. Lewis believes that these early differences may be due to three factors. One possible explanation is biological. Male primates, even rats, show more exploratory behavior than females. Second, parents teach their children sex role behaviors by reward and punishment. Third, children appear to learn rules which guide their sex role behavior.

The Role of Adults in Boy/Girl Play

Although we cannot determine the precise proportion, sex differences in the play behavior of children may, for the most part, be attributed to social learning. From birth, parents selectively reinforce sex-stereotyped behaviors based on cultural norms. This results in subtle differences in behavior during the first year of life. Psychosexual theories offer interesting but unsubstantiated explanations for sex differences in behavior. Recently, due primarily to the women's movement, there has been much discussion in the popular media and professional literature concerning sexism in education and in child-rearing practices. Those concerned with the issue of sexist practices in education point to the fact that, from preschool through secondary schools, girls are directed toward traditional feminine occupations (teaching, nursing, secretarial, homemaking, and so on) and are discouraged from preparing for traditional male occupations (law, medicine, science, engineering, and business). With regard to child-rearing practices, boys are taught at an early age that men must be strong and not to show openly their emotions or affection. In addition, it is acceptable for boys to engage in rough-and-tumble play, but girls are expected to play quietly.

Many well-meaning adults mistakenly be-

Adults do not "teach" sex role behavior. Rather they should provide opportunities for play that include a wide variety of behaviors and roles.

ordinary dress. In addition, the boy's constructions suggested a greater output of energy and more varied use of materials. The girls, on the other hand, portrayed more passive, peaceful indoor scenes using the furniture and family figures.

In studies at the infant laboratory of the Educational Testing Service in Princeton, New Jersey, Lewis (1972) discovered sex differences in the play behavior of one-year-old infants. The girls were more likely to touch, stay closer, and vocalize to their mothers than infant boys. Boys explored their environment more than girls. Girls lieve that it is their duty to actively teach appropriate sex role behavior and to quash what they believe to be inappropriate sex-related behavior. For example, young boys must not be allowed to spend too much time playing with dolls or allowed to dress up in women's clothing for fear that they will become sissies or worse. In order for appropriate sex role identification to develop, it is important to provide opportunities for children to imitate the behaviors of both sexes. By age four, children spend a great deal of time imitating and acting out the adult behaviors that they observe. At this stage of development it is essential for children to observe and act out the behaviors of both sexes. It is through the vehicle of sociodramatic play that children learn and practice sex-related roles of the specific culture in which they live. Adults must be sensitive to this need and provide opportunities for play that include a wide variety of behaviors and roles. It is particularly important that they provide play materials and encourage games representing minority cultures and seek to preserve the cultural identity of minority children.

PLAY AND PERCEPTUAL-MOTOR DEVELOPMENT

Perceptual-motor is an apt term. The hyphen signifies the mutual dependency between perceptual information and voluntary motor activity. Perceptual abilities are learned and depend upon movement as a medium for this learning. Conversely, movement involves a perceptual awareness of sensory stimulation. If both abilities are to develop in a normal fashion, there must be a reciprocal interaction of perceptual information and motor or movement data.

The human body is wonderfully equipped with perceptual modalities for transmitting information to the brain for organization and response. These modalities are auditory (hearing), visual (seeing), tactile (touching), kinesthetic (feeling), gustatory (tasting), and olfactory (smelling). They are developed naturally or informally as children play, they are the subject of formal training as in physical education programs, and they are approached by special remedial and readiness programs.

All of these approaches are expected to enhance or improve perceptual-motor functioning. The formal programs employ specialized activities organized around perceptual-motor qualities and the informal proponents take them into account:

Gross motor activities: throwing, catching, kicking, jumping, swinging

Fine motor activities: cutting, lacing, hammering, buttoning, pouring

Body awareness activities: naming, pointing, identifying, moving, and performing tasks, using body parts

Spatial awareness activities: moving, exploring, locating, comparing and identifying, using walking, running, catching, rolling, tunnels, mazes

Directional awareness activities: moving, stationing, pointing, identifying and imitating, using body, objects, and apparatus

Balance activities: walking, bouncing and clapping, using balance beams and boards, trampoline, and spring boards

Integration activities: hitting moving ball, tracking moving objects, matching visual and motor responses, and responding to auditory signals

Expressive activities: art, music, dance, and dramatic play

Developmental Patterns in Movement

Motor development, like other areas of human development, progresses in a lawful fashion for most children. Sinclair (1971) conducted a longitudinal study aimed at documenting the movement and movement patterns of two- to six-year-old children. The motor characteristics selected for study were dominance, opposition and symmetry, dynamic balance, total body assembly, rhythmic, two-part locomotion, eye-hand efficiency and postural adjustment. The general conclusions were:

• Movement patterns develop according to a predictable timetable
• Development requires effort and practice in a favorable environment
• Basic movement patterns are established in early childhood
• Motor performance and movement development vary with age, sex, and individuals
• Movement prowess tends to be greater for girls at ages two and three and for boys from four to six

Scientific studies of developmental patterns frequently result in the construction of tests to measure, and to formally intervene in, the activities of children. The application of tests and formal programs of instruction, though useful for certain purposes, frequently interfere with normal development. This is nowhere more obvious than in perceptual-motor development.

Perceptual-Motor Training Programs

Over the years a number of perceptual-motor training programs have been developed. Three of the best known are those of Doman-Delacato (Delacato, 1966), Frostig (1969), and Kephart (Chaney and Kephart, 1968). Numerous publications by these people are available. The great majority of studies do not reveal special advantages of these over regular programs.

The American Academy of Neurology (1967) issued a joint executive board statement discussing the lack of controlled studies of the Doman-Delacato method and cases in which the method did not help the patient. Freeman (1967)

listed nine objections to the method. A pediatrician Ottinger (1964) considered Delacato's data to be fallacious, rationale poor, and conclusions untenable.

Klesius (1970) reviewed 28 research studies on the effectiveness of perceptual-motor programs on reading achievement.

1. In general, perceptual-motor programs employing a wide variety of experiences appear to show promise with underachieving intermediate grade children and preschool children.
2. The effectiveness of Delacato- and Frostig-type programs is doubtful.
3. The inclusion of individualized perceptual-motor programs for kindergarten and primary grade children in physical education classes is developmentally appropriate.

Shick and Plack (1976) reviewed 16 studies concerned with Kephart's perceptual-motor training program to conclude:

The Purdue Perceptual-Motor Survey may screen perceptual deficiencies at a gross level but it is not a useful predictive tool.

The only evidence that supports the contention that Kephart's training program enhances academic achievement exists in the form of case studies and these must be interpreted cautiously. Further, studies that use an experimental design do not support the claim.

Nurturing Perceptual-Motor Development

What direction should be pursued in nurturing perceptual-motor development in children. The authors believe (based on case studies and direct observation) that specific programs such as those of Frostig and Kephart are useful in providing guidelines for understanding the nature of perceptual-motor development and for selective application with handicapped and low-functioning

By being sensitive to perceptual-motor abilities at a given point in development, the adult can extend and enrich the child's play and facilitate the transition from one stage to another.

children. But even these children have potential rarely tapped on the sterile playgrounds of America. The exciting adventure playgrounds for handicapped children in London (Chapter 9) illustrate this contrast.

All too frequently, remedial and physical education personnel disregard the value of free play in perceptual-motor development. We are especially concerned that children in the early childhood (preconceptual) period have opportunities to develop naturally through play without the ever-present test-perform-test cycle imposed by the adult whose primary concern is motor development for participation in sports. Perceptual-motor skills are developed naturally during free play on the new creative playgrounds now appearing in greater frequency. Simultaneously, related skills are developing. Our greatest challenges are (1) to make exciting, challenging play environments available to all children both at schools and in close proximity to their homes, and (2) to provide facilitative adult leaders who understand that perceptual-motor development is but one among many important developmental tasks of children.

PLAY AND PLAY OBJECTS

What is the relationship between play and toys and other play objects? Do different toys promote different behaviors? If a toy embodies a particular principle or concept, will that concept be transferred to the child through play? The majority of studies concerned with the relationship of play to play objects have dealt primarily with play as a function of the novelty and complexity of the object. Toy play begins in early infancy.

Toy Play of Infants and Toddlers

Play with toys follows an interesting developmental progression beginning at an early age.

Lowe (1975) observed infants and toddlers (12 to 36 months) as they manipulated a set of miniature objects. The following is a summary of the observation at each age level:

12 months The child uses the eating utensils appropriately. She will "drink" from the cup or "feed" herself with a spoon, or she might place the cup on the saucer and the spoon in the cup. However, the other objects will be used in an inappropriate manner such as waving, banging, or mouthing.

15 Months At this age the child is more likely to "stir" or "pick up" the imaginary food and to link this with the action of self-feeding. She may also extend this self-feeding behavior to other objects, for example, dip the log into the truck and put it in her mouth. The 15-month-old will push the little truck and trailer back and forth on the table.

18 months This is the peak age for self-related activity. The child will feed and comb herself and wipe her face. She now begins to direct more attention to the doll—made to stand, sit or jump, but not yet as a rule fed or combed.

21 months This appears to be a transitional stage at which doll-related activities for the first time equal or slightly outweigh self-related behavior. She will now feed and brush the doll and put the doll on the bed with clear intentions of putting it down to sleep. The child will also place the logs and the little man in one of the vehicles.

24 months Doll-related behavior is now dominant. The child will feed the doll or place it in a meal situation. When putting the doll to bed, she will include the essential elements (doll, bed, blanket) in an integrated manner. More care may go into making the bed than at the previous stage.

30 months The child can now make meaningful use of all elements. The doll will not only be seated on the chair but also pushed to the table, usually with the eating utensils in front of it. She may also search for absent objects that she needs for her play or she may even create these objects herself, for example, fold a piece of cloth to make a pillow.

36 months There is now a marked decline in overt versus implied feeding of the doll; that is, the child is more likely to place the doll at the set table than actually feed it. She will now hook the trailer to the truck.

Novelty, Realism, and Complexity of Toys

The *novelty* of a toy is a primary reason for children to explore it. The introduction of a novel object stimulates the child to get to know its properties. Exploration ceases once these properties are known. At that point play begins. This transition from exploration to play is apparent by a gradual relaxation of mood, evidenced not only by changes in facial expression, but in greater diversity of activities with the object. In play, the emphasis changes from the question of "What does this object do?" to "What can I do with this object?" (Hutt, 1966).

Realism of toys is a second primary factor in children's play. Pulaski's study of five- to seven-year-olds showed that less structured toys (construction and art materials, simple rag dolls) elicited a greater variety of fantasy themes than did highly structured toys (realistic dolls, detailed toy buildings, cars, fully furnished doll house). However, high fantasy children were less influenced by the realism of the toys apparently because tendencies toward fantasy were already well developed.

A third factor affecting exploration, curiosity, and play behavior of children is *complexity* of toys. Four- to seven-year-old children were asked to do anything they liked with a series of objects varying in complexity (Switzky, Haywood, and Isett, 1974). The older children were more curious than the younger children, spending more time exploring the high complexity objects. But, in general, the time spent playing decreased for both the older and the younger children.

Based on the research pertaining to the relationship between play and play objects, it is safe to say that the critical characteristics of a

In general, the simple, raw materials of play are best. As complexity of play materials increases, the amount and quality (creativeness, inventiveness) of play decreases.

play object are its relative degree of complexity and novelty. When a novel object is encountered, it will first be explored and then played with. The intensity of play is related to the degree of the novelty. With regard to the complexity of a play object, the amount and quality (creativeness, inventiveness) of play decreases as complexity increases. Caplan and Caplan (1973, pp. 159–160), the originators of Creative Playthings, aptly point to the fact that "Detail and reality can be a hindrance to free, creative play for the very young child, because he can use the toy only for what it was originally intended."

Toys, Television, and Play

There is considerable concern at present about the probable antisocial effects of television. It is widely believed that American children watch television more than they engage in any other

activity, including time in school and time interacting with parents. Toys enter the picture because they serve as props to play out the scenes depicted on television.

Nursery school children were observed during free play by Turner and Goldsmith (1976). During some sessions the children played with novel toy guns and airplanes in addition to their usual toys. Both the guns and the airplanes increased the rate of antisocial behavior as compared to the usual toys. It appeared that the toy guns elicited greater antisocial behavior because the children associated the guns with violent episodes on television and in the movies in which the firing of guns is paired with verbal threats, fist fights, and other violent actions.

It seems particularly important that adults exert some control over children's television viewing. In 1976 television was introduced to remote Eskimo villages. Within a few weeks

Violence on television breeds aggression in children. Most Americans have yet to learn what many people in other countries already know, personal involvement in play and playgrounds is a wise investment in the future of children.

the nature of children's play was transformed from predominantly tribal games passed down through generations to television-inspired games such as "Six Million Dollar Man" and "Kojak," with a dramatic increase in violence themes. The same play materials can be used for the acting out of positive themes or for the make-believe conduct of horror and violence. Television models are powerful forces in this respect.

Making Decisions about Toys

What are the criteria for a good toy? Do the criteria change with the age of the child? Novelty is a critical element in the child's attraction to the length of time spent playing with a particular toy. However, the interaction between novelty and complexity inhibits sustained creative play. Hutt (1966) has shown that the amount of time children direct toward a par-

ticular play object is a function of the degree of novelty or number of novel elements contained in the object. When children are first presented with a novel toy, they explore the object in an attempt to determine what the object does. Once the various qualities of an object have been thoroughly explored and tested, children begin to play with the object. Once the novelty of the object begins to fade, the amount of time spent with the object also decreases. Complex toys that are very detailed in design are initially novel; however, the novelty soon wears off and the toy is disregarded.

It is part of American folk wisdom that when you buy children an expensive toy, they soon tire of playing with it and discard it in favor of the box it came packed in. Why does this scenario typically occur? As Pulaski (1970) and Switzky (1974) have shown, as the level of object complexity increases, the time spent playing with it decreases. A complex, highly detailed toy co-ops a child's ability to play creatively and imaginatively with the toy because it can only be used for what it was designed. The box in which it came, however, is an unstructured object that can be used as a space station, a hangar, a fort, an aircraft carrier, another spaceship, and so on. The best toys and play materials are those that are relatively simple in complexity and design, thus allowing children to supply the element of novelty with their imagination rather than having it imposed by the structure of the toy. This is true except for very young children who find it difficult to transform more than one object at a time, and who need realistic supports for their sociodramatic play.

This research provides parents and early childhood practitioners with a number of practical implications for the design and use of toys, for assessing the child's level of development, and for providing the child with toys appropriate to that level of development. Lowe's (1975) work sensitizes adults to the scope and sequence of play with objects. By examining her description of age-related play with objects, it is possible to assess whether a child is progressing at a normal rate or is significantly delayed in development (the Bayley Mental Scale of Infant Development is also based on play with objects). By being sensitive to the quality of a child's play at a particular point in development, the adult can model, extend, and enrich the child's play and facilitate the transition from one stage to another. For example, prior to 18 months of age, the child's use of objects has been primarily directed toward herself (combs her hair). However, at about 18–20 months of age, the child begins to direct her play toward dolls (combs doll's hair). Here the adult could engage in play with the child and use her interests in dolls to facilitate receptive and expressive language: "Watch daddy comb the doll's hair. Now you comb the doll's hair."

PLAY AND PLAYGROUNDS

While there has been a moderate amount of research concerning the functional relationship between play and play objects (toys), there has been scant research pertaining to the relationship between children's play and the design of playgrounds. However, since playgrounds may be viewed as a collection of large play objects in close proximity to each other, it seems reasonable to assume that the novelty and complexity of playgrounds would effect children's play much as toys do. Is this indeed the case?

A related issue concerns the function of play equipment and its relationship to the developmental needs of children using it. Typically, the American playground is a collection of single-function equipment—merry-go-rounds, see-saws, jungle gyms, slides, and swings. Such equipment is designed primarily for exercise or functional play. The addition of more of the same would hardly improve the quality or range of play.

Complexity and Variety of Equipment and Play Behaviors

When four- and five-year-old children were allowed to play on two play environments, high complexity and low complexity, the high complexity setting sustained more interaction with play objects and less interaction with peers (Scholtz and Ellis). This study was concerned only with quantity and not the quality of interaction. Many years ago, Johnson (1935) studied the effects on children of varying the amount of play equipment. As the amount of equipment increased, the amount of motor play and play with materials increased, while the amount of undesirable behavior (hitting, arguing, teasing) and social play decreased. As the amount of equipment decreased, there was a corresponding decrease in gross motor play and an increase in the number of social contacts and social conflicts.

Thus it appears that increasing the complexity or variety of equipment has a positive effect on behavior. The author's observations support this assumption. Poorly equipped or sparsely equipped playgrounds force children to ramble aimlessly about getting involved in conflicts and frequently leading to difficulties with teachers. On the other hand, there are relatively few conflicts or discipline problems on the best playgrounds we have seen.

A more pressing issue than interaction, per se, is the quality of children's interaction with play equipment. Frost and Campbell (1977) selected an existing traditional playground (seesaw, merry-go-round, swings, slide, and climbing bars). For contrast they built a more varied creative playground including a play house, wheel vehicle area, sand and water areas, storage for movable parts, and a variety of handmade climbing and swinging structures. Fifty second-grade children engaged in free play for 30 minutes a day for ten weeks, alternating between the two playgrounds every other day.

On the traditional playground the children engaged in exercise (gross motor) play over 77 percent of the time and in dramatic play less than 3 percent of the time. On the creative playground these same children engaged in dramatic play 40 percent and exercise play 43 percent of the time. On the traditional playground over 35 percent of the time was spent in solitary and parallel activity but on the creative playground this activity occupied less than 25 percent of the time. The nature of the equipment on playgrounds makes significant differences in the types of play engaged in by children. The key seems to be the provision of a sufficient range of materials and equipment to allow expression through many types of play. If, for example, dramatic play is desired, it can be stimulated by the appropriate type of equipment.

Traditional, Contemporary (Designer), and Adventure Playgrounds

Traditional playgrounds, which are usually part of schools, housing projects, or neighborhood parks, typically contain swings, slides, seesaws, and climbing bars. Contemporary playgrounds are frequently designed by architects and emphasize novel forms, textures, and different heights in aesthetically pleasing arrangements. Typically, these playgrounds are somewhat sculptured, frequently based on sand or concrete forms. Adventure playgrounds provide children with raw building materials and tools with which they can build their own play structures.

Hayward, Rothenberg, and Beasley (1974) compared the play activities taking place on these three types of playgrounds. At each of the playgrounds the six- to thirteen-year-old group made up a greater part of the playground population at the adventure playground (45 percent), while this school-age group was only a minor proportion of the total number of users at the traditional playground (21 percent) and the contemporary (22 percent) playground. At the traditional playground and contemporary playground, adults were the most predominant age group (40 percent and 35 percent respectively), while preschool children were the most predominant group (30 percent and 35 percent) at the adventure playground.

The most used piece of equipment on the traditional playground was the swing, followed by the wading pool. On the contemporary playground the sand areas were most widely used, followed by the mounds and slides. At the adventure playgrounds, the clubhouse area was the most used. The slides on the traditional playground were rarely used by any age group, while the slides on the contemporary playground were used heavily. The one small and two large slides at the contemporary playground allowed

Adventure playgrounds, which provide children with raw building materials and tools, hold children's attention longer and increase the variety of language when compared to traditional playgrounds.

a variety of ways of climbing to the top. One slide purposely had bumps in it, there was sand and water nearby which could be applied to the surface of the slide, and more than one child could slide down side-by-side.

Another interesting aspect of this study pertained to the nature of verbal interactions between children. At the traditional and contemporary playgrounds, conversations focused primarily on equipment use and mutual play activities. In contrast, at the adventure playground children's conversations reflected a broader focus than the immediate setting and dealt with a wide variety of topics pertaining to their lives outside the playground. The author hypothesized that perhaps the opportunity for small groups of children to achieve some degree of privacy in their clubhouses led to some of this diversity.

There were also significant differences in the length of time children spent at each of the playgrounds. Children stayed the shortest lengths of time at the traditional playground, the next longest at the contemporary playground, and the longest at the adventure playground (median length of stay in minutes = 21, 32, 75, respectively).

The ambiguity of the adventure playground offered the children a potential setting in which to define self as well as space . . . it offered a selection of loose parts (e.g., tires, wood, tools, paint, plants, seeds, and the like) which supplied part of the potential for children to define their own activities. Thus, an important difference in the meaning of the environment to the users was that the built playgrounds were planned by others, they were permanent, and the potential for original combination was minimal; at the adventure playground, the form was created by the users and was only as permanent as they chose it to be (Hayward et al., 1974, p. 166).

The adventure playground with its collection of "loose parts" was by far the most popular of the playgrounds. This setting allowed the children to create their own form and structure and level of complexity. Studies now in progress will help to answer additional relevant questions. For instance, will a collection of loose parts (planks, crates, tires, cable spools, etc.) foster more cooperative play than traditional play equipment? From the observations of the authors, this appears to be the case.

Creative and Commercial Playgrounds

Frost and Strickland (1978) compared the equipment choices of 138 kindergarten, first, and second grade children on a creative playground and two types of commercially equipped playgrounds. The creative playground was an inexpensive mix of handbuilt equipment and loose parts. One of the commercial environments consisted of a massive "unit" structure containing interior and exterior space for climbing and dramatic play, two horizontal tire swings, a slide, and a fireman's pole and ladder. This unit structure, built of western red cedar retails for over $5,000. The second commercial environment consisted of an array of specially treated wood structures including balance beams, chinning bars, obstacle climbers, suspension bridge, slide, jungle gym and related equipment. The entire package retails for over $5,000.

Children's equipment choices during free play were systematically coded during over a period of six weeks. The creative environment was the most popular with 63 percent of the observations broken down as follows: wheeled vehicles 9.93 percent of all observations, organized games 9.63 percent, house and housekeeping equipment 8.20 percent, play without equipment 6.65 percent, complex slide 5.72 percent, loose parts 5.61 percent, old car and boat

4.56 percent, sand areas 4.37 percent, climbing structures 3.67 percent, and movable see-saw 2.44 percent.

In comparison, only 23 percent of all observations were recorded for the commercial unit structure (one-fifth of this play was in the sand surrounding the structure) and only 13 percent of the observations were recorded for the commercial linked structures.

Some general conclusions were: (1) action oriented equipment (equipment that moves) is preferred by children, (2) equipment designed primarily for exercise play is not sufficient to provide for the wide range of children's developmental play needs, (3) children prefer equipment that can be *adapted* to their play schemes, (4) among equipment tested only one type, loose parts, had equal appeal to children across all grade/age levels, and (5) inexpensive play environments can be superior to expensive ones.

SUMMARY

The purpose of this chapter has been to examine the relationships between play and other aspects of human development; to examine the relationships between play, toys, and play environments; and to make suggestions about the role of adults in children's play. Human development refers to the process of acquiring competence in dealing with the physical and social world. From the moment of birth, when children are thrust into an alien universe, they become explorers, attempting to discover through play, the rules by which the universe operates. Powerful forces interact to shape their developmental through the medium of play. Chief among these seems to be culture, supported, of course, by biology.

Culture governs the content of children's play and controls the rate at which they move through the developmental sequence of play. The playing of games aids in the enculturation of children, teaching them to cope with stress and preparing them, particularly in primitive cultures, for adult work roles. In modern societies, technology has complicated adult roles and heavily influenced the play of children.

Play is the chief vehicle for the development of imagination and intelligence, language, sex role behavior, and perceptual-motor development in infants and young children. Development occurs naturally when healthy children are allowed freedom to explore rich environments. Adults can also influence development by becoming involved in children's play. This results in increased verbal fluency, verbal expression, imaginativeness, positive affect, concentration and better performance on intellectual tasks.

Language and play go hand-in-hand. Play promotes imitation of adult speech while speech serves for the management of play in the form of explanations, commands, and discussions. Through play both vocabulary and thought are extended and enriched. The involvement of adults in nonthreatening, facilitative ways increases the range and quality of language during play. In sum, children learn to master their environment through the wedding of play and language.

There is controversy about the relative influences of culture and biology on developing sex roles of children. Sex differences are evident in one-year-old infants at play and continue to be evident in play throughout childhood. There is compelling evidence for biological influences but culture plays the predominant role. Consequently, adults have considerable influence through the behavior modeling of family and community members. In recent years television has taken on greater influence in influencing sex roles.

Perceptual-motor development is a lawful process encompassing the reciprocal processes of awareness and movement. Both formal and informal procedures are employed in fostering perceptual-motor development. These include specific readiness and remedial programs, planned physical education programs, and supervised and/or free play on playgrounds. The appropriateness of specific programs is a subject of considerable professional controversy, and there is need for improvement in physical education programs and the physical state of playgrounds.

Materials (toys, nontoy objects, and playground equipment) are critical variables in children's play. The primary way in which the child learns rules is through operations on objects. From Piaget's rich description of intellectual development, based on a model organism—environmental interchange; we know that when a child acts on an object in the environment, both the object and the child are changed, not in a physical sense, but in a mental sense. That is, play with objects follows a developmental progression and results in the development of intelligent behavior. Three factors, novelty, complexity, and realism, influence children's interest in play objects. Adult models, peer models, and television influence play themes.

The chief focus of this book, outdoor play environments, has been subjected to only limited research. However, the principles about play and development explored in Chapters 1 and 2 are directly relevant to the construction and use of playgrounds. Playgrounds should be developmentally relevant (accommodate various types of play) to the play needs of children. Complexity and variety of equipment influences play types, equipment choices, social behavior, and verbal interaction. The evidence for rebuilding the traditional American playground continues to accumulate. Just how to do this is the subject matter for the remainder of this book.

REFERENCES

American Academy of Neurology: Joint executive board statement—The Doman-Delacato treatment of neurologically handicapped children. *Neurology, 1967, 17,* 637.

Arnaud, S. H. Some functions of play in the educative process. *Childhood Education*, 1974, *51*, 72–78.

Caplan, F., and Caplan, T. *The Power of Play*. Garden City, New York: Doubleday, 1973.

Chaney, C. M., and Kephart, N. C. *Motoric Aids to Perceptual Training*. Columbus, Ohio: Charles E. Merrill, 1968.

Delacato, C. H. *Neurological Organization and Reading*. Springfield, Illinois.: Charles C. Thomas, 1966.

deMille, R. *Put Your Mother on the Ceiling: Children's Imagination Games*. New York: Walker, 1967.

Erikson, E. H. Sex differences in play configurations of preadolescents. *American Journal of Orthopsychiatry*, 1951, *21*, 667–692.

Fein, G. A transformational analysis of pretending. *Developmental Psychology*, 1975, *11*, 291–296.

———, Johnson, D., Kosson, N., Stork, L., and Wasserman, L. Sex stereotype and preferences in the toy choices of 20-month-old boys and girls. *Developmental Psychology*, 1975, *11*, 527–528.

Freeman, R. D. Controversy over "Patterning" as a treatment for brain damage in children. *American Medical Association Journal*, 1967, *202*, 358–385.

Freyberg, J. Increasing the imaginative play of urban disadvantaged kindergarten children through systematic training. In J. L. Singer (ed.), *The Child's World of Make-Believe*. New York: Academic, 1973.

Frost, J. L. (ed.). *Early Childhood Education Rediscovered*. New York: Holt, Rinehart, & Winston, 1968.

———, and Campbell, S. Play and equipment choices of second grade children on two types of playgrounds. Unpublished research report. Austin: The University of Texas, 1977.

———, and Strickland, E. Equipment choices of young children during free play. *Lutheran Education*, 1978, *114*, 34–46.

Frostig, M. *Move—Grow—Learn*. Chicago: Follett, 1969.

Garvey, C. *Play*. Cambridge: Harvard University Press, 1977.

Goldberg, S., and Lewis, M. Play behavior in the year-old infant: Early sex differences. *Child Development*, 1969, *40*, 21–31.

Groos, Karl. *The Play of Animals*. New York: D. Appleton, 1898.

Hayward, D., Rothenberg, M., and Beasley, R. Children's play and urban playground environments: A comparison of traditional, contemporary and adventure playground types. *Environment and Behavior*, 1974, *6* (2), 131–168.

Henniger, M. L. Free play behaviors of nursery school children in an indoor and outdoor environment. Unpublished doctoral dissertation. Austin: The University of Texas, 1977.

Honzik, M. P. Sex differences in the occurrence of materials in the play construction of preadolescents. *Child Development*, 1951, *22*, (1), 15–35.

Hutt, G. Exploration and play in children. *Symposia of the Zoological Society of London*, 1966, *18*, 61–81.

Jacklin, C. N., Maccoby, E. E., and Dick, A. E. Barrier behavior and toy preference: Sex differences (and their absence) in the year-old child. *Child Development*, 1975, *44*, 196–200.

Johnson, M. W. The effect on behavior of variation in the amount of play equipment. *Child Development*, 1935, *6*, 56–68.

Klesius, S. E. Perceptual-motor development and reading. 1970. (E.R.I.C. ED 040 823, microfiche.)

Leacock, E. At play in African villages. *Natural History*, December 1971, special supplement on play, 60–65.

Lever, J. Little girl's play patterns may hinder career. Austin, Texas: *The Austin American Statesman*. Thursday, March 3, 1977.

Lewis, M. Sex differences in play behavior of the very young. *Journal of Health, Physical Education and Recreation*, 1972, *43*, 38–39.

Lovinger, S. L. Socio-dramatic play and language development in preschool disadvantaged children. *Psychology in the Schools*, 1974, *11*, 313–320.

Lowe, M. Trends in the developmental representational play in infants from one to three years—an observational study. *Journal of Child Psychology and Psychiatry*, 1975, *16*, 33–47.

Ottinger, L. The theory from the standpoint of pediatrics. In Claremont Reading Conference 28th Yearbook, 1964, *28*, 123–136.

Overton, W., and Jackson, J. The representation of imagined objects in action sequences: A developmental study. *Child Development*, 1973, *44* (2), 309–314.

Pulaski, M. S. Play as a function of toy structure and fantasy predisposition. *Child Development*, 1970, *41*, 531–537.

Roberts, J. M., Arth, M. J., and Bush, R. R. Games in culture. *American Anthropologist*, 1959, *61*, 597–605.

————, and Sutton-Smith, B. Game training and game involvement. *Ethnology*, 1962, *1*, 166–185.

Rosenberg, B. G., and Sutton-Smith, B. A revised conception of masculine-feminine differences in play activities. *The Journal of Genetic Psychology*, 1960, *96*, 165–170.

Saltz, E., and Johnson, J. Training for thematic fantasy play in culturally disadvantaged children. *Journal of Educational Psychology*, 1974, *66*, 623–630.

Shick, J., and Plack, J. J. Kephart's perceptual-motor training program. *Journal of Physical Education and Recreation*, 1967, *47*, 58–59.

Sinclair, C. A résumé of movement patterns of early childhood. In *Foundations and Practices in Percep-tual-Motor Learning—A Quest for Understanding.* Washington, D.C.: American Association for Health, Physical Education, and Recreation, 1971.

Singer, J. L. *The child's world of make-believe.* New York: Academic, 1973.

Smilansky, S. *The effects of sociodramatic play on disadvantaged preschool children.* New York: John Wiley, 1968.

Switzky, H. N., Haywood, H. C., and Isett, R. Exploration, curiosity, and play in young children: Effects of stimulus complexity. *Developmental Psychology*, 1974, *19*, 321–329.

Turnbull, C. *The Forest People.* New York: Simon and Schuster, 1961.

Turner, C. W., and Goldsmith, D. Effects of toy guns and airplanes on children's antisocial free play behavior. *Journal of Experimental Child Psychology*, 1976, *21* (2), 303–315.

Werner, H., and Kaplan, B. *Symbol formation.* New York: John Wiley, 1963.

3

THE PLAYGROUNDS OF AMERICA

"The fact has to be faced that modern civilization interferes with a hard and heavy hand in the spontaneous play of children."

Lady Allen of Hurtwood*

The outdoor landscapes of America are, in the broadest sense, wherever children may wish to play—the abandoned city lot, the top of buildings, forests and streams, or the more formal playgrounds prepared by adults. These formal playgrounds are found in private schools, church schools, day-care centers, public schools, city and community parks, on the cramped grounds of apartment complexes, and the backyards of private homes.

The history of America's formal playgrounds is relatively brief. There was little need for contrived exercise apparatus during the colonial period, at least for the large majority of

families who shared heavy work responsibilities, adult and child alike. With the advent of the industrial era and increasing affluence of Americans, more and more children were spared the necessity of working to support the family and were sent to school. The early recess period of contrived play and organized games was gradually supplanted by the provision of manufactured equipment, mainly of the exercise variety, for adults viewed play as a way of "letting off steam" and building a strong, healthy body. Until recently there was no widespread sentiment that play was valuable in it's own right or that play was a valuable vehicle for cognitive, social, and emotional, as well as physical, development.

During the extraordinary period of economic growth following the second world war,

---

Planning for Play. London: Thames and Hudson, 1968, p. II.

53

By the end of the 1950s the American playground had become standardized, an area enclosed by a chain-link fence, paved with asphalt, containing a slide, swing, seesaw, jungle gym, and merry-go-round.

American playgrounds rapidly took on the characteristics of the mechanical age. Contrived toys were replaced by replicas of Detroit-type products; natural features were supplanted by mechanically produced equipment; spontaneous play gave way to play guided by the designs of manufacturers. By the end of the 1950s most American playgrounds had become standardized, an area enclosed by a chain-link fence, paved with asphalt, containing a slide, swing, seesaw, jungle gym, and merry-go-round.

During the past decade the authors have examined first-hand both public and private playgrounds in several hundred communities in most states. Our opinion is that, with relatively few exceptions (5 to 10 percent), American playgrounds for children under eight years of age are hazardous, inadequately equipped, and inappropriate to the developmental play needs of the children they serve. The better ones are, for the most part, of recent construction. Some were designed by professional playground designers,

The typical equipment for backyards is a flimsy, poorly installed swing set, containing a wide array of supplementary parts so tightly clustered that active play is inhibited.

some by college professors, others were developed by architects, child development faculties, parks and recreation professionals, and private day-care center operators. Consistently, we found the poorest playgrounds for young children to be those in public schools. This is in part because of a failure to redevelop playgrounds to accommodate the gradual extension downward of age groups in attendance. During the past five years we have seen isolated examples of progress in public school settings, a few dedicated principals and teachers working on a shoestring budget to develop imaginative playscapes for children.

It is a difficult task for the authors to convey their respect for the many skillful, hard-working professionals who work very diligently toward improving play and playgrounds for children and simultaneously to communicate the nature of existing conditions on most playgrounds. Progress *is* being made but we have a long way to go. In the main, school playgrounds are concrete and steel jungles, hazardous, un-attractive to the eye, unsuited to developmental play needs, and oriented to two important but limited forms of play, exercise and organized games.

Homes and community groups offer little to improve on this picture. Backyards are typically designed for adult activities with only casual attention given to the young. The pattern is flimsy, poorly installed swing sets versus elaborate barbeque pits and expensive tennis courts. Community parks offer some respite from this state of affairs. Architects are frequently employed to create mammoth structures that reveal exemplary taste in form and aesthetic appeal, but which are all too frequently lacking in sensitivity to the diverse play needs of young children. It should be noted that architects and designers are limited in their designs by the standards of the groups they serve. So long as community groups are unwilling to provide storage facilities and play leaders for their playgrounds, the structures will continue to be of the mammoth, fixed variety, impervious to vandalism or theft, and limited in adaptation to spontaneous play.

In this chapter we will document the nature and scope of playground hazards in America. We will examine the uses and misuses of standard and creative equipment and we will explore supervisory and maintenance roles. Finally, we will trace the history of proceedings aimed toward the establishment of standards for the manufacture of playground equipment. A central criterion for good playgrounds, appropriateness to the child's developmental needs, is interwoven throughout the discussion and will be dealt with extensively in later sections.

PLAYGROUND HAZARDS

The growing movement to improve play equipment and children's playgrounds is related to the growing body of data on playground injuries and deaths. Prior to the development of the National Electronic Injury Surveillance System (NEISS) information on such accidents was available largely from independent small sample surveys and case studies (e.g., Dale et al., 1969; Franzen, 1958; McFarland, 1969; Watson, 1969). Since methods of study and study sites differ across independent studies, it is difficult to make meaningful comparisons, but there are some general conclusions that appear to agree with data later retrieved from the NEISS system: (1) falls are the most common factor contributing to injury, (2) the head, face, and neck are the body parts most frequently injured, and (3) lacerations are the most frequent type of injury.

The National Electronic Injury Surveillance System Data

With the initiation of the National Electronic Injury Surveillance System in 1971 an important new tool in the field of product safety came into use. NEISS is a national data collection system designed to determine the nature and scope of consumer product safety problems. In the first year of operation—July 1, 1971 to August 31, 1972—the number of injuries related to public and private playground equipment as reported to statistically selected hospital emergency rooms

was 4,350 (Bureau of Product Safety, 1972). Injuries on public playground equipment represented about 42.8 percent of this total or 1,863 cases.

Projections of estimated annual injuries throughout the United States associated with public playground equipment totaled 353,000 related injuries. Combined with private playground equipment, the number of total estimated injuries for the year was over 800,000 (Bureau of Product Safety, 1972):

Table 1 Estimated Playground Injuries by Specific Equipment on Public Playgrounds (1971–1972)

Equipment	No. of Injuries	Percent
Swings	121,000	40
Climbing apparatus	88,000	29
Slides	77,000	25
Seesaws	17,000	6
Subtotal	303,000	100
Other equipment	50,000	
Total	353,000	

On July 1, 1972 the NEISS, operated by the U.S. Consumer Product Commission's (CPSC) Bureau of Epidemiology was fully operational with a computer-based network of 119 statistically selected hospital emergency

Table 2 NEISS Sample: Playground Injuries by Specific Equipment Public and Home Playgrounds Combined

Equipment	1971–1972	1972–1973
Swings	2,229— 56%	1,623— 52%
Climbing apparatus	739— 19%	695— 22%
Slides	802— 20%	642— 21%
Seesaws	177— 5%	147— 5%
Subtotal	3,947—100%	3,107—100%
Other equipment	403— 9%	

rooms located throughout the country (U.S. Consumer Product Safety Commission, 1975). From this sample estimates are made of product-related (playground equipment) injuries treated in all hospital emergency rooms in the continental United States. Table 2 compares two years of NEISS data (July 1, 1971 to August 31, 1972 and July 1, 1972 to August 31, 1973) on equipment-related injuries for public and private (home-type) equipment.

The 1974 (January 1 to December 31) NEISS data (CPSC, 1975) was collected for 4,769 playground equipment-associated injuries. The number of combined home and public playground equipment injuries was roughly the same although, as in previous years, they differed by type of equipment.

Table 3 Injuries by Equipment Category (1974)

Equipment	Public	Home
Swings	21%	70%
Climbing apparatus	35%	7%
Slides	28%	13%
Seesaws	6%	5%
Other	10%	5%

The great majority of home playground injuries are associated with swings. This is probably due to three reasons: (1) swing sets are very common in backyards, probably out-ranking all other types of heavy equipment by a large margin, (2) backyard equipment is typically of very flimsy construction being constructed for low-cost, high-volume purchase, and (3) there is much less supervision of home play than play on public equipment (e.g., play at school).

Climbing equipment is most often associated with injuries on public playgrounds. This appears to be related to the frequency of falls from equipment.

The most frequent hazard associated with playground equipment is falls, particularly from slides and climbing apparatus. Three-fourths of all the injuries (reported by NEISS) were falls to the ground (ground or artificial surface such as concrete and asphalt) or onto other equipment. (CPSC, 1975)

This 1974 data is generally consistent with that collected in previous years. In 1972–1973 falling from equipment compared to other factors resulting in injury occurred with a 3:1 frequency. There was little difference in this ratio between public and home equipment. In three-fifths of the cases the injuries occurred on the surface beneath the equipment, 43 percent on bare ground or gravel, 12 percent on concrete or asphalt, and 2½ percent each occurred on sand and "safety turf" surfaces.

In August, 1978 NEISS estimated that during the previous year 167,000 persons were administered hospital emergency room treatment nationwide for injuries associated with public and home

Table 4 Injuries by Body Part

Member	1971–1972	1972–1973	1974
Head, face, neck	51%	48%	46%
Extremities	40%	42%	45%
Arms	64%	70%	
Legs	36%	30%	
Trunk	9%	8%	9%
Other		2%	

playground treatment (CPSC, 1978). These estimated injuries were broken down as follows: swings, 72,000; climbing apparatus, 45,000; slides, 25,000; seesaws and teeter boards, 8,000; unspecified equipment, 17,000. The report points out that of all injuries studied, three-fourths resulted from falls to the ground surface or onto other equipment.

NEISS data on injuries to body parts (Table 4) shows that the head, face, and neck are the most frequently injured body parts, followed by the extremities (arms and legs), and then by the least affected body parts, the trunk.

The 1974 NEISS estimate of 117,951 injuries (estimated from emergency room samples) on playgrounds was broken down into sex, age, and diagnosis categories. Just over half of all persons injured were males. Five percent of the injured cases taken to emergency rooms were admitted to the hospital. Seventy-eight percent of those injured were under ten years of age with more four-year-olds being injured at home than on public equipment. In the 5–9 age group 10 percent more injuries occurred on public equipment, and in the 10–14 age group over twice the number of injuries involved public equipment than home equipment.

Table 5 indicates that lacerations and contusions/abrasions were the predominant diagnoses among the younger children, roughly equalled in frequency by fractures and strains/sprains among the older groups. The least frequent type of injuries, hematomas and concussions, along with hangings (strangulation, broken neck) are the most frequent cause of playground equipment-associated deaths.

Related Studies

The data on playground equipment-associated injuries available during the 1960s from the National Safety Council (working in cooperation with public school systems) and early data from NEISS prompted the Bureau of Engineering Sciences of the Consumer Product Safety Commission to enter a research contract with the Accident Prevention Section, Institute of Agricultural Medicine at the University of Iowa. The portion of that study dealing with standards for the manufacture of public playground equip-

Table 5 Estimated Injuries by Age and Diagnosis (1974), N = 117,951

Diagnosis	Total	Age			
		0–4	5–9	10–14	15+
Total	117,951 (100%)	37,862 (100%)	54,140 (100%)	20,641 (100%)	5,308 (100%)
Lacerations and contusions/abrasions	71,743 (61%)	28,287 (74%)	31,030 (57%)	9,812 (48%)	2,609 (49%)
Fractures and strains/sprains	37,736 (32%)	6,837 (18%)	19,660 (36%)	8,951 (43%)	2,284 (43%)
Hematoma and concussion	3,905 (3%)	1,467 (4%)	1,620 (3%)	693 (3%)	121 (2%)
Other	4,567 (4%)	1,271 (3%)	1,830 (4%)	1,185 (6%)	294 (6%)

ment is discussed later in this chapter. A portion of the Iowa Study was an analysis of injuries in the Iowa City School District over a five-year period (Table 6).

Table 6 Iowa City School District Accidents (Sept., 1968 to June, 1973)

Equipment	Number	Percent
Swings	13	15
Climbing apparatus	54	60
Slides	16	18
Seesaws	6	7
Total	89	100

Comparison of this data with 1974 NEISS data for public playgrounds (Table 3) reveals the same order; that is, climbing apparatus is ranked first in frequency of injury involvement by both studies (although percentages differ), followed by slides, swings, and seesaws, in that order.

The National Recreation and Park Association (1975, 1976) conducted in-depth studies of playground equipment-related injuries in public parks and recreation areas (not including public schools). The results are shown in Table 7.

Table 7 National Recreation and Park Association Location of Accidents

Equipment	Number	Percent
Swings	30	31
Climbing apparatus	33	34
Slides	15	15
Seesaws	20	20
Total	98	100

Note that climbing apparatus is the equipment most often associated with injury but not by the wide margin found in public playground data previously cited. The factor of supervision may account for this shift. Public parks do not commonly have the quality adult supervision provided by public schools. It appears that as supervision decreases (home to park to school), swings become the most hazardous equipment. For the reader wishing to examine accident data for Canadian playgrounds, a number of sources are available (Ministry of Culture and Recreation, 1976; Vancouver Board of Parks and Recreation, not dated; Toronto Board of Education, 1975; Ontario Ministry of Community and Social Services, 1972). The data from these studies are in general agreement with American studies cited in respect to location of playground accidents by equipment type.

Serious Injuries and Deaths

Serious injury is defined by the National Recreation and Park Association (1976b) as:

Any injury in which, based on medical experience, there is a reasonable chance of prolonged disability or physical damage to the injured party. *Some* examples of injuries considered "serious" under this definition would be brain damage, fractures, deep laceration, amputation, impalement, loss of eyesight or hearing and of course any injury leading to death.

Complete records on serious injuries and death are not available, but the NEISS statistical projections and in-depth studies together with related studies of a smaller scale give some insight into the nature of injuries and causes. There is considerable evidence that the most common cause of serious injury and deaths is falls:

The most common causes of playground accidents are falls and bumps and blows. (Ministry of Culture and Recreation, 1976, p. 22)

Data from the National Recreation and Park Association (1975) indicate that falls and moving impact are the major causes of accidents on all types of equipment. This finding is supported by Canadian data. (Haffney, 1974, 1975)

NEISS data for 1971–1972 indicate that falling is the most frequent factor in playground injuries (three-fifths of these cases resulting from falling onto hard ground surfaces and two-fifths from striking equipment on the way down).

In-depth studies by the National Consumer Safety Commission show that the primary hazard pattern (75 percent of all injuries) involves falls from equipment (NCSC, 1975). From July 1973 through October 1974, 24 death certificates were received for injuries related to playground equipment. Fifteen of these injuries occurred at home and nine in public settings. Eleven resulted from falls and eight from hanging. Hanging is the most common cause of deaths on home playground equipment (probably related to poor quality equipment and limited supervision) and falls are the most common cause of death on public playground. This in-depth report goes further to detail horror stories of strangulations, hangings, entrapments, fractures, hematomas, concussions, amputations, and deaths. For example:

The seven-year-old girl who was killed when she fell from a swing onto concrete, fracturing her skull.

The six-year-old boy who fell from a swing and died from a fractured neck.

The two-year-old and the four-year-old girls who strangled in separate accidents when their ponchos caught on a vertical member of a slide railing.

The ten-year-old girl who lost her grip on a horizontal bar and was killed when her head struck the asphalt paving below.

The eight children of varying ages who were hanged by swing ropes or chains.

The child who died as a result of a swing set collapsing.

The nine-year-old girl whose finger was amputated by an exposed moving part of a merry-go-round.

The five-year-old boy who was killed by a blow to the abdomen when he fell from a merry-go-round.

And the list goes on. The irony of such reports is that there are relatively simple measures that could have been taken to prevent most of these injuries and deaths.

There are three major types of hazards related to playground equipment (Mahajan, 1974, p. 2).

1. Hazards attributable to defects in construction and design.
2. Hazards resulting from improper installation and maintenance.
3. Hazards associated with function (resulting from human error).

Perhaps the most crucial factor in working toward a solution to the first type of hazard, construction and design, is the development and implementation of a national safety standard, mandatory for equipment manufacturers. The final section of this chapter details recent steps toward this end and the initial sections of Chapters 4 and 7 illustrate applications of a proposed standard (Appendix A).

It is highly unlikely that a federal standard for installation and maintenance will be developed since enforcement would be virtually impossible. Education of consumers seems to be a more appropriate solution.

Hazards associated with human error represent the most complex of the categories. Both physiological and psychological causes are involved and, in addition, human error is compounded by product defect and with improper installation and maintenance. To illustrate the complexity of these factors, consider the major cause of accidents, falls. First, most victims fall all the way to the ground surface. It is a design defect to fail to install a resilient surface underneath equipment. It is a maintenance error to fail to keep the surface in proper condition (e.g., replenish worn-away sand). But it is a function or use error when the child is pushed by another child, is too weak to hold on, the equipment is slippery from rain, the child perceives the situation incorrectly, or the child misjudges his or her ability.

The responsibility, then, for safety on playgrounds is a shared one involving manufacturers, designers, installers, and supervisors. The major responsibility is a local one. Well-designed equipment is now available and bad equipment will probably always be available so intelligent choices must be made. Installation and maintenance are local decisions and, increasingly, skillful assistance can be found. Proper use of play environments begins with education of adults who are in charge of playground activity.

THE TRADITIONAL PLAYGROUND

Let us examine in detail some of the most common problems on traditional American playgrounds. First of all, schools may provide adequate space and equipment for important, organized athletic activities such as basketball and baseball for older children (elementary through high school), but they provide the usual concrete/steel jungle for younger, elementary school children (ages 3–8). The equipment for the elementary school usually consists of swings, slide, jungle gym (monkey bars), seesaws, and a merry-go-round. The popularity rankings of playground equipment in order of most to least likely to exist on the preprimary/primary playgrounds of one state (Texas) as reported by Vernon (1976) are: monkey bars (existing on 80 percent of playgrounds), swings (58 percent), slides (51 percent), seesaws (44 percent), and merry-go-rounds (40 percent). Materials that are adaptable for creative purposes are virtually nonexistent; for example, wood-working materials are available on only 6 percent of Texas's

preprimary/primary playgrounds, water play materials (6 percent), sand boxes (21 percent), play houses (9 percent), climbing ropes and nets (11 percent), and movable equipment such as barrels (6 percent). Typical examples of the principals' views about their playgrounds (Vernon, 1976, p. 9) are:

Need more outdoor gym equipment, merry-go-rounds, tunnels, slides, swings and see-saws.

We prefer the outside learning area with very little equipment. A good teacher and a clean area will and can develop children.

Many of the fun-type items—tunnels, sandpiles, construction activities—do not meet with acceptance of maintenance departments; therefore they are not included in the standard lists. P.T.A. members and parents want these type items, but no one is available when maintenance and daily care are concerned (sic).

There is nothing inherently evil or hazardous about monkey bars, seesaws, and the other common manufactured paraphernalia, and perhaps no one, least of all the authors, desires a playscape so sterile that there is no risk, no daring, no extending, and no chance for injuries. On the other hand, we do not believe that playgrounds should be deliberately designed which cripple, maim, and kill children. We will examine some of the problems associated with the most common equipment.

Climbing Equipment

Climbing equipment (monkey bars, and so on) can be constructed from wood or metal. Wood, splinters and all, has certain advantages over metal. It is not as hot to bare skin (Southern climates) and it is softer. The problem of splinters can be reduced, almost eliminated, by selecting high quality hardwoods and refinishing frequently with a high grade exterior filler and/or enamel. Monkey bars, like all other common equipment, are available in various sizes. One of

Climbing equipment is frequently mismatched to the size of children, too tall for safe use, or improperly installed. In these pictures concrete footings are exposed or the entire area underneath the equipment is paved with asphalt.

The usual school playground slide is tall and narrow with little protection from falling off the side.

the most obvious, yet often overlooked, preventive measures in accident prevention is matching the size of equipment to the physical size and abilities of children who will use that equipment.

Exposed, protruding bolts are common on almost all commercial metal equipment. Some efforts have been made to install smooth protective caps over bolts, but these are generally poorly secured and falls have resulted from the caps pulling loose in the grasp of children. Another and more promising approach is to countersink or indent for protruding bolts. Sharp, jagged edges and protruding ends of pipes often trap children's clothing or cause cuts and bruises. But the most serious criticism of monkey bars is the existence of a steel bar jungle waiting to catch the child who falls from the top. For existing equipment we recommend building alternating wooden platforms from bottom to top so that the child cannot fall over three feet from any point on the equipment. An additional advantage to this is that then the monkey bars will have dramatic play functions (house play,

etc.) also. If you do not presently have a jungle gym, invest your money more wisely in a geodesic dome or arch climber.

Slides

The usual school playground-type slide is tall (up to 16 feet high), and narrow (less than 2 feet wide) with almost no protection from falling off the side (most accidents occur here). There is no safety platform for the critical "transition zone" from the ladder to the slide so the younger child, growing in coordination, performs a delicate balancing act as she attempts to swing her legs and torso from the rear (ladder) to the front (slide). At this point the slightest push can mean a fall to the ground or equipment below. A number of newer types of slides are now available that incorporate alternate access and exit routes; wide, fenced areas in critical height zones; and platforms for movement from ladder to slide. These are available in varying heights and sizes.

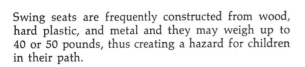

Swing seats are frequently constructed from wood, hard plastic, and metal and they may weigh up to 40 or 50 pounds, thus creating a hazard for children in their path.

Swings

Swings and swinging apparatus are involved by various surveys in about 25 percent of the injuries on playgrounds. Being hit by a swing seat is perhaps the most common hazard. Despite the ease of eliminating this problem by replacing wooden and heavy seats with canvas or rubber belts, an analysis of company catalogues (Butwinick, 1974) showed that swing seats are constructed from rubber, canvas, polyethylene, wood, aluminum, and other metals and they weigh from two to 56 pounds. Two situations account for most of the swing seat-related accidents. The child falls from the swing and is hit on the head by the return sweep of the seat and the child runs or walks into the path of a moving swing. These accidents are particularly frequent for younger children who have not yet developed sufficient cause-effect thinking required to anticipate hazardous events. The swing is out of sight in the other direction so the temporarily unoccupied space may be considered safe by the prelogical thinker. A survey of accidents in an urban and a suburban system (Butwinick, 1974) found that 22 percent of the equipment injuries in the urban system that used wooden seats occurred on swings, but, in the suburban system, which used only canvas belt-type seats, only 9 percent occurred on swings.

The rigid swing seat, unlike the canvas or rubber belt, encourages standing in the swing thus increasing the likelihood of falling or hitting an adjacent swing or vertical equipment leg. Swings are typically set too close together, often as close as 12 to 17 inches, making it difficult to swing without collisions. Seat heights range from just above the ground to three or more feet high, rarely being fitted to the sizes of the children.

The most common cause of serious injuries or deaths related to swings is falling onto hard surfaces.

Combination swing-slide sets are common in backyards. They are usually quite flimsy, made of the cheapest material with every possible space loaded with exercise apparatus—slide, swings, glider, chinning bars, etc. Such equipment is often overloaded. It may be poorly installed, often secured to the ground by driving a heavy wire through a hole in the bottom of each leg into the ground. Constant motion may loosen this in a short time. Further, using improper tools to erect the set may result in its being placed into use in a loose, movable state, thus increasing the risk of structural collapse. The S hooks on this equipment often pinch fingers and hands and the small, flimsy chains do not provide a proper grip for holding on. Within a relatively short time the swivels supporting swing chains at the cross-bar tend to wear out, allowing the seat (and child) to fall to the ground. It is particularly important that all

Swivels supporting swings tend to wear very quickly and should be inspected regularly.

Many merry-go-rounds now in use are of antiquated design. Children can run inside the structure, bolts protrude, and axles are sufficiently worn to allow amputation of fingers.

moving equipment or moving parts be inspected regularly for wear.

Merry-Go-Rounds

Many people question whether merry-go-rounds should be used at all. They have a reputation for being hazardous and for having limited play function. Available accident data do not support the contention that they are among the most hazardous playground fixtures, but they are more limited in play function than some other types of equipment. The injury rate on merry-go-rounds could be reduced by wise selection, proper installation, built-in speed controllers, and some degree of supervision. Many existing

merry-go-rounds are indeed demons. Many have open spaces in the platform large enough for children to fall through, weak axles that bend, foundations that give way to the extent that arms and legs can be trapped underneath, and protruding bolts that can increase the severity of injury.

Butwinick's (1974) survey of an urban school system of 80,000 elementary school pupils over a 10-month period noted 21 accidents associated with merry-go-rounds. Five of these were caused by the equipment being too close to the ground, allowing feet to be caught underneath. Still other merry-go-rounds have exposed moving parts at the spindle-axle connection that invite intrusion. This can and does

The areas around merry-go-rounds are frequently catch basins for water and mud, or they may be paved with concrete, creating a hazard for children who fall from the structure.

cut off fingers. The manufacture of some is so shoddy that railings break off after limited use, exposing jagged edges and eliminating the protection of hand-holds.

Seesaws

The seesaw is functionally narrow as a vehicle for play. The child can go up, down, or fall off—that's all. No dramatic play is involved, no constructive play is involved, the child's thinking is minimally enhanced, no impact on the equipment is made—nothing is created. The same is true for a wide range of springy equipment given such names as "jumpy horse," "buckybout," "kangaroo hop," "bucky bronco," and "poppy porpoise." They consist of a spring base with a plastic animal body for the child to sit on. The primary play function is jumping up and down. They stand idle on well-equipped playgrounds where interesting choices are available, and they represent a questionable investment of money.

Ground Cover

Among all the variables contributing to playground hazards, ground cover is number one.

And, ironically, ground cover is among the easiest variables to manipulate or change. Beginning with the design of a new school, park, or home site, particularly school sites, the prevailing line of reasoning can best be described as "bulldozer mentality." From design through construction to finished plant, everyone seems bent on destroying every blade of grass, every tree, every natural feature of the terrain in a

Seesaws installed too close together allow children to collide. Improper selection for size of children is also a critical factor on many playgrounds.

Adult creations such as concrete or plastic animals capture little attention from children and serve extremely limited play functions. Similarly, "jumpy horses" and "springy pelicans" are of little value on the playground.

seemingly insatiable urge to scrape everything into a sterile, smooth moonlike surface, devoid of all life.

As soon as the natural terrain is destroyed the "concrete mentality" takes over. Someone remembers that a school is being built and that children attend schools. So vast areas are covered with asphalt and/or concrete and marked off into ball courts. Virtually no maintenance will be required and children can do what they are supposed to do—build strong healthy bodies and provide good material for the high school athletic teams. At most (not all) schools for young children, conscience prevails and com-

(Courtesy Columbia Cascade Timber Company)

Among all the variables contributing to playground hazards, ground cover is number one. Many inner city play areas are paved before the site is selected. Rubber mats provide some degree of protection for falls from equipment. Other sites are sandy to begin with but concrete foundations are exposed by wear and erosion.

mercial equipment is purchased and installed. Again the most troublefree surface is concrete and asphalt, so the equipment is either installed on an out-of-the-way chunk of the existing slab or separate, smaller slabs are poured under and around each piece of equipment. However, there are options. When the budget is extremely limited or when hard surfaces must be reserved for "sports," playthings for young children are simply stuck into postholes in the ground and secured by concrete.

Children and the rains arrive, cutting

ditches, washing and wearing away top soil, exposing rocks and concrete foundations around the equipment and adjacent sidewalks and destroying half-hearted efforts at seeding (rarely sodding) the remaining clay and rock cover. The hot sun beats down in summer and the teachers and children retreat to the shade of the building or into a nearby park, escaping the searing hot metal of slides and monkey bars and the reflected heat rays of concrete, asphalt, and barren ground.

Eventually the PTA comes to the rescue, a beautification project is initiated, trees are planted, a small plot is set aside for gardening, several truckloads of top soil are hauled back in to cover the most eroded areas and to provide new concerns for the custodian when it turns to mud. Some school personnel (principals and teachers) seem oblivious to the entire scene (Vernon, 1976):

We have scheduled time in our activity building with our P.E. aides for grades 1–5 and don't need outdoor space.

With half-day programs I do not feel the children are being denied a total education because of no outside equipment and space.

Need asphalt under all equipment to improve maintenance.

Would like games painted on concrete.

Need more sequential skills leading to soccer, baseball, etc. (games to develop each specific skill).

We use the city parks playground.

But many teachers are alert to the play needs of children as illustrated by their comments from Vernon's study.

Many materials and equipment are needed for pre-primary—tricycles, wagons, etc. We have nothing.

Have only a patio with three tree stumps for practicing nailing with hammer. We need outdoor play equipment and space badly.

I feel that teachers and parents should have an important part in planning outdoor equipment and play areas, instead of someone in the administration who does not know what children need for proper development.

I would like a fenced in area close to my portable building. I would like the space to have grass, sand and a planting area. I would want the children to be responsible for keeping their own area clean and neat.

Throughout this entire saga, replayed over and over again in American schools, few seem to question the *method*. Play, perhaps the most important avenue for learning in early childhood, is given only marginal attention in the design and construction of school plants. The exceptions, of course, are two of the several important forms of play—namely exercise and games with rules. And even in planning for these forms, the errors are shameful—given minimal understanding of play development and playground construction.

It is both simple and smart to retain the natural, wooded terrain in areas surrounding proposed schools. It is quite another matter to replace it once it has been destroyed.

Similarly, it is simple and smart to provide a resilient surface under all climbing and moving equipment on the playground. In April 1973 a seven-year-old girl was tragically killed on a public school playground in Ogden, Utah when she fell from climbing bars onto the hard surface below. Consequently, two months later the Ogden School District purchased 10,560 square feet of one-inch thick rubber matting at a cost of $17,000 (cost in 1978 would be $31,680 for material alone) for installation under potentially hazardous equipment.

National standards presently under development (Appendix A) will undoubtedly call for the provision of certain types of resilient surfaces under and around climbing and moving equipment, but the most appropriate types from both economic and safety perspectives have as yet to be determined. Engineering Consultants of La Mirada, California conducted a study, "Dynamic Impact Tests on Three Types Protective Cushioning Mats, Vinyl, Rubber and UNIMAT," and determined that their ranges of satisfactory protection for falls from heights were respectively, 4 feet, 5 feet, and 11 feet. Limited as this seems, the protection afforded can save lives and reduce serious injuries.

In 1951 the Los Angeles school system had the last of 11 playground deaths reported in a 20-year period with the fall of a 6-year-old boy from a swing onto an asphalt surface. In 1955 the system installed rubber surfacing under its playground equipment. No further deaths were reported during the entire next decade (Underwriters Report, October 7, 1965, p. 25) and the incidence of fractures and concussions was reduced from 1.25 per school in 1951 to 0.47 in 1965 (Safety, May–June 1966, pp. 8–11).

The high cost of commercial matting and the merits of such materials as compared to such inexpensive materials as sand and tanbark presently tip the scales in favor of the more inexpensive route. A commonly overlooked factor in the installation of commercial matting is that it requires an expensive smooth, hard base such as asphalt or concrete for the more expensive mat. Through the use of community volunteers it is possible to develop a complete creative playground, using inexpensive materials, at less cost than that required for surfacing alone (base and resilient matting) on the all-commercial playground.

Creative Play Materials

The reader will recall that Vernon's (1976) study of Texas's preprimary/primary public school playgrounds showed that only a very small percentage made provisions for the more creative types of play—dramatic (role playing, make-believe, etc.) and constructive. Sand play,

water play, wheeled vehicle play, house play, and play with movable equipment (barrels, crates, rope nets, tires, etc.) were relegated to a minor role indeed. As the reader will see throughout this book, such restriction of play opportunity is perhaps the greatest single error in playground design and use. Play is fun time and exercise time, but it is also learning time. Time for learning about the roles of adults in society, time for learning social skills, how to get along with self and others, and time for learning complex cognitive skills of discriminating, classifying, numeration, conservation, cause-effect relationships, space and time relations, and time for sharpening one's language abilities. For these learnings, children need play materials that are flexible and adaptable, materials that they can make an impact on, materials that are open to creative actions.

Creative materials are everywhere, in the cast-off junk of homes, schools, and industries, in the natural terrain of undeveloped woodlands, and even in the five and dime stores of every shopping center. They need not be expensive and they need not be unduly hazardous.

Given the paucity of creative materials on playgrounds, survey accounts of injuries while using them are obviously skewed, yet it is of interest to note their frequency. In Vernon's (1976) study, 68 percent of the teachers never allowed their children to engage in water play, one-half never provided for sand play, one-fourth never provided for dramatic play, and one-half never provided for construction play. Vernon found that 93 percent of all playground accidents were related to climbing apparatus, swings, slides, seesaws, and merry-go-rounds while all other categories, including play with creative materials, accounted for only 7 percent of injuries. National statistics by the United States Department of Health, Education and Welfare (1972) supports these findings. In 824,000 estimated playground equipment injuries requiring medical treatment per year for the entire nation, climbing apparatus, seesaws, slides, and swings account for 88 percent (not including merry-go-rounds) of all injuries while all other equipment accounts for only 12 percent.

Supervision and Maintenance

In the relatively small number of injuries in other categories, most appear to be caused by errors of maintenance rather than to defects in equipment. For example, most documented sandbox injuries are caused by objects (such as broken glass) in the sand. Broken tricycle parts, other wheeled vehicle parts, protruding slivers of wood in stacking materials, and misuse of equipment are also cited in accident reports.

Misuse of equipment is related to the natural tendencies of children to extend themselves, to be daring, to show off, to engage in rough housing. Butwinick's (1974) survey found that 21 percent of accidents are caused by such factors as fighting, pushing, inattention, blind running, and foreseeable misuse. All of these factors are at least indirectly tied to the nature of supervision available for the playground. The U.S. Consumer Product Safety Commission (1975) noted that in-depth investigations of 54 playground injuries and deaths showed that an adult was present in only 4 cases. In 38 cases the victim was with 1 or more children and in 12 cases the child was alone when the injury occurred. It would appear that the presence of adults is a very relevant factor in the safety of children on playgrounds.

But how far should adult supervision go? Where is the dividing line between free, creative, meaningful play and overstructured routine? The authors believe that risk taking is an essential ingredient of creative play, absolutely essential for growth of self-assurance and personal power to do and control. Risk taking, daring to do and be, can and should take place in a rich

context of alternatives after the obviously taboo ones are omitted. The way in which the taboo alternatives are reduced or eliminated is quite important. A simple rule, "We will not chase a ball into the street," might be appropriate enough for a twelve-year-old but completely inadequate for a group of four-year-olds playing on an unfenced playground adjacent to a busy street. The removal of this particular alternative, running into the street, is ensured by constructing a fence. Four-year-olds do not live by rules alone, but they are learning to adjust to a system of social and cultural codes.

All too frequently adults expect rules to make up for poorly designed equipment, improper installation, poor maintenance, improperly sized equipment, sterile equipment. Consider the "Student Behavior Guidelines" developed by a group of preprimary/primary teachers (four- to eight-year-olds) to be applied on their playground. Reflect on the apparent condition of the playground and the scope of equipment. In these guidelines both the rule and the punishment option(s), coded by number, are noted.

1. No fighting, pinching and hitting.
   Example-Discipline Option 6: If a child fights at recess, he may lose the privilege of going outside.

2. No throwing rocks or other dangerous items.
   Example-Discipline Option 9: If sticks or rocks are thrown toward other children, spanking may be immediately administered.

3. The misuse, abuse and/or destruction of outside play equipment will not be allowed.
   Example-Discipline Option 6: If riding toys are run into the fence, the student will not be allowed to use them.

4. Students may climb only on playground equipment.
   Discipline Options 3–8.

5. *Swings*-Only one child on a swing. Child must sit down. Child will swing in a straight line.

Many injuries are the result of failure to maintain equipment. Broken or missing equipment seats are one common problem. Broken parts can also reduce the play function of equipment.

6. *Slide*-Child must use ladder to climb up. Only one child on slide and one on ladder. Child must sit down facing forward. No dirt, rocks, etc., may be placed on slide.

7. *Dome* (not present on playground)-Children are not to hang by their knees. Children are not to play inside dome. As soon as the child drops to the ground he must climb out. Children are not allowed to pull on those who are hanging.

8. *Walking bridge* (not present on playground)-Children may walk on the top while holding on. Only one child on the bridge at a time. Form one line while waiting to use the bridge.

9. *Vehicles* (not present on playground)-Bus: Four children may ride and two may push. Boat: Two children may ride and two may push. Wagons: One child may ride and one may pull. Tricycles: One child may ride at a time.

Discipline Options 1–11 for rules 5–9.

Thus, rigid rules and patterns of discipline are unsuccessfully substituted for the creation and maintenance of a creative playground. Imagine the sterility of child play resulting from such impossible rules—a group of little robot-zombies standing in line to engage in a brief mechanical activity, total absence of physical contact, fearful to extend themselves lest the wrath of discipline rules one through nine be exacted. What complete and callous disrespect such rules betray for the powers of children to assist in responsible decision making and acting when treated with respect and skill by adults.

PROCEEDINGS FOR THE DEVELOPMENT OF STANDARDS FOR PLAYGROUND EQUIPMENT

On September 13, 1972 the United States Food and Drug Administration's (FDA) Bureau of Product Safety (BPS) issued a report, *Public Playground Equipment* (B.P.S., 1972) that was

to set in motion a complex series of events aimed toward the eventual establishment of mandatory standards for playground equipment. The FDA report used as its major source statistics on playground injuries reported through the National Electronic Surveillance System between July 1, 1971 and August 31, 1972. This report, stimulated by the interest of various public, industry, professional and trade associations and individuals, revealed a not-so-rosy picture of playground hazards and resulting injuries in the United States. Playground equipment ranks eighth on the Consumer Product Hazard list.

The involvement of the Consumer Product Safety Commission was initiated at about the time of the FDA's 1972 report when they supported an original request of the Food and Drug Administration that the University of Iowa (McConnell, et al., 1973) undertake a study of safety problems surrounding public playground equipment. The Iowa Study, issued in October 1973, revealed that an abortive attempt was made by the Committee on Accident Prevention of the American Academy of Pediatrics (1969) in 1969 to develop equipment design standards. The apparent intent of this document was to provide a set of standards for voluntary adoption by industry. True to tradition, however, the standards were not adopted, no legislation was passed (or proposed), and the effort stalled with the initial draft. The standards, though brief, dealt with children's outdoor home playground equipment including swinging, revolving, rotating, seesaw, climbing, sliding, and related equipment. Specific sections made recommendations for design, testing, durability, assembly, installation, and special safety features. The Academy's effort was abandoned in 1971.

The Iowa Study was relatively thorough. Data were collected on injuries from the National Safety Council, NEISS, and numerous in-depth investigations available from the Consumer Product Safety Commission. Their search for existing standards for playground equipment which brought to light the American Academy of Pediatrics Standards also revealed that neither the National Association of Children's Home Playground Manufacturers nor manufacturers of public playground equipment had a basic standard.

The Iowa Study is important for its recovery and analysis of accident/injury data, but the study also delved into the critical area of child development in respect to play, specifically in the areas of child behaviors contributing to accidents (misuse of equipment) and anthropometric data (physical size relationships between children and equipment). The recommendations of the report influenced efforts on several fronts. For example, subsequent reports and proposed standards dealt with the critical factor of ground cover, the single most common element in injuries and deaths on playgrounds. Playground surfaces must eventually and inevitably be energy absorbing. Studies to determine standards for energy-absorbing surfaces were begun as were studies on anthropometric data and strength of children at the University of Michigan.

During the same period of the Iowa Study, the Playground Equipment Manufacturer's Association, a section of the National School Supply and Equipment Association, was developing a set of proposed standards. Working in conjunction with a safety task force of the National Recreation and Park Association, they produced a draft, *Proposed Technical Requirements for Heavy Duty Playground Equipment Regulations* (Consumer Product Safety Commission, 1973), intended to be used by industry as a *voluntary* standard.

Criticism was directed toward the work of this group by one of its members, Elayne Butwinick (1974, p. 10). In a petition to the Consumer Product Safety Commission in April 1974 she said, "I find the standards are being drawn up by industry with only token input by other members. The Task Force has only met twice ... At the October (1973) meeting the standards were not discussed directly, and at a later industry meeting they were, only one member who was not from industry (from about 15 non-industry members) was present."

Beginning in 1974 and continuing in their 1976 catalogue, the voluntary standards (with modifications) were used by one company, Game Time by Toro. On page 3 of their 1976 catalogue is the statement:

For the past two years and for the coming year, Game Time playground products have been tested by an independent testing and engineering laboratory to certify that each complies with the proposed industry safety standards developed for recreational equipment for use in public parks and playgrounds.

Game Time deserves commendation for its effort to upgrade the design and manufacture of playground equipment. True to American industry's marketing ingenuity, however, is the obvious advertising appeal of placing the essence of the above quote in bold, stand-out type on almost every double-page spread of the playground equipment section of the catalogue. A much-needed service *is* included in recommending that "safety surface be placed around base (of equipment) to cushion accidental falls."

Despite the voluntary status and limited nature of the voluntary standards, the continuing work toward the establishment of *mandatory* standards appears to be stimulating additional manufacturers to adopt voluntary regulations. Miracle/Jamison's equipment is "safety-certified to meet or surpass Proposed Industry Safety Standards." Their standards are printed in their catalogue:

• No wood board swing seats; all safety strap seats.
• No high slides without safety canopies at the top.
• No climbers designed with metal under metal. All climbers are "fall free" design. (On this point Miracle takes a step ahead of other manufacturers.)

- No dangerous protrusions, sharp edges, flimsy ladders, open "S" hooks or guard rails.
- No platform equipment more than four feet high without guard rails.

Meager as they are, such standards represent an important step in the movement to make playgrounds safer places while enhancing their play value. Manufacturers are beginning to assume greater responsibility toward these ends as will be illustrated in Chapter 7.

A great deal of additional work remains to be done before the United States has a comprehensive, feasible set of standards. The Consumer Product Safety Commission (1974, pp. 9–10) cited a long list of inadequacies of the voluntary standard being applied by at least one company including the following examples:

1. Nebulous terms such as "adequate" and "accessible" are used without specific explanatory criteria.
2. More detailed testing methods for structural integrity, durability and resistance to deterioration are needed.
3. A wider use of performance tests is needed to determine whether specified standards have been met.
4. Certain specifications may create or perpetuate hazards. For example, the allowable bolt protrusion length.
5. Certain standards may discourage the use of new advances. For example the exclusive requirement of "welded" links for suspension chains.
6. Additional specifications are needed in some instances. For example, the matter of swing chair lengths and swing weights.

In April 1974 the Consumer Product Safety Commission received two petitions for actions leading to mandatory guidelines. Butwinick (1974) petitioned to commence the development of standards for both playground equipment and playground surfaces under the Consumer Product Safety Act. This petition was later endorsed by the Americans for Democratic Action and Consumers Union. The Commissioners of the CPSC granted the Butwinick petition "in substance" on June 20, 1974. The second petition, submitted by Theodora Sweeney (1974), chairperson of an ad hoc playground committee of Coventry School PTA in Cleveland Heights, Ohio was used by the commissioners in support of the Butwinick petition and was not considered as a separate petition.

Later in 1974 it was learned that the Federal Hazardous Substance Act rather than the Consumer Product Safety Act is the appropriate legal mechanism for regulating playground equipment. The CSPC Commission developed a Federal Register notice calling for offers to develop a standard that will cover both home and public playground equipment. The National Recreation and Parks Association was the only bidder. They formed a committee of citizens and representatives from industry and formulated a draft, *Proposed Safety Standard for Public Playground Equipment*. A summary of this document is found in Appendix A.

SUMMARY

The playgrounds of America are found in private and public schools, public parks and recreation areas, apartment complexes and backyards of private homes. With few exceptions they are poorly planned, hazardous, unattractive, and inappropriate to the broad developmental needs of children. The typical playground contains one or more slides, jungle gyms, seesaws, swings, and a merry-go-round.

Conservative estimates indicate that about 1,000,000 children are injured on public and private playgrounds each year. Incomplete data by the Consumer Products Safety Commission reveals that 118,000 children received treatment in emergency rooms from playground injuries in 1974. The most common causes of serious injuries and deaths are falls onto hard surfaces and striking stationary or moving parts of equipment.

There are no mandatory standards for the manufacture of playground equipment. Designs are frequently unsafe, out of character with children's developmental needs, and installation is often faulty. The present efforts to develop standards for manufacturers are bogged down in bureaucracy; feedback available from the early proceedings indicates that efforts were dominated by representatives of the manufacturing industry. Some manufacturers are placing their companies under voluntary standards and, very recently, a few designers with expertise in child development have entered the business of developing and marketing play equipment. These points will be elaborated in Chapter 7.

REFERENCES

Bureau of Product Safety. *Public Playground Equipment.* Washington, D.C.: Food and Drug Administration, September 13, 1972.

Butwinick, E. Petition Requesting the Issuance of a Consumer Product Safety Standard for Public Playground Slides, Swinging Apparatus and Climbing Equipment. Washington, D.C.: United States Consumer Product Safety Commission, 1974.

Committee of Accident Prevention of the American Academy of Pediatrics. *Proposed Voluntary Standard for Children's Home Playground Equipment.* Evanston, Illinois: American Academy of Pediatrics, 1969.

Consumer Product Safety Commission. *Hazard Analysis: Playground Equipment.* Washington, D.C.: Bureau of Epidemiology, April 1975.

———. *Proposed Technical Requirements for Heavy Duty Playground Equipment Regulations.* Washington, D.C.: The Commission, November 14, 1973.

———. "Public Playground Equipment Proceedings to Develop Safety-Related Requirements Under the Federal Hazardous Substances Act." Washington, D.C.: The Commission, 1974.

———. "Special Summer Safety Issue." *CPSC Memo.* July/August, 1978.

Haffey, H. "Causes of Injury—1973." Report prepared for Toronto Hospital for Sick Children, Toronto, 1974.

———. "Causes of Injury—1974." Report prepared for Toronto Hospital for Sick Children, Toronto, 1975.

Mahajan, B. J. "Recommendations for a Safety Standard for Home Playground Equipment—Swing Sets." *Interim Report NBSIP 74-563.* Bethesda, Maryland: Consumer Product Safety Commission, United States Bureau of Standards, 1974.

McConnell, W. H., J. T. Parks, and L. W. Knapp, Jr. *Public Playgrounds Equipment.* Iowa City: College of Medicine, October 15, 1973.

National Recreation and Park Association. "Summary of In-Depth Accident Studies Received from 1-9-74 to 6-17-75." Arlington, Virginia: National Recreation and Park Association, 1975.

———. "Background and Rationale for Proposed Public Playground Equipment Safety Standards." Prepared for the Consumer Product Safety Commission. Arlington, Virginia: National Recreation and Park Association, 1976a.

National Recreation and Park Association. "Proposed Safety Standard for Public Playground Equipment." Developed for the Consumer Product Safety Commission. Arlington, Virginia: National Recreation and Park Association, 1976b.

Ontario Ministry of Community and Social Services. "Case studies." In *Creative Play Resources Bank.* Toronto: Youth and Recreation Branch, Ontario Ministry of Community and Social Services, 1972.

Sweeney, T. "Petition to the Consumer Products Safety Commission." Cleveland Heights, Ohio: Coventry School PTA, May 1974.

Toronto Board of Education. "Report to the Chairman and Members of the Community Programs Committee. Toronto: Office of the Director of Education, 1975.

United States Department of Health, Education and Welfare. "Staff Analysis of Playground Equipment Injuries." Washington, D.C.: Bureau of Product Safety, March 22, 1972.

Vancouver Board of Parks and Recreation. "A Comprehensive Listing of Accidents Occurring at Community Centres and Playgrounds in Vancouver during 1970, 1971 and 1972." Vancouver: Board of Parks and Recreation, not dated.

Vernon, E. A. A Survey of Preprimary and Primary Outdoor Learning Centers/Playgrounds in Texas Public Schools. Unpublished doctoral dissertation. Austin: The University of Texas, 1976.

4

FUNDAMENTALS OF PLAYGROUND DEVELOPMENT AND SUPERVISION

"Too much money and uninformed thought is often spent on fixed play apparatus. It must not be forgotten that this is only furniture and no matter how ingenious it may be, it alone does not make a playground."

Arvid Bengtsson*

Changing patterns of American families, particularly increasing proportions of one-parent families and working mothers, are gradually leading to shared, community responsibility for children. There is no single, simple pattern for child care, no single form of schooling, and no simple solution to providing for the play needs of children. Families, family-care centers, day care-centers, public and private schools,

churches, and community parks and recreation agencies share the responsibility. All of these groups, sometimes working together but usually working alone, construct playgrounds. But whether the concern is for the development of a backyard playground for two or three children, a public school playground for children in early childhood education, a private nursery school playground for infants and toddlers or a public park playground for all age groups, toddlers through old age, attention to certain needs is, in most cases, fundamental. These needs are selecting and preparing the site, selecting

---

*Arvid Bengtsson. *The Child's Right to Play.* Sheffield, England: International Playground Association, 1974, p. 88.

No effort should be spared to preserve the natural features of a play space. Only underbrush and poisonous plants should be cleared. *Below*—Rich top soil is hauled in and spread in open spaces that will become grassy areas for organized games.

permanent equipment, zoning the playground, and safety, maintenance, and supervision.

SELECTING AND PREPARING THE SITE

Not so many years ago American children grew up in a relatively uncomplicated, uncrowded environment, largely rural, with ready access to natural terrain—woodlands, creeks, wild animals, hills, rocks, grass—and an extended family of adults who encouraged movement,

exploration, and responsible work roles. It was easy to play for healthy children need only opportunity and interesting objects. Play is as natural for children as flying is for birds. And nature extends beyond the play motive of children to their play objects. It is quite a challenge for modern adults to equal the natural playscapes and the more natural human relationships that existed for children during the colonial period. Today's adults must compete with television, traffic, concrete, limited space, bureaucracies, playground tradition, and the bulldozer mentality (described in Chapter 2) afflicting many administrators, planners, and builders.

To get right to the point, the primary, and in the long run most economical criterion for the provision of a creative playscape is to retain the original natural features of the site. From the initial conception of a building or area that will accommodate children, no effort should be spared to prevent the destruction of hilly terrain, trees, grass, top soil, and streams. Fortunately more and more people are becoming conscious of the need but far too few are doing anything about it. Parents and teachers must apply pressure on groups such as school boards to guard against the wanton practice of demolishing many acres of natural terrain for each relatively small school building. This can be done through organizations such as Parent Teacher Associations. Win this battle and the playground is well under way. Except for space for the buildings and organized games, the rule is firm—not an unnecessary tree, not a yard of top soil is to be moved. The appropriate clearing of underbrush (such as poisonous plants) can be done carefully and by plan after the builders have completed their work. Local environmentalists (garden clubs, science centers) are usually eager to assist in proper preservation and development of such sites. Children themselves can and should be deeply involved in such activities. After all, it is their site too.

Unfortunately, most playground development projects get underway long after the site has been cleared and considerable additional expense and effort is required to make the playground a creative place for children. Several factors enter into planning, not necessarily in the order to be discussed.

Space

There is no simple rule of thumb for determining the optimum space for a playground.

Mounds of earth increase the effective use area of the play space and add challenge and interest to play activities.

Such factors as numbers of children, type of soil, type and number of natural features (e.g., trees and streams), and types of structures available tend to influence the user/space ratio. It is not realistic to assume that a playyard that will accommodate thirty children at one time will do so repeatedly for group after group throughout the day. If grassy areas are desired, there can only be so many small feet per time unit. Some soils support grass better than others and some grasses are more resistant to traffic than others. Further, in extremely limited spaces multiple-platform climbing structures and dirt mounds effectively increase play area per child without increasing yard area. A very general approximation is that some areas of grass can be retained and appropriate equipment can be provided for four- to eight-year-old children on spaces of 50 to 100 square feet for each actual child user per day. This means that a playyard of 5,000 to 10,000 square feet would accommodate 100 to 300 children using the area in groups of 20–60 for thirty minutes to one hour each day. Obviously, infants and toddlers require

Grass is a highly desirable ground cover for most areas except fall zones under equipment. It must be tended regularly.

considerably less space and 8- to 12-year-olds require much more space for organized games such as baseball, tennis, and basketball.

We have seen very good playyards with extremely limited space and should point out that clever design and use patterns can compensate for limited space. This is particularly important in cities where space is scarce and expensive.

Ground Cover

The most desirable ground cover for the open spaces on a playground is grass. It is highly desirable for organized games. In selecting or organizing the site one of the initial tasks is to select a relatively level area for this purpose. In most contexts this portion of the playground requires least supervision and can be located in an area farthest from the building. If grass is already present the required care may be simply periodic watering and fertilizing. The grassy area requires the same tender loving care that well-to-do suburbanites give to their lawns. In most parts of the country a thorough soaking every Friday afternoon during dry periods will provide the needed moisture and will allow time

for sufficient drying before children arrive on Monday. Fertilizer should be applied according to the recommendations of experts (nursery operators, etc.) in the locale. Generally three to four applications each year are appropriate. Application at the beginning of holiday periods followed by soakings with water will allow the fertilizer to dissipate into the ground before children begin using the area.

If the area must be seeded or sodded, a thick bed (8–12 inches) of rich top soil should be spread evenly over the area to encourage future dense growth. The area must be declared off limits or fenced until heavy growth has begun. While equipment and labor are available for preparing the top soil, it is wise to inquire about the installation of a sprinkler system for the area. This greatly reduces the work and cost of caring for the grass in future years.

The type of grass to be used varies from region to region but the best all around variety (cost, appearance, durability, disease resistance) is usually the most common type found on lawns in the local area, generally some type of Bermuda or St. Augustine. Seeding may be done if time is not an important factor. Strip sodding, like seeding, is relatively inexpensive

(Gullett School, Austin, Texas)

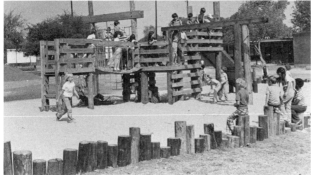

Sand is inexpensive and provides a reasonable degree of protection when children fall from equipment. It must be bordered by a retaining wall to prevent scattering. Utility poles, railroad ties, and natural stone make excellent retaining walls.

but requires a full growing season to form a solid blanket. Blanket sodding is more expensive but it is the most rapid way to secure a complete ground cover. In addition, blanket sodding of the entire area in question prevents erosion under usual conditions and limited use of the area can begin in three or four weeks.

It will not be possible or desirable to retain grass on certain areas. All areas within the fall zone (five to six feet) of moving and climbing equipment must be covered with a highly resilient material such as sand, tanbark, or small pebble gravel. We have found common concrete sand to be best for this purpose. It is inexpensive and provides a reasonable degree of protection when children fall from equipment. Since

such material tends to scatter easily, retaining walls must be provided. These can be formed with railroad ties or telephone poles placed horizontally or vertically into the ground and projecting above ground according to a variety of designs to be described later. If sand is used it should be 8 to 12 inches deep and periodically re-spread to ensure coverage in areas of greatest use. Manufactured pads of rubber or similarly resilient material can be used but the expense is great and the protective qualities are questionable.

Finally, certain areas can simply remain dirt or mud areas for digging, water play, or gardening. These should be located near a water hydrant. No particular care or maintenance is in-

Paths for wheeled vehicles should have gentle slopes and gradual curves to prevent undue speed and tipping over and to add excitement and challenge.

volved in a mud or digging area. Provided with some simple tools (shovels, etc.), children will know what to do.

Drainage

Ideally the playyard will slope gently away from the building, gutters will be properly installed on the adjacent building to channel run-off water away from the play area, and steep, sloping areas will have enough vegetation to prevent erosion. Steps to correct drainage problems should be taken before zoning and constructing play equipment take place. Low areas where water collects and settles should be filled with top soil. If water runs toward the building, dirt fill should be placed to reverse the direction of flow or drainage tile can be installed, perhaps with the advice of a parent who specializes in such work. Permanent equipment should not be installed in low areas for steady pounding of feet will accentuate the ground depression and create a catch basin for water and mud.

Areas for water play should have a natural slope to an outlet for run off. A ditch outside the playyard, or a drainage pipe with a ventilated cover, are sufficient for this purpose. Since water and sand play tend to go hand-in-hand, the sand play areas are located near a hydrant. Of course, equipment for house play, especially cooking, also fit within this general play area.

Additional Site Preparation

Certain additional preparation of the site may be desirable. If the site is flat, truckloads of dirt can be hauled in and graded into low, rolling inclines for wheeled vehicle (tricycles, etc.) paths. Great care should be taken to ensure that the inclines are not so steep that tricycles pick up dangerous rates of speed. A grade of 12 running feet from beginning (top) to end (bottom) should not exceed approximately 10 degrees in slope. The longer the slope the smaller the degree of rise should be. This means that the hill would not exceed about three feet in height (measured vertically from level ground).

Steeper hills can be constructed during this preliminary stage. Culverts that are three to four feet in diameter can bridge hill to hill and also serve as tunnels for imaginative play. Tunnel length should be kept sufficiently short for clear, unobstructed vision and of sufficient diameter to allow easy entry by adults. The greater the diameter, the greater the allowable length. Hills are made more inviting and functional by the addition of slides and of steps constructed from railroad ties.

The site preparation stage is the best time to provide one or more drinking fountains and hydrants. These should be located next to the building or fence, out of the line of traffic, and away from active play areas. Usually, a water line already exists in a convenient location. This is also the best time to install plumbing for additional bathrooms that might be added in the future. Some schools build storage sheds sufficiently large to accommodate facilities for both boys and girls. Separate facilities in buildings designed for the purpose are common in community parks.

If the playground is to accommodate older children, selected areas are leveled and prepared for the installation of asphalt or concrete areas for organized games during this early stage.

SELECTING PERMANENT EQUIPMENT

Once the site preparation is complete, attention is directed to selecting and installing permanent equipment such as fencing and storage.

The Fence

A fence must be constructed around playgrounds for children through the primary grades and also for older children if play space is immediately adjacent to a hazard such as a busy street or a drop off (ditch, wall, etc.). The fence should be at least four feet high with gates that can be locked. (Very young children do not always remember rules or admonitions about wandering away). The fence can be constructed from chain link or other materials such as wood. Basic chain-link fences cost about one-half as much as wood fences with wide variations in cost reflecting geographical areas of the country, difficulty of installing posts in the ground, and the irregularity of terrain.

Gates for walk through (three to four feet wide) should be installed in appropriate traffic areas such as entry to buildings and entry to adjacent open spaces that will be used for organized games. An additional gate (12 feet wide) is needed for truck delivery of sand and other

materials or equipment. A path leading to sand pits and other areas to be served by trucks must not be obstructed with permanent equipment.

In addition to providing a measure of safety, the type of fence selected will determine what children will be able to see and, to some extent, what they will hear. Solid wood fences (use cedar or redwood for durability) cut down traffic or other undesirable noise to some extent but, simultaneously, they may also prevent the children from viewing activities relevant to conceptual development. So the developer should examine carefully the range of visual and auditory stimuli available before deciding on the type of fence to be constructed. Regardless of the type selected, growing plants should be used to overcome the barren effect and to provide visual and auditory boundaries as needed. Their care becomes the children's responsibility through cooperative planning with adults.

Storage

Storage facilities are an absolute requirement for good playgrounds for young children because "loose parts" (Nicholson, 1971) are the major content for young children's play. The most valuable, creative materials are those that children can make an impact on. They can move them, build with them, stack, arrange, tear down, rearrange, use them as props for imaginative play, create their own structures for gross motor activity, and even incorporate them into games with rules. In short, every major form of play uses loose parts. The creative applications of most fixed structures are far more limited.

The location of storage facilities is critical. If children and/or teachers must carry everything from the classroom for each play period, it is doubtful that a wide range of play activities will be accommodated. Storage must be directly accessible to the outdoors for outdoor equipment. Ideally there will be several facilities, each

This storage house has several important features: double doors for easy entry and exit, drinking fountain attached, bathrooms, and easy access to the wheeled vehicle path. Its barn-like appearance is also appealing. Animals are housed in the adjacent pen.

(Briar Patch School, Austin, Texas)

serving the particular area of the playground that best accommodates the use of the equipment stored there. For example, wheeled vehicles are stored adjacent to the bike paths, sand and water play equipment near the sand and water areas, construction materials and carpentry tools near the space designated for construction play, gardening tools and pet supplies near the farm area, art supplies near the creative arts area, and so on. Several smaller storage bins are usually preferable to a single large storage house because it is easier to organize and locate the contents and less carrying of equipment is required.

The type of facility is a matter of choice. We prefer wooden bins or buildings constructed from rough cedar because of their natural appearance. Application of exterior sealer or a natural stain is all the treatment needed for cedar is extremely resistant to decay. Series of hooks and shelves are arranged to accommodate the type of equipment being stored and to make it easy for the children to locate, remove, and return. Teachers or adults do not put away equipment for children. They plan with children for the clean up that follows each play session.

Alternative types of storage facilities include aluminum, steel, or wood prefabricated buildings commonly sold along major thoroughfares of American towns and cities. Prices begin at $200 to $300 for an 8' × 8' building (1978) and go up depending on size and type of material and construction. These are usually water tight but somewhat less durable and attractive than a custom-constructed storage shed. A second alternate type is the relatively flimsy sheet metal, prefabricated shed sold by department stores at about $200 each (8' × 10'). The major difference between this type and those mentioned above is the absence of wood framing and the resulting weakness of construction. These should be considered for temporary use only. A third alternative is modification of packing crates, adding a door and roof, to form a series of sheds to be placed in select areas. Properly prepared and maintained, these can serve quite effectively for several years.

Playground developers may have their structures branded "eyesores" or "public nuisances" by the neighborhood busybody or the community fathers. The simple way to avoid this is to involve the community from the beginning. People are not likely to reject a project they understand and help develop. Every public playground should be a community, or at least, a neighborhood project. The involvement of children is a must because they throw themselves into playground construction with unbelievable interest and energy. Involvement also cuts down the possibility of vandalism. The following is a sample list of materials frequently found in storage structures.

Wheel Vehicles

tricycles
wagons
wheel barrows
fire engines (pedal cars)
road signs
spare parts

Sand and Water Play

shovels
rakes
assorted containers
screens
cooking utensils
water hoses
funnels
soap bubbles

Construction

assorted wood blocks
interlocking plastic
　blocks
coke crates
lumber
saw horses
wood
cable spools
plastic electrical spools
packing crates
assorted tires

Assorted toys

hula hoops
lemon twist
can stilts

Dramatic

folding chairs and
　table
sheets of plastic
dress up clothes
refrigerator boxes
　(folded)
puppets
puppet stage
parachute
mats
folding screens

Nature

animal feed
bird feeders
nets
magnifying
　glasses
binoculars
gardening tools
seeds
watering hose

Creative Arts (optional
　indoors or outdoors)

paints
brushes
art paper
clay
pottery wheel
handicraft materials
assorted art supplies
rhythm band
　instruments

Carpentry

hammers
saws
screwdrivers
nails, nuts,
　washers, bolts
wrenches

carpentry table
vise
paint and brushes
scrap lumber
clamps
brace and bits
sandpaper
portable tool kit

ZONING THE PLAYGROUND

At last, preliminary work is at an advanced stage and it is time to begin the construction and installation of equipment according to a previously planned format which we refer to as zoning the playground. Zoning is a critical step for it is in this process that one's philosophy and factual knowledge of play are clearly revealed. We believe that there are certain universal forms of play, developmental in nature, that occur naturally and spontaneously when children have freedom to move and interesting objects to explore. These forms, described in detail in Chapter 1, are commonly categorized as social or cognitive. The social forms are solitary, parallel, associative, and cooperative. The cognitive forms are functional or exercise, constructive, dramatic or symbolic and games with rules or organized games. Each form is important in the enhancement of social, cognitive, and motor development.

Play Development and Zoning

An understanding of play development is essential for effective playground zoning. If children are to have the tremendous developmental advantages afforded by play, the environment must be capable of stimulating and supporting every form of play naturally engaged in by the participating children. For the early childhood context (ages three to eight) this means every form.

The various forms of social play are accommodated by the provision of private, out-of-the-way places for quiet solitary play or for reflecting and observing and a variety of places for cooperative and sociodramatic play. There are times when all children will prefer to be alone. The fact that play is essentially developmental in nature, that children engage in solitary play before they grow into cooperative play, does not mean, necessarily, that the seven-year-old who chooses to play alone is socially retarded. Children do not give up earlier forms of play as new forms are learned, rather they build new, more interesting, or more advanced features into a particular form. The solitary three-year-old stacks his blocks indiscriminately while the solitary eight-year-old builds elaborate castles, garages, and space stations. Gradually the child with many opportunities to interact with other children in free play contexts will develop more socialized behavior. The solitary play of the two- to three-year-old will phase into parallel, associative, and eventually the cooperative play of four- and five-year-olds. The accessibility and arrangement of playground equipment influences this development. Barren or dead areas, predominance of fixed equipment, relative absence of loose parts, restriction of play flow, and lack of natural materials hamper development by restricting the range of child-to-child interactions.

Provision for optimal social development is linked to provision for optimum cognitive development. The functional play of infants and toddlers is frequently carried on in solitary but often with an adult figure. A great deal happens during this social interaction and it works in two directions. Mother is socializing baby into childhood and baby is socializing mother into motherhood. The fantastic range of messages being conveyed through primitive verbal utterances and body language have their effect on both individuals. Baby and mother play because it is intuitively and biologically right to do so. The motive is intrinsic. In their game of peek-a-boo or shake-the-rattle, primitive functional-cooperative play is the vehicle or process for social and cognitive development and the object in question is the content of their play. Social and cognitive, indeed motor activities too, become one piece in the complex play and development act. The play environment for one form of development sustains and lends force to other forms even in infancy.

Just as the social forms of play merge into one another as development proceeds (simpler forms integrated into more complex forms), the cognitive forms are seen to become more complex and differentiated with the advanced development of the child. Dramatic play can and usually does incorporate both functional and constructive play. Frequently the observer must listen carefully to the language of the children to determine what form is going on. Stacking a set of blocks and spools next to the bike path may be interpreted as mere constructive play until one overhears a plan to use the structure as a gas station and incorporate it into the play of drivers passing by—all with their knowledge of course! Sociodramatic play, incorporating constructive play, is going on.

Some Factors to Consider

There are certain fundamental factors to consider in equipping and zoning the playground. First, *simple, single-function structures are generally not as useful as complex, multiple-function structures.* Simple structures can be arranged, of course, to form complex structures. If loose parts are plentiful, children will do this without prompting by adults. For example, the large fenced platform on a simple slide becomes a complex structure when children stock it with dramatic play props. The same slide can be made complex when adults attach a swivel and horizontal tire swing to the understructure.

(Brooke School, Austin, Texas)

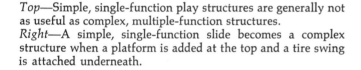

Top—Simple, single-function play structures are generally not as useful as complex, multiple-function structures.
Right—A simple, single-function slide becomes a complex structure when a platform is added at the top and a tire swing is attached underneath.

Second, *there must be a sufficiently broad range of equipment to accommodate every form of play naturally engaged in by available children.* For exercise or gross motor activity: climbing structures, swings, loose parts such as tires, cable spools, stacking materials, etc. For constructive play: carpentry tools, blocks, lumber, dirt, sand, etc. For dramatic play: wheeled vehicles, play houses, crates, road signs, kitchen equipment, pots and pans, dirt, sand, water, dress-up clothes, etc. For organized games: balls, nets, paved and grassy areas, etc.

Third, *structures and equipment are arranged for integration of play between structures.* Dramatic play frequently has a mushrooming effect. As exciting activities begin to form, others join in and are taken up in the action. The activity gains intensity and begins

to spill over to adjacent areas or structures. We observed the drama of a pirate ship being played out in an old boat. The captain sat on the front while the crew rocked the boat back and forth in the heavy seas. Sharks arrived and one enterprising fellow ran to a nearby pile of large plastic spools and, assisted by a volunteer, carried a half dozen or so back to the boat where they were thrown overboard to feed and appease the angry sharks. Land was sighted and half the pirates disembarked to set up quarters in an adjacent platform structure that became the home base for pirates entering and leaving town. The close proximity of these structures and parts allowed a smooth, natural integration with play theme, generating wider involvement and creativity in language, purpose, thought, and action. Although dramatic play can and does

Right—Structures and equipment should be arranged for integration of play across playspace and between various equipment.

Below—Play zones should be defined by boundaries that set them apart functionally and visually and that integrate them spatially with adjacent zones.

(Naud Burnett, design)

(Pease School, Austin, Texas)

take place at one point or another on almost every structure on the playground, it is more likely to be fostered by certain equipment and this equipment should be zoned into a relatively compact but functional area. The same principle applies to gross motor and construction play, to organized games, and to work/play activities such as gardening and animal tending.

Fourth, *these play zones should be defined by boundaries that set them apart functionally and visually and integrate them spatially with*

adjacent zones. These boundaries may take numerous forms: the low horizontal, partially buried railroad ties bounding the huge sand pit encircling the array of climbing, sliding, and swinging structures; the staggered array of vertical telephone poles bounding a portion of the dramatic play area with an opening and low, stepping column extensions leading into the construction area; the one-third buried vertical truck tires forming a tunnel to offer a choice (with the path) from the dramatic play struc-

Space should be arranged to allow alternate movement within and between zones. Here the child has the option of climbing over, crawling through, or walking around.

As the child contemplates a complex structure, he or she may find a number of entry and exit routes, a slide, fireman's pole, ladder, ramp, and cargo net.

tures to the nearby sand and water areas, and so on. Thus, two broad functions are achieved: one, the nature of the structure itself tells the child what it can be used for; and, two, the proximity and spatial arrangement of adjacent structures with their boundaries stimulates and directs the child, visually, motorically, and cognitively, leading to diversity and creativity. The designers of Disneyland and Disney World must have had such concepts in mind when they arranged the various entertainment areas of their glittering funscapes.

Fifth, *space should be arranged to invite movement within zones, between zones, and between points of entry and exit.* In most enclosed playyards there will be three gates, one for service entrance and two for people. The service gate is positioned for unobstructed access from a street and ready access to areas of the playground where service will be needed, sand for sand areas, etc. One of the people gates is conveniently located for entry and exit into the building (school), and the other is usually located all the way across the playyard to allow

ANDERSON MILL

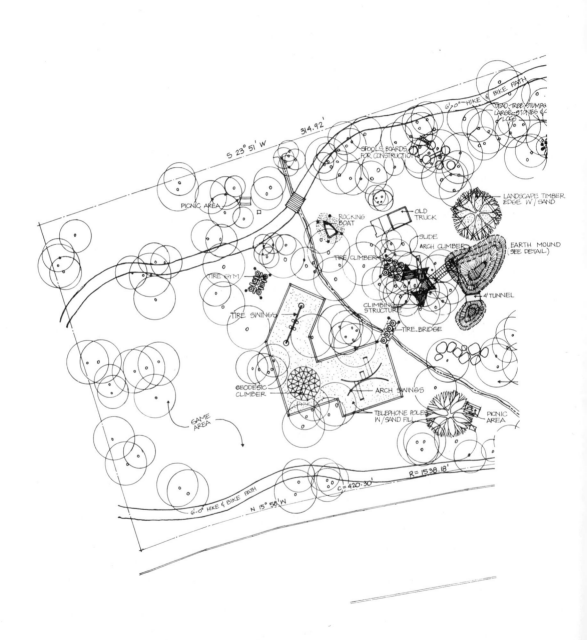

PARK PLAYGROUND

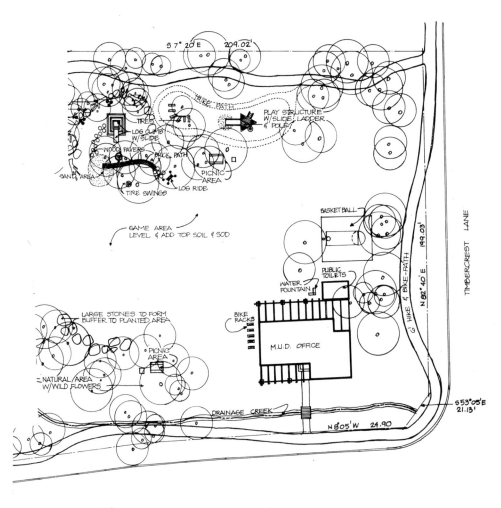

S 7° 20' E   209.02'

TREE PATH

TIRES

LOG CLIMB W/ SLIDE

PLAY STRUCTURE W/ SLIDE, LADDER & POLE

WOOD PAVERS

BRICK PATH

SAND AREA

PICNIC AREA

TIRE SWINGS   LOG RIDE

GAME AREA
LEVEL & ADD TOP SOIL & SOD

BASKETBALL

PUBLIC TOILETS

WATER FOUNTAIN

6' HIKE & BIKE PATH

N 82° 40' E   199.03'

TIMBERCREST LANE

LARGE STONES TO FORM
BUFFER TO PLANTED AREA

BIKE RACKS

PICNIC AREA

M.U.D. OFFICE

NATURAL AREA
W/ WILD FLOWERS

S 53° 05' E
21.13'

DRAINAGE CREEK

N 8° 05' W   24.90

MILLWRIGHT PARKWAY

DESIGNED BY JOE FROST AND HETTIE WORLEY   PLAN   NORTH   SCALE 1" = 25'-0"   SHEET 1

REDEEMER LUTHERAN PLAYGROUND

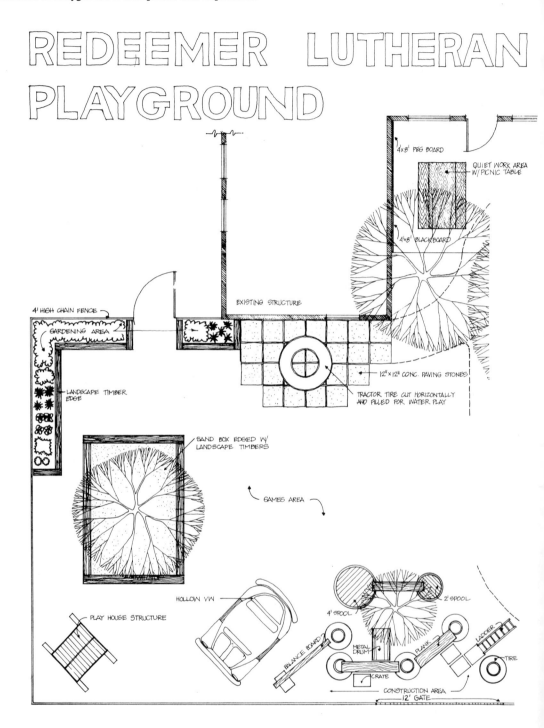

4'x8' PEG BOARD

QUIET WORK AREA W/ PICNIC TABLE

4'x8' BLACKBOARD

EXISTING STRUCTURE

4' HIGH CHAIN FENCE

GARDENING AREA

LANDSCAPE TIMBER EDGE

12" x 12" CONC. PAVING STONES

TRACTOR TIRE CUT HORIZONTALLY AND FILLED FOR WATER PLAY

SAND BOX EDGED W/ LANDSCAPE TIMBERS

GAMES AREA

HOLLOW V/W

PLAY HOUSE STRUCTURE

BALANCE BOARD

4' SPOOL

2' SPOOL

METAL DRUM

PLANK

LADDER

TIRE

CRATE

CONSTRUCTION AREA
12' GATE

PRE·SCHOOL

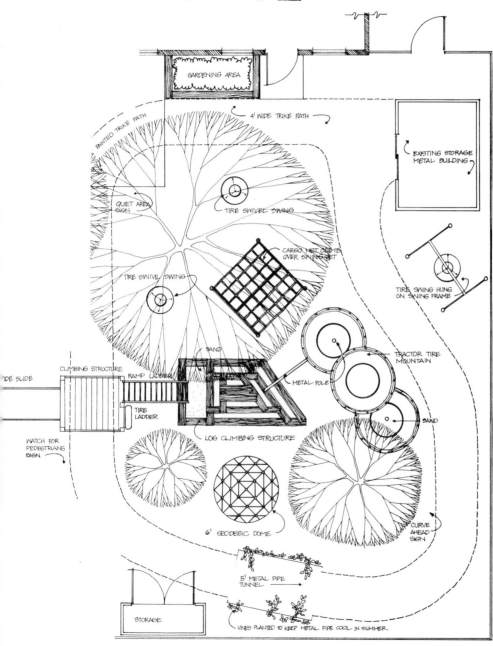

GARDENING AREA

PAINTED TRIKE PATH

4' WIDE TRIKE PATH

EXISTING STORAGE
METAL BUILDING

QUIET AREA
SIGN

TIRE SWIVEL SWING

TIRE SWIVEL SWING

CARGO NET CLIMB
OVER SWING SET

TIRE SWING HUNG
ON SWING FRAME

TRACTOR TIRE
MOUNTAIN

SAND

METAL POLE

SAND

IDE SLIDE

CLIMBING STRUCTURE

RAMP LADDER

TIRE
LADDER

LOG CLIMBING STRUCTURE

WATCH FOR
PEDESTRIANS
SIGN

CURVE
AHEAD
SIGN

6' GEODESIC DOME

5' METAL PIPE
TUNNEL

STORAGE

VINES PLANTED TO KEEP METAL PIPE COOL IN SUMMER

DESIGNED BY JOE FROST AND HETTIE WORLEY

SCALE ¼" = 1'-0"
PLAN SHEET 1

exit to retrieve wayward equipment, such as balls, and/or for access to adjacent areas, such as open space for organized games or a nature area. An individual would be able to follow a more or less direct path along the triangle formed by these three gates.

Once inside the play area, children should find challenge and alternate access to any of the play zones. The open space, the visual boundaries, and the lines of invited movement (e.g., balance logs) carry them naturally from one zone to another. It should be noted that equipment for invited movement between zones does not replace open space. Children are merely given a choice of whether to walk, run, or climb through a tunnel, over steps, or walk a balance beam from one zone to another.

With regard to movement on equipment proper, a similar principle is used. As children contemplate a complex climbing structure, they may find a number of access routes—arch climber, ladder, suspended rope, or tire climber. Upon gaining access they may have numerous exit possibilities—all of the entry points plus a slide or fireman's pole. Further, they find various on-equipment play possibilities, areas for privacy, dramatic houseplay, or mastering built-in climbing obstacles. Such a complex structure occupies a central position in the gross motor zone and is often called a superstructure.

Zoning for Individual Differences

When children of widely varying ages or developmental levels (for example, infants through eight- to nine-year-olds) are occupying the same general play area, certain modifications are built into the zoning arrangement. Infant and toddler areas are fenced off from older children's areas, but within the infant-toddler area certain zones are created. Gerry Fergeson of Pacific Oaks College starts her youngest infants in a relatively simple zone that is adjacent to gradually more

difficult ones according to the motor skills involved. These zones are bridged by series of steps or staggered surfaces and a tunnel. As infants gain motor skill they gradually begin to explore and eventually master these boundaries. Soon they become active in more complex zones.

The "graduated" principle can also be applied to individual play structures. Increasing the difficulty factor involved in scaling a climbing structure decreases the number of children able to try or succeed. Installing steps or platforms at successively wider intervals, allowing access only by a rope climber, and so on, effectively regulates activity. This also builds in a safety factor by prohibiting access to areas too high for younger children. Some considerations about zoning and equipment design for handicapped children will be treated in a following section.

Work/Play Areas

Additional outdoor zones or areas are created (especially in warmer climates) for activities not quite meeting the definitions of free play or those for the teacher-directed, didactic activities of the classroom. We choose to call these work/play zones. They allow the teacher to integrate outdoor work/play activity with the indoor curriculum—creative arts, science, math and social studies. We will not attempt to name or discuss all the possibilities but will identify some of the more common ones.

A relatively full range of creative arts activities can be conducted out of doors. The most convenient location for this may be directly adjacent to the indoor environment. This location facilitates the flow of art materials between the indoors and the outdoors. It is more likely to be near a ready source of water and, perhaps most importantly, this location allows for free movement of activity—the indoor-outdoor continuum. This is particularly enhanced by the provision

(Naud Burnett, design)

The infant-toddler area contains relatively simple materials of gradually increasing complexity. Texture and challenge are woven together.

of direct openings between the classroom and the playground. There are no readily identifiable limits to the range of creative arts activity that can be conducted outdoors. Weather is perhaps the most crucial factor. The variety may include painting, pottery, sculpture, handicrafts, weaving, music, drama, and dance.

The possibilities for science activity are virtually endless. Corrals and pet houses allow children to care for their own animals. A great deal of cooperative planning can be conducted with children about the proper care of animals. Too many school-related pet projects are exercises in animal abuse. In many areas wild animals such as birds, squirrels, and deer can be attracted by locating feeders near the play area. Areas for gardening and growing plants and flowers are essential to every school-related playground. Children can learn basic principles of forestry, geology, and ecology by caring for a wild area of woodland, ponds, streams, and native wildlife. Social science concepts are developed through the establishment of small villages, streets, stores, signs, and the use of vehicles. These and additional possibilities are summarized below.

Animals

Corrals
Feeders
Cages
Bird bath
Fish pond
Observation shelter
Bird houses
Habitat area

Forest and Plants

Vegetable garden
Local flora

Climbing trees
Rock and fern garden
Natural trail
Marsh and pond
Picnic site
Compost area
Amphitheater

Other

Weather station
Photography
Preserving historical
sites

SAFETY, MAINTENANCE, AND SUPERVISION

Children play wherever they must—in well-designed city parks or on crowded streets, in backyards or on deserted lots, on schoolyards or on roof-tops, in abandoned houses or in natural woodland. Many such places are potentially hazardous, especially for young children, for they involve heights, broken glass, deep water, busy traffic, and deep holes. Most American children play outside the supervision of their parents at some time during the day. They need planned, supervised playgrounds. Provisions for the safety of children at play begin with the rules laid down by a community reflecting its concern for the young. No major housing facility should be allowed that fails to incorporate into its design facilities for play and standards for maintenance and supervision. This includes schools, apartment complexes, housing developments, and public parks. Communities need minimum standards and regulations for playgrounds that are equivalent in quality to their rules for property zoning, construction, health, and other vital human services.

Safety on the playground is a complex matter. No set of standards can prevent all accidents. There will be bruises, cuts, abrasions, and occasional fractures. Risk taking is an essential part of the growth process. We argue for playgrounds that are exciting, pose challenges, and allow creativity but that do not introduce features that are blatantly foreign to safety sense, for example, broken glass, hard surfaces under climbing and moving equipment, broken equipment, unnecessary, unprotected heights, poorly designed equipment, direct access to traffic, deep pits, deep water, or inadequate supervision.

The major tasks of playground personnel in respect to safety are: (1) Selecting and/or developing criteria for selection and installation of equipment. One list is presented in Chapter 5. (2) Involving community people (including children) in the development of the playground. Our experience shows that involvement promotes pride in creation and results in better care of the play area by the community. (3) Providing regular maintenance. Responsibilities for maintenance will vary from group to group. On school grounds the regular custodian usually takes care of minor clean up and repair with major repairs being requisitioned through the central maintenance office in large schools. Many schools have

no apparent provisions for care of playgrounds (many have little or no equipment). City parks personnel usually care for public parks. Special citizens committees may personally care for, or hire staff to care for joint venture playgrounds found in some major residential subdivisions. Whatever the context, careful attention must be given to playground maintenance.

Some of the common maintenance tasks are as follows:*

1. Maintain resilient ground cover (sand) around major pieces of equipment.

2. Provide a resilient surface such as sand or tanbark under and around all climbing equipment and fixed equipment that moves (e.g., merry-go-rounds).

3. Pad metal legs of large equipment, swing seats, and other surfaces that may cause injury on impact.

4. Remove, replace, or repair all broken or worn out equipment.

5. Declare off limits to younger children all equipment designed for older children or equipment that is temporarily unsafe.

6. Smooth all jagged or rough edges.

7. Inspect all moving parts (e.g., swing swivels) of equipment regularly.

8. Plan with children to remove glass, loose rocks, cans, and other trash.

9. Develop buddy systems and provide constant supervision whenever pools or other deep water is used.

10. Enclose slides with platforms or attach slides to hills and mounds to prevent falls from the top.

---

*Adapted and expanded from Joe L. Frost and Joan Kissinger, *The Child and the Educative Process.* New York: Holt, Rinehart and Winston, 1976, pp. 343–344.

All equipment should be inspected regularly for wear and unsafe features. Playground maintenance is never finished.

11. Plan with children to rake sand areas regularly to extract foreign material such as glass and rocks.

12. Clean and paint or apply appropriate preservative to equipment regularly to prevent deterioration.

13. Clean out drains and dig trenches to drain standing water.

14. Work with other adults or professionals to develop optimum schedule for use of playground.

15. Plan with other concerned adults for the continuing development of the playground. The best playgrounds are never finished.

16. Discuss essential safety rules with children so that they understand the limits of their play. Reasonably controlled conditions are the middle ground between oversupervision and complete freedom in children's play.

Most of the activity on good playgrounds is free, unregulated play, children doing what comes naturally. Nonetheless, adult supervision is essential. The qualities of a good free play supervisor are not a result of training so much as biological/intuitive. He or she must be warm, friendly, energetic, love children, and preferably have a broad experiential base in such areas as nature, mechanics, carpentry, gardening, and so on. The person must be able to get involved, talk, question, and listen without being obtrusive. He or she must share and plan with the children. The type of person who will *not* do is the one who is concerned primarily with such matters as evaluating all the four-year-olds on gross motor skills, running races under the watchful eye of the stop watch, or choosing up sides for a competitive event. The shy, retiring, "don't get dirty" type will not do either. Children deserve more than an adult who sits under a shade tree directing his or her charges to abide by this or that rule.

Supervisors do intervene on occasion. Bullying or deliberate abuse of others is not allowed. Children do not venture into prohibited areas

The play leader or supervisor needs to have a broad experiential base but most importantly, must be interested in involvement with children. Learning does go on during play.

Play leaders do intervene on occasion. Children are not allowed to bully or physically abuse one another, nor are they allowed to venture into hazardous areas such as busy streets.

(streets, etc.). Direct intervention is rarely necessary for adults who understand the value of taking time to evaluate and plan with children. In addition, good playgrounds are sufficiently challenging to occupy the attention of children who would be more likely to create disturbances on poorly equipped areas.

Making the playground safe for children is only one side of the safety picture. Making the children safe for the playground is the more important factor. What we intend to say here is that safety consciousness and safety ability are developed in children. These traits develop from repeated risk-taking experiences on a playscape carefully designed for gradually increasing complexity of movement. Children learn to exercise good judgment in risk taking by having many opportunities to risk at their present level of ability. The playground is so designed that younger or new children will have many experiences with easy to master equipment before they

Making the playground safe for children is only one side of the picture. Making children safe for the playground is a role of the play leader who is present to suggest, model, and support early efforts.

As children are learning new skills (social or motor), the sensitive adult is available to establish a supportive attitude for children to emulate.

try their wings on the more difficult. Interestingly, when a wide range of equipment and materials is available, most children are remarkably able to make wise choices. Others, especially when exposed to peer pressure, may need sensitive assistance by an adult.

One of the most compelling observations in our years of work with play groups is the apparently remarkable judgment and physical dexterity of children who enjoy regular, extensive periods on creative playgrounds. Newcomers to such groups, having no equivalent experiences, require careful supervision to prevent serious injury. Some do not seem to know how to play, having missed opportunities for play and involvement with adults. Children need

adults who participate in their play, who provide the role models and the encouragement essential to creative activity on the playground.

SUMMARY

Playgrounds are developed for children in a wide variety of contexts, but there are common fundamentals of design that should be taken into account in all public contexts.

A great deal of later effort can be avoided by careful selection and preparation of the site. Ideally, planners of public buildings such as schools and apartments will include the playground in original site plans long before buildings are started. This activity should be done

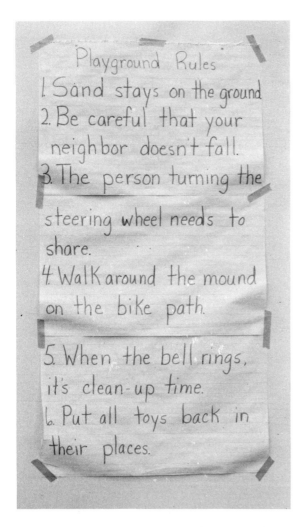

Playground Rules
1. Sand stays on the ground
2. Be careful that your neighbor doesn't fall.
3. The person turning the steering wheel needs to share.
4. Walk around the mound on the bike path.
5. When the bell rings, it's clean-up time.
6. Put all toys back in their places.

Children plan cooperatively with the play leader or teacher for conduct on the playground. They may tape their rules on the storage room door as a reminder during play.

with careful attention to preservation of natural terrain—shrubbery, streams, and trees. Preliminary planning also takes into account child/space ratios, ground cover, drainage, and site preparation.

Before play equipment is placed on the site, permanent equipment is installed. This includes the fence, storage facilities, water lines, water fountains, and hard-surfaced areas such as wheeled vehicle paths and areas for organized games. In some areas artificial structures for shade will also be built.

Following these steps the playground is zoned to provide for the range and arrangement of equipment to be used. Some major factors taken into account are: (1) providing complex, multiple-function structures, (2) providing sufficient variety of equipment to allow every form of play naturally engaged in by the children, (3) arranging structures and loose equipment to allow for integration of play across two or more structures, (4) defining play zones by functional and visual boundaries that allow the integration of zones, and (5) arranging space to allow and invite movement within zones, between zones, and between points of entry and exit.

The playground is also zoned to accommodate special needs. Individual differences in ability are taken into account, allowing various age groups and ability levels to use the area. Zones are created to facilitate work/play such as creative arts and natural activities. These activities are arranged to allow a smooth uninterrupted flow of indoor-outdoor participation.

Finally, safety, maintenance, and supervision are important elements in assuring that children's play is relatively safe, that the playground is maintained in a usable state, and that children learn during play. Children are involved in planning for the care and use of the outdoor environment just as they participate in similar indoor activity. This is viewed as an important process in learning to assume responsibility for the welfare of self and others. The play supervisor or leader gets involved with the children without being "bossy" or didactic. He or she assists in planning to make the playground safe for children but sees the major responsibility as making the children safe for the playground. This is accomplished by providing continuous rich, challenging play experiences for children.

SUGGESTED READINGS

Allen, M. A. *Planning for Play*. London: Thames and Hudson, 1968.

Bengtsson, A. *Environmental Planning for Children's Play*. New York: Praeger, 1970.

Dattner, R. *Designs for Play*. New York: Van Nostrand Reinhold, 1969.

Friedberg, M. P. *Play and Interplay: A Manifesto for New Design in Urban Recreational Environment*. New York: Macmillan, 1970.

Frost, J. L., and M. L. Henniger. "Making Playgrounds Safe for Children and Children Safe for Playgrounds." *Young Children*, 1979 (in press).

Ledermann, A., and A. Trachsel. *Creative Playgrounds and Recreation Centers*. New York: Praeger, 1959.

Kritchensky, S., E. Prescott, and L. Walling. *Planning Environments for Young Children: Physical Space*. Washington, D.C.: National Association for the Education of Young Children, 1969.

Nicholson, S. "The Theory of Loose Parts." *Landscape Architecture*, October, 1971.

Seymour, W. N. *Small Urban Spaces: The Philosophy of Vest Pocket Parks*. New York: New York University Press, 1969.

5

PLANNING FOR PLAY: INVOLVING PARENTS, CHILDREN, AND COMMUNITY GROUPS

"For a playground to succeed, its ultimate users must be its builders. This does not mean only that the adults of a community must build and be responsible for that community's playground; it also means that the children must be involved. . . . I used to think that I wanted to build playgrounds for people; then I thought that I would build with people; but now I see that by far the best—though most difficult—way is to encourage people to build for themselves."*

Paul Hogan

The playgrounds of a society are a visible expression of the esteem granted children by their elders. When adults care, really care, they dig

*Paul Hogan. *Playgrounds for Free.* Cambridge, Massachusetts: The MIT Press, 1974 (introductory comment).

beyond the superficiality of letting others decide what children need or of merely *buying* gifts for their children. This modern American way is not the most sensitive, compassionate, or artistic way, and in respect to playground development it is not the most fruitful way. Our history says that the playscapes that adults are willing to settle for and what children need are worlds apart. The truth of the matter is that only a handful of Americans have paid any attention to children's play and these often do so at great personal sacrifice.

Few Americans are willing to commit one valuable natural resource (land) to the preservation and enhancement of the greatest natural resource of all—children. Many of America's "finest" neighborhoods have set aside no space for children's play. City councils budget substantial funds for parks and recreation but little for playgrounds specifically. Many public schools are constructed and children are enrolled with no budget for a playground. Play, one of the richest vehicles for human development, is an estranged appendage in the educative process. Teachers, untrained in play process, see the play period as a time for children to let off steam, "trained" physical education supervisors see it as a time to "teach" specific motor skills, administrators see it as a time for teachers to have a break and parents agree with teachers. All agree that play should not detract from the academic program.

When adults carefully examine children's play they reflect back in disbelief at their earlier naiveté. A little understanding goes a long way. Parents and teachers frequently remark after a workshop or PTA session on play, "How could we have been so blind," "I'm going home and blow up my backyard," "My whole attitude toward play has changed." But what we are really listening for are those who ask, "What can I do about the playground at my school?" "I'm a contractor, could you use my crew on a Saturday afternoon?" "How could I help my child fix up our backyard?" "What can I do to help?" These questions reflect the cooperative spirit that we hope to stimulate and use in the planning and development of a playground. It means that teachers and principals, custodians and cooks, moms and dads, boys and girls are going to be working together for the welfare of children. It means that tradition is not going to build this playground. It means that this playground will be built with children in mind, that the practice of "socking it to kids on the playground" is over, at least in this neighborhood. A new attitude about play is being formed. Just how to go about creating this new attitude and putting it to work with parents and community groups is the subject of this chapter.

GETTING THE IDEA

Before any movement to improve playgrounds can get off the ground, someone must get the idea that something needs to be done. At the present time the play and playgrounds theme appears to be on the verge of movement proportions. Articles and books are being written by professionals. Researchers are entering the play scene in increasing numbers and a growing number of skillful, enthusiastic professionals are conducting workshops, speaking at conferences, and giving direct help to community groups in playground development. These professionals, fortunately, represent a wide range of professions, including education, child development, psychology, physical education and recreation, creative arts, and architecture. Such diversity is stimulating rich, new insights into the play needs of children. We treasure the "Creative Playgrounds Share-A-Thon" session that we shared with Gerry Fergeson (Pacific Oaks College), Reba Southwell (Mississippi College for Women), Jay Beckwith (San Francisco designer), Libby Vernon (Texas Education Agency), and Jack Mahan (Palomar College) at the 1976 Conference of the National Association for the Education of Young Children in Anaheim. A packed audience kept the session alive from early afternoon until sundown when we called time from exhaustion.

We believe that a creative playgrounds movement is in the cards because we have observed tremendous interest and excitement about children's play in our university classes, in workshops and conferences, among community groups and virtually everywhere that the topic is introduced. The Scandanavians have set the challenge with their exciting adventure playgrounds, perhaps the finest in the world. The North Americans are about to take up the challenge, in their own way, of course.

We first got the idea in 1971 while team teaching an extension course at the Region XIII Education Center in Austin, Texas. The students in the class, teachers from area early childhood centers and elementary schools, asked to visit an exemplary playground. The resulting search in central Texas uncovered no good ones, much less exemplary ones (we have since learned that one good playground did exist). According to our criteria, the existing playgrounds ranged from bad to horrible. Our personal observations, since extended to most states, revealed a similarly gloomy picture nationwide.

With the teachers in this class we planned to select one early childhood center (a preschool for children of migrant workers) and set about constructing a creative playground. An architect was brought in to assist with designs and a blueprint was completed. The next step was to contact the superintendent of schools for the area that included the selected site. We proposed:

1. To construct the playground with no charge for professional assistance

2. To solicit the assistance of community helpers at PTA

3. That we would provide inservice training on the use of the playground for teachers at the school selected

4. That the superintendent would construct a fence around the playground site

The next step was to talk to parents at a PTA meeting about the value of play, to show slides of various playground structures and to present the proposed design. We then handed out a list of junk materials that could be used and a pledge form soliciting materials and labor. During the social period following the discussion, pledges for materials and labor were received. The parents of this small, two-room migrant school dumped and stacked the following materials on the playground site during the next few days:

6 railroad ties	5 quarts of enamel
2 clothesline poles	3 spools 18 inches
2 children's swing	in diameter
sets	9 2-inch drain pipes
6 oil drums	22 1-inch pipes
9 tractor tires	14 drain pipes
2 spools 66 inches	21 car tires
in diameter	assorted plywood &
3 spools 49 inches	masonite
in diameter	3 large crates
1 door	1 bookcase
1 boat	assorted carpet samples
29 gallons of auto	2 quarts of house paint
paint	2 yards of sand

The work was scheduled on a Saturday. Over 30 parents and teachers came with their tools and set about to build the piles of junk into the structures on the blueprint. Our first lesson came early in the morning. The materials on hand did not match in every respect the materials required by the design. So the building process took on a great deal of creativity with materials being substituted, some structures being modified, and others being replaced with new structures.

The work day moved slowly until we realized that the workers expected direct supervision, someone to take charge, give instructions, and check on progress. Once we assumed this role the work was intense for the remainder of the day. Lunch time was special with everyone sharing dishes, tamales, tacos, sandwiches, and

With little assistance from adults, children become involved in every stage of playground development, from planning through construction.

finally ice cream sent over by the owner of a nearby drive-in. As each new structure was completed, the children, ages 3 to 16, moved in to "evaluate" it. One of the most exciting observations of this entire project was discovering, during later showings of slides, the *intense involvement of children in the construction process*. We had not made a special invitation to children, had not really thought about their possible contributions to playground construction, and did not realize just how active they had been until the work day was over. Practically every slide showed children working side by side with adults, taking the initiative on some tasks. The 4 slides showing sequential stages in the construction of a railroad tie sand pit showed: (1) 3 men measuring and staking off the area with one teenage boy and a younger girl handing out stakes; (2) 2 men and 2 boys (about 7 and 14) digging in the hard-packed

ground; (3) 2 sides completed, 3 boys and 1 girl digging the remaining sides. The adults had abandoned this difficult task to the children who were working with eagerness and obvious pleasure (perhaps adults' work can be children's play!); (4) the sand pit completed, sand installed, 7 children, ages 4 to sixteen playing in the area. Needless to say, children have figured prominently into our plans from that point.

The result of this initial effort was a hybrid adventure-creative playground. The climbing and swinging structures, the sand pit, and a wide range of loose parts were functional, though of cheap construction. A group of people got the idea that their children needed a relatively safe, creative place to play and set about to make the idea into reality.

This first effort was especially meaningful to us because it was the beginning of a series of projects for helping people design and construct their own playgrounds. The effects have mush-roomed and are currently influencing, directly and indirectly, the development of various types of playgrounds in a variety of settings ranging from backyards to schools and public parks. As a result of working in these projects, we have refined our views about involving parents and community groups in planning and development.

ORGANIZING

After someone in a community gets the idea that children deserve a better break on playgrounds, the next step is to organize. As in any organization, someone must be in charge. This person should be selected for motivation, organizational ability, and ability to motivate others. The playground design skill can be secured from other sources. Some larger communities now have architects, designers, and consultants who specialize in playground design and construction. Groups in smaller communities may need to look to larger communities or to universities for assistance. Professional assistance should be secured as early as possible, preferably before a site is cleared but certainly before design and construction begin. In making the choice of consultant, be sure to ask for photographs, slides, and blueprints of previous work and take the working committees to visit sites developed by your potential consultant as well as all other promising playgrounds in your area. Throughout these initial contacts, seek clarification of the consultant's philosophy of play and its relation to playground development.

THE WORKING COMMITTEES

The core working committees should be organized as early as possible, but the membership should be considered tentative and incomplete to allow for modification to meet new needs and to allow new members to join. There should be a working role for everyone who volunteers.

There is no set committee organization that will meet the needs of all projects. The typical playground organization has three committees initially, each responsible to the group at large. The *arrangements committee* serves a mediating, public relations role, making appropriate contacts with officials, scheduling meetings, and handling publicity. The people on this committee need human relations, organization, and legal skills. The *design committee* is responsible for primary contacts with consultants, collection of media on play and playground development, site visitations, building materials, and continuous interaction with the consultant and community on actual playground design. This committee needs to solicit some members who have professional skills related to play and playgrounds. Useful people might include teachers, psychologists, architects, carpenters, contractors, pediatricians, etc. The *funding committee* begins its work as early as possible. Their job is to raise money for playground construction. The range of possible fund-raising activities is virtually endless including PTA and community events such as garage sales and more sophisticated methods such as developing proposals for possible funding from agencies and foundations. The *general chairman* makes official contacts with community officials, coordinates the work of all three committees, and takes steps to keep the community appraised and involved.

THE COMMUNITY MEETING

After preliminary organization has been accomplished and tentative plans have been developed, it is time for a special community meeting. In the case of school playgrounds this may be a PTA meeting. For public park playgrounds a meeting may be held in a public building, church, or school. The meeting should be widely advertised in the community newspaper, through posters, and through announcement at regular community functions. It is wise to schedule the playground discussion with a brief entertainment function such as a performance by children. The enthusiasm for playgrounds comes as a result of the meeting and is rarely present in advance. A typical meeting format is as follows:

1. Entertainment by children (children stay for the playground presentation)—15 minutes

2. Introduction to playground project by general chairman—5 minutes

3. Slide presentation, informal presentation on play and playgrounds by consultant—30–40 minutes

4. Presentation and discussion of tentative plans for playground project—10–15 minutes

5. Hand out lists of needed materials, labor pledges, and suggestion form

6. Social with refreshments; take up forms

All designs, agreements, and committees should be considered tentative before the community meeting. If the project is to be cooperative, participants must know that their contributions count. The pledge forms collected (Figure 1) and the comments and suggestions at the community meeting are all carefully weighed by the committees as soon after the session as possible. The committees may conduct a session immediately after the social to evaluate, make modifications on assignments and committee structure, and project plans for next steps.

The pledges give invaluable information but their proper use requires careful follow up by the arrangements committee. Each person pledging is contacted to confirm the pledge and to confirm when and where donated materials are to be delivered. Materials should be delivered within two to three weeks after pledging so

that each successive step can be accomplished within a reasonably brief time schedule. After pledges are evaluated, a work day can be tentatively scheduled within six to eight weeks, allowing time for delivery of material, refinement of design, arrangements for additional material, and needed contacts with workers and community officials. The work day should not be formally established until after all such arrangements are complete.

The list of free and inexpensive playground materials (Figure 2) is duplicated and handed to parents along with the pledge form. The list is not all inclusive and may need revision for some projects. It may be necessary to establish the approximate quantity of given materials needed. For example, the design may call for 10 telephone poles and a representative of the telephone company has over 100 available or a given individual may be able to donate any one of several items. Careful coordination is needed in securing materials.

DESIGNING

Preliminary planning was going on well in advance of the community meeting but now, with the broad input from the community available, formal planning, leading to a final design can proceed. The first step is to measure the playground site and develop a scale drawing. One-fourth inch to one foot of actual area is a workable scale for the average size playground. All existing features (trees, boulders, hills, streams, existing structures) should be drawn initially. Then draw the various pieces of equipment roughly to scale on posterboard or durable paper, cut out flat, place on the scale drawing, and arrange as desired. The approximate scale of various pieces of equipment can be determined by checking dimensions for manufactured equipment in catalogues or by measuring with

Figure 1 Playground Pledge

NAME _____ PHONE _____

BEST TIMES TO CALL _____

ADDRESS _____

WHAT MATERIALS DO YOU THINK YOU WILL BE ABLE TO SUPPLY (see list)?

Name of Material	*Quantity*
1. _____	_____
2. _____	_____
3. _____	_____
4. _____	_____
5. _____	_____
6. _____	_____
7. _____	_____
8. _____	_____

DO YOU HAVE ANY TOOLS YOU COULD LEND FOR THE CONSTRUCTION OF THE PLAYGROUND?

1. Carpentry (saws, hammers, tape measures, extension cords, etc.) _____

2. Digging (shovels, picks, posthole digger, etc.) _____

3. Mechanics tools (wrenches, vise grips, etc.) _____

4. Heavy equipment (backhoe, grader, bulldozer, etc.) _____

5. Hauling (dump truck, pickup, etc.) _____

6. Special (chainsaw, welder, heavy wood-drilling equipment, etc.) _____

7. Other _____

WOULD YOU LIKE TO HELP IN THE CONSTRUCTION OF THE PLAYGROUND?

YES _____ NO _____

WHAT DAY OF THE WEEK WOULD BE BEST FOR YOU? _____

WHAT TIME? _____

WHAT IDEAS, HINTS, COMMENTS, ETC. DO YOU HAVE CONCERNING THE DESIGN OR CON-
STRUCTION OF THE PLAYGROUND?

Figure 2 Playground Materials

The following is a list of free and inexpensive materials that may be used in the construction of playgrounds for young children:

lumber, new or used	ladders	old boat
wooden packing crates	parachutes	airplane
old furniture	paint (exterior)	water hose (to be repaired)
plastic wading pool	burlap	repairable swing sets
old tires (truck, tractor, car)	metal poles and pipes	small tools
barrels (wood, metal, plastic)	dead trees (inspect for shape,	cargo nets
old doors	soundness)	paving blocks or bricks
wooden telephone cable spools	short lengths of drain pipe	shrubbery
plastic electrical spools	concrete sand	slides
carpet scraps (indoor-outdoor)	soft drink crates	conveyor belts
heavy rope	saw horses	wheels
large nuts and bolts	discarded toys (repairable)	pulleys
nails	old car body (or truck)	boulders
telephone poles	caboose	fill dirt

Sources

utility companies	paint stores	railroad companies
tire companies	nurseries	electrical contractors
service stations	government surplus	building contractors
wrecking yards	parks and recreation depts.	bridge contractors
factories	tree-service companies	lumber yards
hardware dealers	sand and concrete companies	lumber mills

tape or "stepping off" equipment on existing playgrounds.

For even greater clarity of detail a three-dimensional model may be built. The base of the model can be a piece of plywood, fiberboard, or similar light-weight but durable material. Spacing of models in proper perspective is facilitated by taping graph paper over the surface of the base. The designer need only count the number of squares (one inch or appropriate fraction) to determine proper spacing. Natural features such as hills and trees and permanent structures such as buildings are constructed and positioned first, then models of equipment are added. The model may be constructed from scrap and inexpensive materials, sand and white glue, cardboard, styrofoam, balsa (climbing structures), strips of cloth, life savers (tires), wire, string (rope), cardboard cylinders (tunnels), cardboard boxes (houses), old necklaces (chains), toy cars, screen wire (fence), wood dowels (telephone poles), pipe cleaners, white tape (wheeled vehicle path), very fine sand, plastic plants (shrubbery), bits of moss (shrubbery), Play-dough (tree trunks, boulders, and a wide range of additional adaptations).

In assessing the site and designing the playground a number of questions should be asked: What age ranges are to be accommodated? What forms of play will be involved? How will the

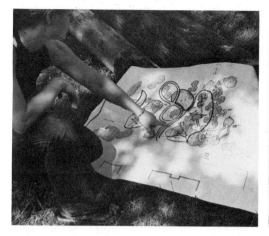 

The first step in designing the playground is to prepare a scale drawing. Then a three-dimensional model is built for additional clarity.

playground relate to the indoor curriculum? How much time and money can be invested? What should be done first? What are the priorities?

Criteria for the Playground*

Assuming that the playground is being designed for the early childhood range (about 3 to 8) in a school setting, the following criteria are suggested. Each should be considered throughout the design process and rechecked again upon completion of the plan.

Environmental Criteria. The playground is designed to:

1. Encourage play

    Inviting, easy access
    Open, flowing, and relaxed spaces
    Clear movement from inside to outside
    Appropriate equipment for the age group

2. Stimulate the child's senses

    Change and contrasts in scale, light, texture, and color
    Flexible equipment
    Diverse experiences

3. Nurture the child's curiosity

    Equipment that the child can change
    Materials for experiments and construction

4. Allow interaction between . . .

    The child and the resources
        Systematic storage that defines routines
        Semi-enclosed spaces to read, work a puzzle, or be alone
    The child and other children
        Variety of spaces
        Adequate space to avoid conflicts
        Equipment that invites socialization
    The child and adults
        Easy maintenance
        Adequate and convenient storage

*Adapted from Joe L. Frost. *Playground Rating Scale.* Austin: University of Texas, 1977. See Appendix B.

Organization of spaces to allow general supervision
Rest areas for adults

5. Support the child's basic social and physical needs
   Comfortable to the child
   Scaled to the child
   Free of hazards

6. Complement the natural forms of play engaged in by the child
   Functional, exercise, gross motor, active
   Constructive, building, creating
   Dramatic, pretending, make-believe, social
   Organized games, games with rules

Generally, the following elements should be included in a play area:

a. A hard-surfaced area with space for games and a network of paths for wheeled toys
b. Sand and sand equipment
c. Dramatic play structures (play houses zoned near complementary equipment such as an old car or boat and sand/water areas)
d. Climbing structures (with room for more than one child at a time and with a variety of entrys, exists, and levels)
e. Mounds of earth for climbing and digging
f. Trees and natural areas (including weed areas)
g. Low walls for climbing and sitting (these can protect planting areas or trees)
h. Water play areas with fountains, pools, and sprinklers
i. Construction area with junk materials such as tires, crates, planks, boards, bricks, and nails. Tools should be provided and demolition allowed.
j. An old vehicle—train, boat, car—that has been made safe, but not stripped of its play value. (This item should be changed or relocated after a period of time to renew interest.)

k. Equipment for active play: a slide with a large platform at the top (best if slide is built into side of a hill); swings that can be used safely in a variety of ways (old tires as seats); climbing trees (mature, dead trees that are horizontally positioned); climbing nets.
l. A large grassy area for organized games.
m. Small private spaces at the child's own scale: tunnels, niches, playhouses, hiding places.
n. Fences, gates, walls, and windows that are adaptable as opportunities for learning/play.
o. Natural areas that attract birds and bugs. A garden and flowers sited so that they are protected from play but with easy access for the child to tend them.
p. Provisions for the housing of pets.
q. A transitional space from outdoors to indoors. This could be a covered play area immediately adjoining the playroom areas which will protect the children from the sun and rain and extend indoor activities to the outside.
r. Adequate protected storage for outdoor play equipment, tools for construction area, and maintenance tools. Storage can be separate: wheeled toys stored next to the roadway, sand equipment near or next to the sand enclosure, tools in the workshop area. Or storage can be the lower level of the climbing structure or separate structures attached to the building or fence. But storage should aid in pick up (that is, make it easy for children to put equipment away at the end of each play period).
s. Easy access from outdoor play areas to coats and toilets.
t. Places for adults, parents and teachers, to sit within the outdoor play areas. Shade structures with benches can provide this as well as seating for children.
u. Landscaping of playgrounds is extremely im-

portant. There should be hedges planted as windbreaks; trees to provide shade and cool, as well as protection on the west from direct sun; changes in surface materials (grass, gravel, sand, hard surfaces, weeds, and flowers) to add variety as well as protection from sun glare. In hot climates the transition from air-conditioned interiors to playgrounds should be buffered in some way; either with natural shade or structures covered with vines. Growing plants, well watered, provide cool areas as a relief from the heat. In cold climates, children are protected by warm clothing, outdoor fires and, ideally, by providing large heated areas for play.

v. The playground should continuously change.

THE WORK DAY

At last the most satisfying part of the entire process is about to happen. The "happening" is a time when people, young and old, men and women, professionals and laborers, cooperate to build a tangible expression of their concern for children and the free spirit inherent in play and playgrounds. It is not a free-wheeling happening for long hours of hard work and planning have set the stage. The community has contributed to the design and the materials and is about to assist in the actual construction. The design is complete, the materials, tools, and equipment are on hand, and the workers are ready.

There is a leader, someone with the skills to interpret the design and the know-how to give detailed instructions for construction. We have seen successful leaders from such roles as school principal, architect, university professor, and playground consultant. It is wise to select someone with a record of success in such projects. The work-day leader is selected by mutual consent early in the design stages of the project.

There is a leader, someone with the skills to interpret the design and the know-how to give detailed instructions for construction.

He or she must be familiar with every detail because the work day is the "acid test" of careful planning and skill. It must move rapidly and smoothly and the workers must have confidence in what they are doing. There is little time for second thoughts or indecisions.

The leader has thought through and discussed with the committees in advance just which tasks are to be given priority. Tasks should be selected that can be completed in one day so that the participants will go away feeling successful. If a series of work days are planned, the first may be for cleaning up the site, installing a fence, constructing storage facilities, and constructing hard-surface areas such as wheeled vehicle paths. On the second work day one group can build a climbing structure, another can construct a sand pit, and another can

Power tools can be dangerous. Careful preparation should be made for using them: proper tools in good repair, skilled operators or instruction for those unskilled in use.

repair and paint loose parts. Subsequent work days are planned (at least two a year) to further develop the playground and to repair old equipment. *Playgrounds are never finished.*

The arrangements committee makes contacts to ensure that everyone is prepared to share food and conversation during the lunch break. There should be common sharing of food (cultural dishes) but special treats (desserts, drinks) can be solicited from local businesses. This friendly sharing helps to solidify positive feelings about the mutual project and carries over in preventing or resolving special problems that frequently arise.

Special Problems

Beginning with the community meeting and extending through work day, special problems arise and are dealt with promptly. There is frequently a negative soul in the crowd who "doesn't want his neighborhood to become an eyesore." The thought of having an old car in a public park brings up visions of a roadside junk yard piled high with wrecked vehicles. These feelings are usually dispelled by showing slides of carefully prepared scrap materials, made functional and maintained through careful planning and regular maintenance. We have never had an old car removed from a playground.

A second frequent concern is allowing children to play in sand, dirt, or mud, "Cats and dogs have played there and the children are likely to get worms." We simply point out in no uncertain terms that this is one of the risks that we are willing to take. A small risk indeed in relation to the values to be derived from the activity. A playground cannot at the same time be both hazard free and a creative arena for children's play. We are also willing to assume the minor risks of splinters from wood construction, reasonable heights for climbing apparatus, drinking from a public fountain, and riding Big Wheels without a helmet. In our estimation these are not points worthy of time-consuming argument and should be dismissed promptly. If an operator of a small day-care center or a mother concerned about the cats in

PHOTO ESSAY: THE CREATION OF TWO PLAYGROUNDS

Both the authors teach graduate classes on early childhood play and playgrounds. In conjunction with these courses, dozens of playgrounds have been designed, some have been constructed and others are in the development process. Two playgrounds, built from scrounged materials during 1977, are the subject of this photo essay. The first is located at Ortega Elementary School in Austin, Texas. The principal designers and coordinators were two teachers at that school, Kathy McCord and Pamela Pearce, and a fellow graduate student, Debbie Johnson.

The second playground is located at Allison Elementary School in Austin, Texas. Principal designers and coordinators were Joel Hodges and Faye Inglis, teachers at that school.

The Ortega playground is relatively small and inexpensive ($600), while the Allison playground is more elaborate and more costly, having involved extensive earth work and construction of elaborate structures. The total cost of this playground, however, will be quite small compared to an equivalent commercial site. In addition, it is a community effort.

The Ortega Story

Kathy and Pam have a talk-it-over before the workers arrive.

Debbie (second from left) orients volunteer workers to the work day activity.

Even four-year-olds do their part. All age groups can contribute.

 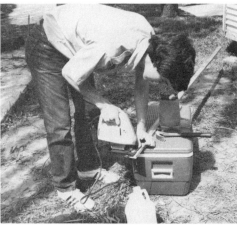

With caution and occasional instruction, various types of tools are used effectively by unaccustomed hands.

Little is wasted. Grass sod is taken from the sand pit area and placed in the wheeled vehicle area.

Bill gets help from his friends in building the tire swing.

The climbing structure takes shape:

Laying out the framework,

Attaching the decking,

Levelling and setting posts,

Installing the cargo net and other means of entry and exit.

After twelve weeks of planning and construction, including several work days, opening day has arrived.

The wheeled vehicle path (donated)

The storage shed (cost, $280)

The sand and water play area (cost, $10)

The tire swing (cost, $28)

The climbing structure (cost, $195)

The tire climber (cost, $25)

The playground (total cost, about $600; total construction time, 316 person/hours)

The old car (cost, $5)

The celebration.

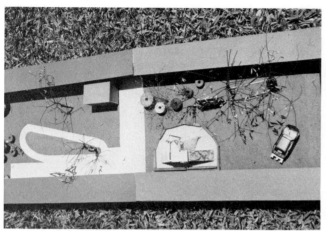 

The Ortega Model

How We Did It, by Debbie, Kathy, and Pam

Design. We consulted available literature and planned according to the limited funds we would be able to raise, taking into account our available space. The playground was designed for five- and six-year-olds. The model was constructed on a ¼ in. equals 1 ft. scale. Materials used to construct the model were plywood, tagboard, felt, balsa wood, aluminum foil, sand paper, wire screen, spools, assorted everyday items. Construction of the model required 38 person/hours.

Planning with Parents. Kindergarten students performed for parents at a PTA meeting and a guest speaker was invited to discuss the need for early childhood playgrounds. Pledge sheets were passed out asking for time and materials. Materials were collected and parents were called to remind them of the work day. The playground model was discussed with parents to gain additional suggestions for improvement.

Fund Raising. Parents from all grade levels donated cupcakes every Friday for seven weeks. Fourth and fifth grade teachers organized programs and proceeds were donated to the playground project.

Materials Collection. The majority of the materials were donated or sold to us at a reduced price. Sources: paint stores, hardware stores, heavy equipment companies, city electric company, lumber yards, junk yards, tire dealers. Parents donated materials specified on the pledge sheet: pipe, lumber, tractor tires, paint, paint brushes, tools, and cable spools.

Construction

Storage shed. Plywood base on cinder block foundation, yellow pine frame, galvanized metal siding—cost $280.

Sand and water play. Sand, heavy equipment tires, water containers, household items—cost $10.

Tire climber. Pipe frame, rope (polypropylene), Sakrete, tires—cost $25.

Old car. Junk body, paint, steering wheel, Sakrete, duct tape—cost $5.

Tire swing. Railroad ties, Sakrete, 4 in. × 6 in. beam, swivel, chain, squeeze links, tire—cost $28.

Movable parts. Cable spools, crates, pallets, tires, wheeled wooden toys, mounted steering wheel —cost $10.

Climbing Platform

Playhouse. ½ in. exterior plywood—cost $7.

Ramp. ¾ in. exterior plywood, cleats, paint, 2 in. × 6 in. and 4 in. × 4 in. frame—$20.

Ladder. 2 in. × 6 in. for railing, 2 in. doweling for rungs (donated).

Slide. Galvanized pipe, galvanized sheet metal, 4 ft. × 8 ft. plywood, 4 in. × 4 in. legs—cost $64.

Cargo net. 6 ft. × 8 ft. cargo net (donated by a sea food restaurant), rope—cost $4.

Fire pole. 2½ in. galvanized pipe, Sakrete, 2 in. × 4 in. lumber—$5.

Platform. 4 ft. × 8 ft. L-shaped platform, 5 ft. above ground—$86.

Miscellaneous. Lag bolts, nails, etc.—$9.

Total cost of climbing platform—$195.
Total cost of playground $600.
Total construction time—316 person/hours.

The Allison Story

The processes used at Allison School for raising money, involving parents, and securing materials were similar to those used at Ortega School. There were major construction differences. Preparation of the Allison site was much more extensive. The school district provided heavy equipment, hauled in dirt and sand, and provided several workers for site preparation. The task of building structures was left to the designers, teachers, parents, and children.

Faye shows the Allison plan to visiting teachers.

Joel goes over details with the heavy equipment supervisor.

Being careful not to damage trees,

areas for sand pits are excavated.

Railroad tie barriers are installed.

Sand is hauled in.

Newly created mounds are sodded. This one is for the amphitheater.

and notched.

The area for climbing structures is staked off.

Holes are dug by machine.

Supporting members are drilled

Posts are set

and bolted.

The redwood deck is nailed on.

The fireman's pole is installed.

The climbing platforms are extended.

The clatter bridge is built.

Break time!

Yet to come is the area containing the cargo net, old car, boat, and obstacle course (center in photo).

The extensive climbing structures (central) will be bounded by a figure eight wheeled vehicle path (foreground) and a water play area (far background). Space for gardening is also included.

her backyard sand box persist, suggest that they cover it up when not in use and continue to more important matters.

During work day there will invariably be forgotten items and details that must be dealt with immediately. Someone should be desig-nated to run errands, pick up extra bolts, lumber, or tools. A charge account at a lumber/hardware store or cash should be made available in ad-vance. This errand runner will need a pick-up truck for hauling bulky or long items.

On occasion someone will inquire whether

the appropriate officials have granted permission for the project. This is an extremely pertinent point. The appropriate levels of bureaucracy must be consulted early in the conceptual stages of the project. In a public school the initial contact is with the school principal who participates in the next step, consulting the superintendent of schools who usually refers the group to the superintendent of buildings and grounds for further planning. It is wise to confirm all major decisions by letter. This helps to prevent later misunderstandings. In many public parks projects, an organized procedure for activities such as playground development is already formalized. In private day-care centers, directors need to consult state standards and local building codes to ensure that planned developments meet legal requirements.

Finally, the general chairman should meet with the committees immediately after the first and all later work days to reassess and formalize plans for future activities. Notes of appreciation should be sent to all parents (and children) who participated in work day. They should be encouraged to volunteer their ideas for further development and alerted to the date for the next activity. Additional parents can be encouraged to participate in future work days by showing slides of the initial activity at the next PTA or community meeting.

The first step in planning for community involvement is organizing working committees. These may include arrangements, design, and funding. A general chairman or leader coordinates the total activity. These committees begin their work immediately. The next step is conducting a community meeting to disseminate information, generate interest, and secure pledges for material and labor.

A preliminary design for the playground may be developed in advance of the community meeting to conserve time. Ideas for modification are secured at every opportunity before actual construction begins. The stages in design include the assessment of the site, development of a scale drawing and eventually a three-dimensional model. A comprehensive set of criteria is employed to ensure high quality and inclusion of all appropriate equipment and areas.

After the design is completed and materials are on site, work days are planned. A selected leader coordinates the work of parents and other interested parties. Children are encouraged to participate and socializing is stimulated through sharing of work roles and a midday meal.

Development of the playground is viewed as a continuing process with periodic work days to add new and repair existing equipment.

SUMMARY

The American public, parents and professionals, is entering a rapidly expanding era of interest in playgrounds for children. Community groups across the nation are "getting the idea" that they can join together to assist in the design and construction of playscapes that are more imaginative, more economical, and safer than the standard.

6

CREATIVE, COMMUNITY-BUILT PLAYGROUNDS

"The true creator is necessity, which is the mother of our invention."

Plato

Playground. What visions does this word conjure up? Close your eyes and envision the playground that you played on as a child. In your minds eye you probably saw swings, slides, merry-go-rounds, seesaws, and monkey bars. As we have seen in Chapter 3, these traditional playgrounds are often hazardous and do not take into account the play needs of children. However, the play scene in America is rapidly changing. A revolution in playground design and construction is underway due largely to a dedicated group of artists, early childhood educators, psychologists, landscape architects, and community-minded people who all share one common concern: providing quality play experiences for children.

A creative playground is constructed primarily from scrounged materials such as tires, lumber, telephone poles, railroad ties, cable spools, and scrap pipe. The construction often incorporates existing commercial equipment and purchased or gift equipment. The playground includes permanent equipment, provisions for sand and water play, and an array of loose parts to accommodate all forms of play. Areas for special activities such as art, gardening, and caring for animals are often included.

PLAYGROUND POWER

The most unique aspect of a creative playground is that it is a community venture, planned and constructed by parents, teachers, and children, often with the help of a playground specialist. A creative playground is an expression of the unique ideas and needs of the adults and children who build and play on it. The playground typically grows out of a desire to do something positive for children, an economic need, and an unwillingness to leave something as important as providing a play space for children to the bureaucrats. The authors, who have been involved in over 100 creative, community-built playgrounds, never cease to wonder at the excitement generated before, during, and after construction. The excitement comes from a sense of pride in doing something assertive to improve the quality of life in the community. It comes from a feeling of *déjà vu:* of reliving pleasant childhood memories or of fulfilling unrealized childhood dreams. It comes from the joy of children as they explore the newly constructed equipment.

Good vibrations continue long after the sounds of hammering and sawing have stopped. It has been the experience of the authors that the construction of a playground serves as a catalyst for other community projects and improvements. Typically, after being involved in the construction of a school playground, parents demonstrate a greater interest and participation in all aspects of the school program. Children who have been involved in the construction of a playground are less likely to vandalize it. Playgrounds bring people together and create a sense of powerfulness among community members.

The construction of a playground is a true creative act because common materials are used in novel and innovative ways. Each time the authors have worked on the construction of a playground, someone has always come up with a new use for scrap materials or a new way to put things together. The maxim that there is "nothing

new under the sun" does not pertain to creative playgrounds. The purpose of this chapter is to share our ideas, plans, designs, and technology for playground construction. While each playground will have its own distinct personality, there are some basic hints for putting things together. The reader should refer to the two previous chapters for information pertaining to involving parents, organizing the work day, criteria for design, sources for free and inexpensive materials (see Chapter 5), and space utilization, site preparation, zoning for specific play activities and safety (see Chapter 4).

BUILDING WITH TIRES

The most versatile of all play equipment is free and litters the cities and countryside by the millions—tires. Go to any dump, service station, or tire dealer and you can usually haul away a truckload of old tires. Tires come in many shapes and sizes ranging from automobile tires, to truck tires, to tractor tires, to huge earth mover tires. The possibilities for utilizing tires in playground construction are limitless. Each time the authors build a new playground, someone comes up with a new idea. Some of the ideas we have used include the following.

tire swings	tire jumpers
tire tunnels	tire gyms
tire climbers	tire bridges
tire rafts	tire planters
tire walls	tire sand boxes
tire pyramids	tire trees
tire mountains	tire animals

Of course there are dozens of variations for each of these tire themes. For example, tire swings may include the traditional tire suspended from a tree limb, a tractor or truck tire suspended horizontally from the ground from a frame or pole, or several tires bolted together and suspended by cable or chain from telephone poles.

Tires free for the taking. There are enough tires in this pile to equip 20 playgrounds.

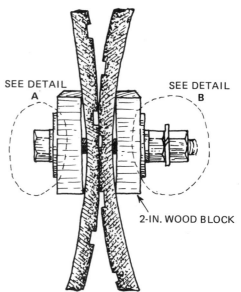

SEE DETAIL A

SEE DETAIL B

2-IN. WOOD BLOCK

A 1 in. countersinking bore is ideal for drilling drainage holes in tires.

DETAIL A

1-1/2" STEEL WASHER

1/2" FENDER WASHER

1/2" x 6" MACHINE BOLT

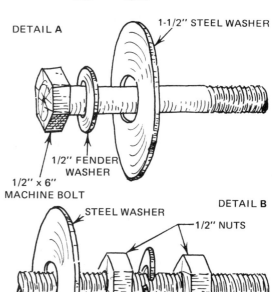

STEEL WASHER

DETAIL B

1/2" NUTS

LOCKWASHER

An auger bit should be used for drilling holes in the tire tread when bolting tires together.

Figure 1 Joining tires, tread to tread.

Joining Tires

When constructing tire rafts or tire climbers, the tires are bolted together tread to tread (see Figure 1). The following hardware is needed for each joint:

> One ½ in. hex head carriage bolt
> Two ½ in. nuts
> Two 2 in. × 4 in. × 6 in. hardwood blocks
> Two ½ in. fender washers
> Two 1½ in. steel washers
> One ½ in. lock washer

Tools needed to tighten joints include a ratchet handle and deep-well socket wrenches and a box wrench. Joining tires is a difficult, time-consuming job requiring two or more people.

Drilling Tires

Tires are difficult to drill and a light-weight ¼ in. electric drill which is great for fixing things around the house is not adequate for drilling tires. Use a heavy duty ½ in. drill. An ordinary wood bit stretches the rubber and does not leave a clean hole, making it difficult to push the cap screw through. A ⁹⁄₁₆ in. auger bit or countersinking bore will make clean holes. Use a 1 in. auger or countersinking bit for making drainage holes.

Suspending Tires

Tires can be suspended with rope, cable, or chain. Rope is the cheapest but least durable, followed by cable, and then chain which is the most expensive. The following chart will be helpful in determining what materials to use and in estimating costs:

Materials	Safe Load Limit	Cost Per Foot
½ in. Polypropylene rope	715 lbs.	$.11
¾ in. Hemp rope	1000 lbs.	.25
½ in. Nylon rope	3000 lbs.	.18
¼ in. Cable	5000 lbs.	.50
⁹⁄₁₆ in. Cable	2500 lbs.	.40
¼ in. Chain	1200 lbs.	.50
⁵⁄₁₆ in. Chain	1700 lbs.	.70

Building With Giant Tires

Giant tires from earth-moving equipment may be incorporated into the playground in a variety of ways. The huge tires, which may be from 6 to 8 feet in diameter and weigh a ton or more, can be obtained free of charge from construction companies and tire companies specializing in large tires. Getting the tires to the playground site is a problem and will require the use of a large flatbed or dump truck. Once there, a crane or large wrecker will be needed to lift and place the tires.

Singly, the tires may be used as sand boxes or planters. They may be stood on end and buried vertically to form tunnels (bury the tires ⅓ of their height) or they may be stacked to form tire mountains or constructions. Because of their great weight, the tires must be bolted securely together when stacking them; 8 in. sections of inch-threaded rod work nicely. After they have been stacked and securely bolted, drill 1 in. drainage holes. If the tires are stacked, the ground surrounding the structure should be covered with 10–12 in. sand to cushion falls.

Giant tires also make great sandboxes and planters. Do not forget to drill 1 in. drainage holes.

A truck wrecker or crane is needed to stack earth-mover tires which may weigh a ton or more.

Use 8 inch sections of ½ in. threaded rod to bolt the tires together. Two bolts should be used at each junction. Since the sidewalls are three inches thick, a ½ in. auger bit should be used.

Giant tires may be arranged in a variety of patterns. This structure is appropriate for preschool and primary school aged children.

Eight earth-mover tires were used to construct this tire mountain. The structure will be framed with cross-ties and 12 in. of sand will be added to cushion falls.

Tire Swings

The first rubber automobile tire to be discarded was probably made into a tire swing. A tire suspended from a tree branch by a stout piece of rope is part of most people's childhood memories.

In constructing a tire swing that will be used by a large number of children, a truck or tractor tire is suspended horizontally from the ground by chain. This will promote social play by allowing a number of children to safely swing together. A car tire will accommodate three children. Attaching the chain to a swivel will prevent the chain from twisting and will allow the tire to both swing and rotate. Heavy-duty swivels are available from local heavy equipment outlets, but these generally have a short lifespan. The best commercial swivels are available from playground equipment manufacturers.

This commercially manufactured tire swivel allows the tire to swing and to rotate 360°.

This cantilever swing was constructed by sinking a telephone pole into the ground at a 45° angle and attaching the chain to a universal joint.

This tractor tire swing can accommodate six preschoolers at the same time.

This tire swing was made by cutting away much of the tire tread.

The load on this unique structure is supported by ½ in. chain. One child swinging or bouncing on a tire affects the others. ▼

A tire swing can be incorporated into a play structure.

A combination tire swing and climber built with 6 in. × 6 in. timbers. The tires are suspended from the ridge pole.

Eye bolts threaded through a block of wood are used to construct this sturdy tire swing.

Constructing a tire raft or climber

A tire climber attached to a platform can accommodate a large number of active preschoolers.

Tires are first laid out in the pattern they are going to be hung, drilled, and then bolted together.

4 in. × 24 in. treated posts are used to anchor the tire raft to the ground. The posts are set at an angle slanting away from the climbing structure to prevent them from pulling out of the ground. The entire post is buried in the ground.

A pickup truck is used to pull the tire raft taut before it is anchored to the post buried in the ground.

A ½ in. × 6 in. lag bolt with large washer and 2 in. × 4 in. wood block is used to anchor each of the tires on the bottom row of the tire raft to posts sunk in the ground.

The final step in constructing a tire raft is to drill 1 in. drain holes in each tire.

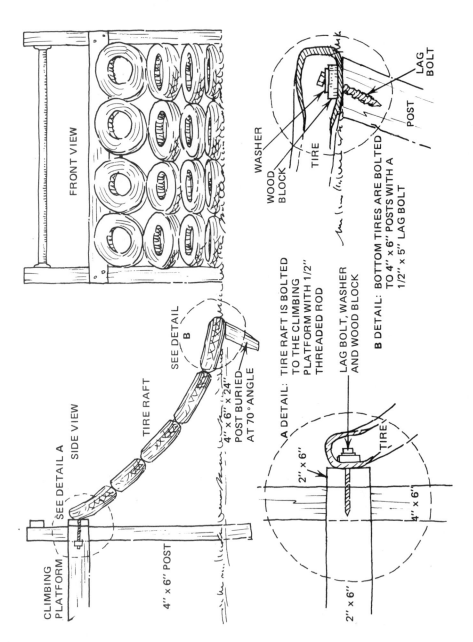

FRONT VIEW

WASHER

WOOD BLOCK

TIRE

LAG BOLT

POST

B DETAIL: BOTTOM TIRES ARE BOLTED TO 4″ × 6″ POSTS WITH A 1/2″ × 5″ LAG BOLT

A DETAIL: TIRE RAFT IS BOLTED TO THE CLIMBING PLATFORM WITH 1/2″ THREADED ROD

LAG BOLT, WASHER AND WOOD BLOCK

SEE DETAIL B

TIRE RAFT

SIDE VIEW

SEE DETAIL A

CLIMBING PLATFORM

4″ × 6″ POST

4″ × 6″ × 24″ POST BURIED AT 70° ANGLE

2″ × 6″

TIRE

4″ × 6″

2″ × 6″

Figure 2   Tire raft

Tire bridges are relatively easy to construct and may be used to connect play structures or may be free standing as in this example.

In constructing a tire bridge lay out three rows of tires and attach a length of ½ in. chain which will support the structure. Next, bolt the sidewalls of the outer verticle tires to the treads of the inner horizontal tires.

Cross-ties, telephone poles, or 6 in. × 6 in. posts secured in concrete may be used to support the tire bridge.

This tire gym was constructed by suspending tires both horizontally and vertically with ¼ in. chain.

This combination tire gym and climber has the advantage of being portable.

To construct this tire teepee, first bolt the tires tread to tread, then suspend the structure with chain.

Tire Climber: These tires are suspended with ½ in. nylon rope.

More Tire Ideas

This tire tunnel was constructed by bolting ten truck tires together and burying them up to the sidewalls.

Tires bolted to the supporting post of a play structure. Metal plates inside the tires help to hold the tires securely.

This tire pyramid was formed by bolting tires of varying sizes together.

By leaving a number of loose tires on the playground, children are able to create their own tire structures.

SLIDES

The typically commercially manufactured slide found on most playgrounds is hazardous because it is too high and narrow, and, once at the top, there is only one way down. A preschooler typically finds herself at the top of a narrow 12-foot high slide with a long line of children behind her clammering for her to go down. Older children will exceed the design limitations by using the slide in ways that it was not designed to be used: riding a bicycle down the slide, climbing up while others are sliding down, sliding down standing up and so on. A four-foot wide slide attached to a play structure with alternative exits or a slide that hugs the side of a hill eliminates many of these problems.

Constructing a wide slide

A 4 ft. × 10 ft. supporting structure is constructed using ¾ in. exterior plywood and 2 in. × 3 in. cross supports.

A 4 ft. × 10 ft. sheet of 22-gauge stainless steel or galvanized sheet metal is bent under and bent over the ends of the frame.

Side rails: 2 in. × 10 in. rails are bolted to the frame. Notice how the rails extend beyond the frame so that the slide may be bolted to the main structure.

Attaching the slide: The final step is to bolt the slide and supporting structure to the main play structure and to the ground support.

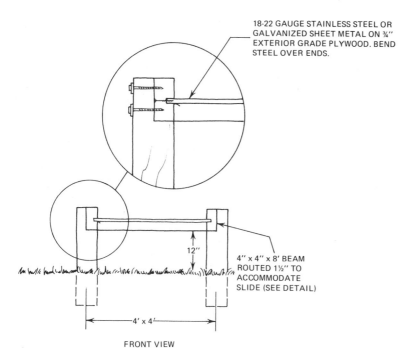

18-22 GAUGE STAINLESS STEEL OR
GALVANIZED SHEET METAL ON ¾"
EXTERIOR GRADE PLYWOOD. BEND
STEEL OVER ENDS.

12"

4" x 4" x 8' BEAM
ROUTED 1½" TO
ACCOMMODATE
SLIDE (SEE DETAIL)

4' x 4'

FRONT VIEW

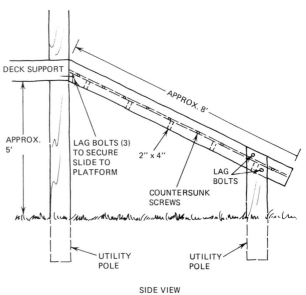

DECK SUPPORT

APPROX. 8'

APPROX.
5'

LAG BOLTS (3)
TO SECURE
SLIDE TO
PLATFORM

2" x 4"

LAG
BOLTS

COUNTERSUNK
SCREWS

UTILITY
POLE

UTILITY
POLE

SIDE VIEW

Figure 3 A 4' by 10' slide

This double slide is appropriate for preschool handicapped children. Cross-ties were terraced into the side of a mound to form steps. The slides were then bolted to the ties. The sand pit provides a soft landing area.

This extra-length handmade slide is appropriate for older children.

An old slide may be adapted nicely to fit a climbing structure.

BUILDING WITH CABLE SPOOLS, BARRELS, AND CONCRETE PIPES

Cable spools come in a variety of sizes ranging from 12 feet to 2 feet in diameter. The larger spools may be bolted together to form play structures (see the Palomar Discovery Playground), and medium-sized spools can be used as picnic tables. The smaller spools can be used along with other "loose parts" such as boards, barrels, and boxes, which children use to form their own constructions. Figure 4 shows how a cable spool fort may be constructed by bolting two large spools together.

Cable spools combined with other "loose parts."

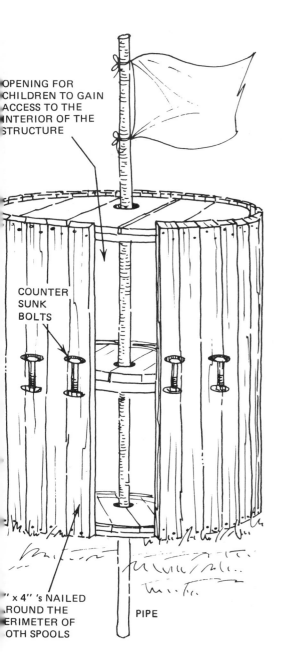

OPENING FOR
CHILDREN TO GAIN
ACCESS TO THE
INTERIOR OF THE
STRUCTURE

COUNTER
SUNK
BOLTS

" x 4" 's NAILED
ROUND THE
ERIMETER OF
OTH SPOOLS

PIPE

Figure 4 Cable spool fort

Cable spools of varying heights used as stepping stairs.

Cable spool seesaw

145

A cable spool obstacle course.

Wooden barrels and 50-gallon metal drums have a variety of uses on the playground. Barrels may be used to construct animals or used in conjunction with other loose parts. Metal drums may be welded together to form tunnels and slides, set into frames, or incorporated into play-structures.

A suggestion about using concrete pipes—don't do it. Concrete pipes frequently have rough, jagged edges, and even when covered with earth mounds are hazardous. Children fall against the exposed edges and the mound may soon be worn and washed away. There is enough concrete in the world today without making it a major element on playgrounds.

This structure was built with 3 cable spools, an old ladder sawed in half, and several 2 in. × 4 in.

Barrels may be set in frames or simply left loose on the playground.

Concrete pipe: Don't.

BUILDING WITH CROSS-TIES AND UTILITY POLES

Railroad cross-ties and utility poles are free materials having a variety of uses in playground construction. They may be used to frame a sand area, serve as corner posts for play structures, used to support tire climbers and swings, used as stepping stones, or bolted together to construct forts and climbing structures.

Railroad ties can usually be obtained from railroad yards and utility poles from power companies. The Georgia Power Company has been especially helpful in providing poles to community-built playgrounds in the Atlanta area. Poles and ties that have recently been soaked in creosote should not be used because creosote can burn skin and eyes. Older poles and ties usually do not present a problem but, if in doubt, nail a smooth redwood or cedar 2 in. $\times$ 8 in. or 2 in. $\times$ 10 in. over the exposed seating surfaces of railroad ties. Protruding splinters may be removed with a machine sander.

Come see our fort.

An enclosed corner of the playground can be converted into a utility pole fort.

Sand boxes are out—sand areas are in. Poles set at varying heights are used to enclose the sand area. Sand areas will accommodate a larger number of children and facilitate more varied activities than a smaller sand box.

A railroad tie balance beam and sand box form a pleasing design.

This climber was bolted together with threaded rod. It has been worn smooth from use.

Poles bolted together to form a climbing structure.

Two cross-tie forts connected with a bridge.

This horizontal ladder was built by bolting two sections of a ladder to railroad ties. The frame surrounding the structure will be filled with sand to cushion falls.

A utility pole balance beam.

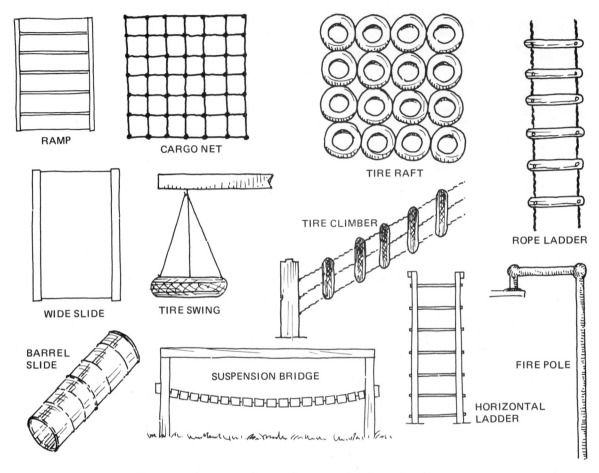

RAMP

CARGO NET

TIRE RAFT

ROPE LADDER

WIDE SLIDE

TIRE SWING

TIRE CLIMBER

BARREL SLIDE

SUSPENSION BRIDGE

HORIZONTAL LADDER

FIRE POLE

Figure 5   Apparatus that can be suspended from play structures

PLAY STRUCTURES

A play structure is a self-contained play environment. The structures are typically composed of a series of overlapping and connecting platforms of varying heights, shapes, and dimensions. A variety of swinging, sliding, and climbing apparatus are suspended and attached to the platforms of the structure (see Figure 5).

Play structures are especially useful on small playgrounds where the space is limited. However, large elaborate structures may be built if space permits. Large playgrounds may contain a series of play structures linked together with ramps and bridges. Different designs create different patterns of movement (see Figures 6 through 12). The relationship between the structure and the rest of the playground should be carefully considered in the design and placement of the structures. Howard Minsk, a playground designer and builder in Atlanta, has constructed a number of playgrounds throughout Georgia. One of the out-

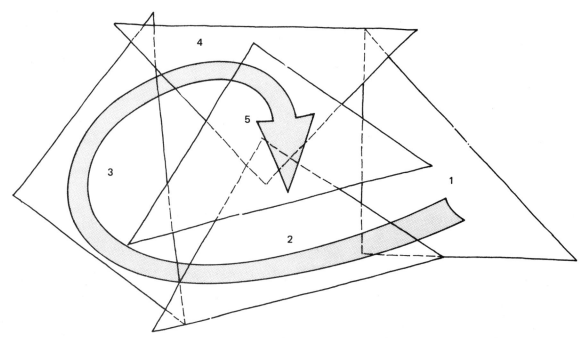

Figure 6 Play structure composed of overlapping triangles. Platform # 1 is at the lowest level and # 5 is at the highest level.

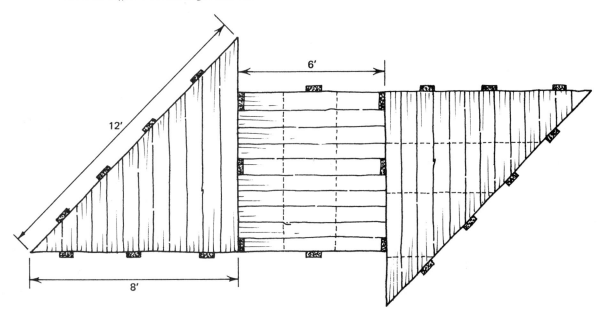

Figure 7 Play structure showing construction detail

This bridge may be used to link structures of different zones of the playground. Notice the tire tunnel under the structure.

Examples of how overlapping triangles may be used to form a spiral (l) and to connect sections of a structure (r).

This play structure resembles a dock complete with boats. The fiberglass boat was an experimental model donated by the Austin, Texas, manufacturer.

A horizontal ladder can either extend from a single structure or can be used to link structures.

This suspension bridge was constructed by drilling two ½ in. holes in segments of 6 in. × 6 in. post and stringing the posts together with ½ in. cable. The structure is suspended with ½ in. chain.

This structure was designed for a day-care center that has a very limited play area in a courtyard.

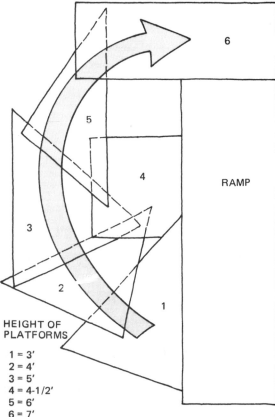

HEIGHT OF
PLATFORMS

1 = 3'
2 = 4'
3 = 5'
4 = 4-1/2'
5 = 6'
6 = 7'

Figure 8 Spiral and platform

standing features of Minsk's playgrounds is the intricately designed play structures. The structures are quite striking in appearance and are an art form in their own right, but at the same time are totally functional. Minsk believes that designing a play structure is a matter of providing children with alternatives for action.

A play environment should encourage children to actively explore their surroundings. Children are constantly searching, feeling, and experimenting. During exploration the play environment must provide a chance for success and a chance for failure, but most of all there needs to be constant feedback on which the child builds concepts of self. A play environment must also provide a number of choices for the child to make. By maximizing play alternatives the child uses his imagination and puts together a flow of activity. The child's imagination is challenged while he is an active participant in his environment. (Personal communication with the authors)

(Gullet School, Austin, Texas)

Multilevel platforms connected with ramps.

An attractive log ladder.

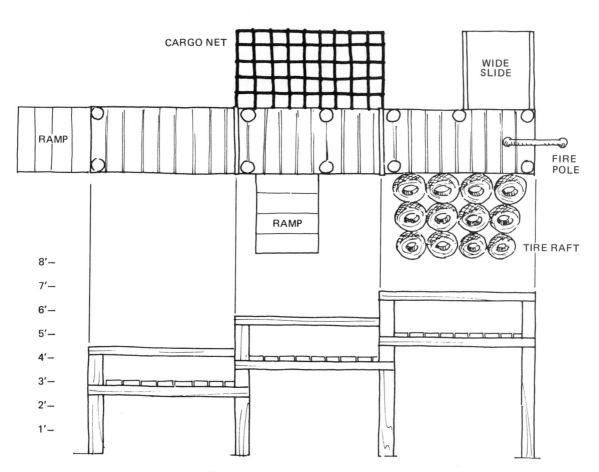

CARGO NET

WIDE SLIDE

RAMP

FIRE POLE

RAMP

TIRE RAFT

8' —
7' —
6' —
5' —
4' —
3' —
2' —
1' —

Figure 9 Multilevel linear design

155

Overlapping creates private spaces.

A play structure should have a variety of ways for entry and exit. (Designed by Howard Minsk)

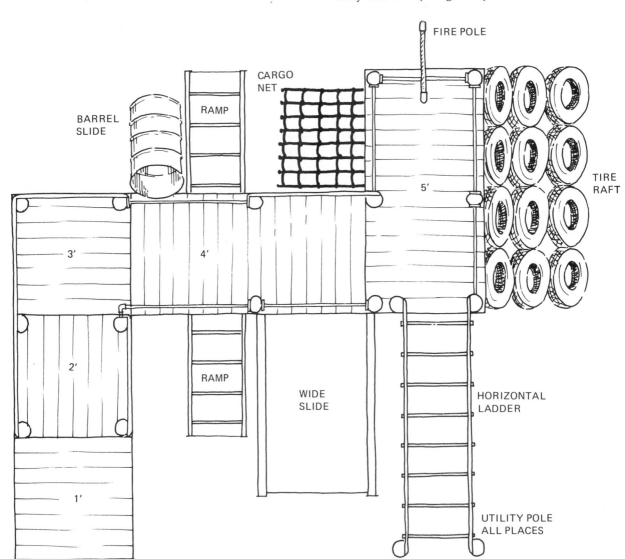

FIRE POLE

CARGO NET

BARREL SLIDE

RAMP

TIRE RAFT

5'

3'

4'

2'

RAMP

WIDE SLIDE

HORIZONTAL LADDER

1'

UTILITY POLE ALL PLACES

Figure 10 Multilevel zigzag design

156

Intricate play structures provide children with a wealth of alternatives for exploration and movement.

(Govalle Austin, Texas)

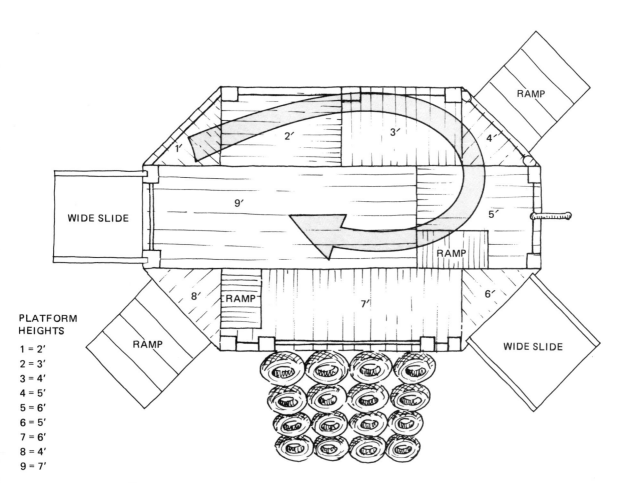

PLATFORM
HEIGHTS

1 = 2'
2 = 3'
3 = 4'
4 = 5'
5 = 6'
6 = 5'
7 = 6'
8 = 4'
9 = 7'

Figure 11 Multilevel octagon composed of nine separate platforms

A smaller, more simply, designed play structure designed by teachers in a play course.

(Redeemer School, Austin, Texas)

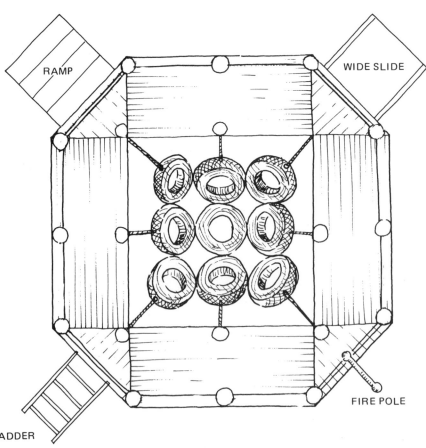

Figure 12 Closed design

Play houses can also be incorporated into the structures.

This utility pole structure is a sturdy, attractive, and inexpensive support for swings.

This ampitheatre, under construction, will be used for group activities, such as art, discussion, lunch, etc. Note the railroad tie base and the redwood decking. Vertical utility poles form the boundary. (Lady of the Lake Children's Center, San Antonio, Texas)

Children at Redeemer Lutheran School in Austin, Texas enjoy their ampitheatre.

The High Meadows Play Structure

High Meadows is an early childhood center secluded in the Woods of Roswell, Georgia. The
school program is based upon the discovery approach which emphasizes play as a vehicle for
learning and for fostering social and emotional
development. The staff draws heavily upon the
natural environment for teaching as well as a
variety of animals such as horses, goats, chickens,
cats, dogs, rabbits, and guinea pigs. The children
also plant and tend vegetable and flower gardens.

The parents and teachers of High Meadows
constructed a large play structure using packing
crates, telephone poles, cable spools, and scrap
lumber. The multilevel structure was built on the
side of a hill and incorporates the terrain into
the design.

Packing Crate Play Structures

This cargo net was built with 1 in. hemp rope woven
around heavy timbers.

The play structure is all things to all children: a
place to relax, a fort to be defended, a place to
socialize.

Dead trees may be incorporated linked with the
structure.

The structure promotes sociodramatic play as well as sophisticated solitary play.

There is more than one way to exit.

Packing crates make a great place to hide

The Palomar College Playground

Dr. Jack L. Mahan, professor of child development at Palomar College in San Marcos, California, constructed one of the finest examples of a creative playground. The architectural firm of Stegen and Marca developed the initial design and, with the help of many community volunteers, children, parents and teachers, Dr. Mahan refined the design and built the play environment using donated material. Total expenditure was under $800.00 for rope and hardware to bolt the equipment together.

San Diego Gas and Electric Company donated power poles, cable spools, and cross arms that made up the major portion of the material used. Power poles (about 12 in. in diameter) were sunk 6 feet into concrete. The cable spools (up to 8 feet in diameter) were dismantled, cut, lowered into place (like a collar) with a crane, and supported in place with crossarms.

The discovery structure, which forms a Y-pattern on the ground 40 feet in each direction, is comprised of 6 major areas: a rope-climbing structure, two dramatic play towers, an elevated activity space, a moving-log bridge, and a swing area. Each is designed for various types of emotional, social, and movement behavior (Mahan, 1976).

Mahan teaches courses on children's play and environmental design and believes that children learn best when allowed to freely explore a rich environment.

As with adults, the young child discovers truly meaningful and significant learnings not primarily through formal instruction but rather through creative commerce with the complexities of his various environments. From each challenge posed by the realities of its environments, the child creates alternative feelings, acts, solutions, and self-attitudes. Wisdom, knowledge, self-respect and creativity, therefore, are products of environmental challenge— the consequences of each act re-create both the environment and the child. (Mahan, 1977)

(Photos courtesy of Jack Mahan)

(Photos courtesy of Jack Mahan)

(Photos courtesy of Jack Mahan)

TOOLS

Only heavy-duty, professional-quality tools should be used in playground construction. Lightweight tools typically found in the home will not get the job done and will be ruined by heavy use. To avoid accident and injury, all volunteer builders should be instructed and checked out in the proper use of power tools and tools with sharp edges. An experienced builder should be appointed safety supervisor to ensure that tools are being used correctly. Providing an adequate source of electrical power is often a problem because the construction site is typically some distance from the nearest outlet. In providing electrical power to the construction site, use only heavy-duty, grounded extension cords with three-pronged plugs. The best source is a box outlet, connected by three-wire (grounded) cable. Never use power tools on wet ground.

Chain cutter.

Belt sander.

This drill bit saves effort by both drilling the bolt hole and countersinking.

Heavy-duty, reversible power drill.

Heavy-duty power saw.

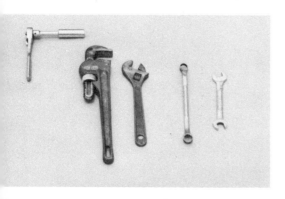

Wrenches (l-r) socket wrench and ratchet handle, pipe wrench, adjustable wrench, box wrench, open-end wrench.

THE EVOLUTION OF A PLAYGROUND

The development of a creative, community-built playground is an evolutionary process that strives toward perfection but is never completely finished. After a structure or piece of equipment is initially built, children should be observed playing on it for a period of time. Their behavior will give you clues as to how the equipment can be modified to greater enhance their play. Swing-

Measuring tools: (l-r) framing square, tape measure, chalk line and plumb bob, adjustable protractor, combination square, carpenter's rule.

Wood working tools: (t) wood rasp, (l-r) plane, chisels, mallet.

ing and climbing apparatus and loose parts should be periodically exchanged to ensure continued novelty. Children's ideas should be actively elicited concerning playground improvements. A committee of parents and teachers with rotating membership should perform periodic preventive maintenance and make modifications. An ever-changing, evolving playground provides continuous challenge and new opportunities for mastery. The creation of a community-built playground is a bold act requiring a great deal of time and hard work. However, the end results are well worth the effort. The challenges met and mastered, the concepts learned, the good feelings derived will follow children for the rest of their lives.

SUGGESTED READING

Bengtsson, A. *Environmental Planning for Children's Play*. New York: Praeger, 1970.

Dattner, R. *Design for Play*. Cambridge: MIT Press, 1969.

D'Eugenio, T. *Building with Tires*. Cambridge: Early Childhood Education Advisory Study for Open Education, 1971.

Ellison, G. *Play Structures*. Pasadena, Calif. (91105): Pacific Oaks College and Children's School (714 West California Blvd.), 1974.

Friedberg, P. *Handcrafted Playgrounds: Designs You Can Build Yourself*. New York: Vintage Books, 1975.

————. *Play and Interplay*. New York: Macmillan, 1970.

Helick, R. M., and Watkins, M. T. *Elements of Preschool Playyards*. Swissvale, PA.: Regent Graphic Services, 1973.

Hewes, J. J. *Build Your Own Playground*. Boston, Mass.: Houghton Mifflin, 1975.

Hogan, P. *Playgrounds for Free: The Utilization of Used and Surplus Materials in Playground Construction*. Cambridge, Mass.: MIT Press, 1974.

Lederman, A., and Trauchsel, A. *Creative Playground and Recreation Centers*. New York: Praeger, 1968.

Licht, K. F. Safe playground design. *American School and University*, 1975, 4, 23–25.

Mahan, J. *The Palomar College Discovery Structure Learning Environment*. Escondido, CA. (92027): Behavioral Science/Design (1982 Craigmore Avenue), 1976.

————. Playgrounds as learning environments. In L. Golubchick and B. Persky (eds.), *Early Childhood Education*. Dubuque, Iowa: Kendal/Hunt, 1977.

Rudolph, N. *Workyards: Playgrounds Planned for Adventure*. New York: Teachers College Press, 1974.

7

FORMAL PLAY ENVIRONMENTS: COMMERCIAL EQUIPMENT AND DESIGNERS' PLAYSCAPES

Playyard of Buchanan School, Washington, D.C. M. Paul Friedburg, Designer.

"No more static seesaw! No more immutable concrete turtles! Instead, a dynamic, ever-changing and exciting environment, one in which a child can participate. Participate, be involved with, contribute and learn. This may sound farfetched, visionary and utopian; the only thing that I find farfetched is the fact that it doesn't exist now."

M. Paul Friedburg*

The work of manufacturers and of designers/architects is explored together in this chapter for three reasons: (1) The work of both groups has advanced significantly in recent years both in terms of safety and functional design. (2) Some of the country's leading playground designers and architects are also employed by

*Playgrounds for City Children. Washington, D. C.: Association for Childhood Education International, p. 11.

equipment manufacturers and common themes are present in the equipment on their personally contracted playgrounds and those they design for manufacturers. (3) Many designers/architects with no direct ties to commercial companies integrate commercial equipment into these playgrounds. (4) Both groups are primarily concerned with formal, professionally designed products.

On the other hand, several manufacturers employ full-time designers who engage in no independent play equipment design and many designers/architects create their own independent play equipment and playground designs and have no ties to commercial manufacturers. Consequently, original creations are emerging from both groups and there is great diversity of ideas and practices.

One intent of this chapter is to illustrate and contrast features of commercial playground equipment and formal playgrounds in current use, ranging from the fixed traditional steel and concrete playgrounds to the creations of contemporary architects. This study will be illuminated by focusing upon such factors as types of material, functions of equipment, equipment-space relationships, aesthetic qualities, and safety. The *Proposed Safety Standard for Public Playground Equipment* developed by the National Recreation and Park Association (1976) may be used as a tentative standard for weighing progress in safety features. The theory and research of Chapter 1 coupled with personal experience will temper our observations on both function and safety. In addition we have used a report prepared by the Creative Play Committee of the Ontario Recreation Society for the Ontario Ministry of Culture and Recreation (Wilkinson and Lockhart, 1976) entitled *Safety in Children's Formal Play Environments.*

A second intent of this chapter is to present the philosophies or points of view of selected manufacturers, designers, and architects and to illustrate the nature of their designs.

DEVELOPMENTS IN SAFETY OF PLAYGROUND EQUIPMENT

In a previous chapter it was pointed out that there are no mandatory standards for the manufacture of playground equipment in the United States. Under contract to the United States Consumer Product Safety Commission, the National Recreation and Park Association completed a

draft, *Proposed Safety Standard for Public Playground Equipment*, on May 1, 1976. A condensed version of this proposed standard is found in Appendix A and should be reviewed by the reader at this point. The reader and potential user of this standard (and of the analysis in this chapter) should take careful note of several factors:*

1. Serious problems were discovered as the standard was subjected to extensive testing by the Consumer Product Safety Commission and the Bureau of Engineering Sciences.

2. There is considerable controversy about whether standards should be adopted or extensive public information and education programs should be used to reduce playground injuries.

3. The details of the proposed standard, particularly numbers and dimensions, are extremely tentative in nature and should not be misinterpreted as an absolute and acceptable standard for all instances.

With these reservations in mind, the proposed standard does give an idea of what to look for in safety hazards and it provides a base for further work and modification. Those contemplating the construction of any of the major types of playgrounds, formal or informal, should become familiar with its content.

The item by item illustrated safety analysis to follow shows new safety features and also reveals certain evolutionary features of design related to play function and aesthetic appeal.

Equipment should be designed for a specific developmental range and should be used by the group for which it is developed. This is particularly relevant to fixed, formal equipment such as climbing structures, slides, and swings.

---

*Appreciation is extended to Robert D. Buechner of the National Recreation and Park Association for his help in illuminating these concerns.

Three- to five-year-old children may be exposed to undue hazards (maximum height, gripping surface of ladders, step heights) on equipment designed for nine- to twelve-year-olds. There are several means of accommodation to this standard: (1) Select a wide range of equipment to accommodate widely mixed age groups but develop rules for use. (2) Design equipment for graduated challenge; that is, make equipment for older children uninviting to younger children by increasing difficulty of use through such means as providing wide gaps between ladder rungs. (3) Construct separate play areas for different developmental groups. For example, the elementary school may provide one play area for kindergarten through second grade and a second for third through sixth grade. This arrangement also provides for greater use (larger numbers of children involved in a given time period) and duplication of certain types (different scale) of equipment cuts down on its wear.

Materials used in construction of playground equipment must be durable. Materials selected should have a demonstrated record of durability or they should be tested. Increasingly, manufacturers are subjecting their products to load tests after they are fully assembled. This is necessary for determining whether parts linked together, such as a swing seat, linkages, chains, and swivel, will collectively and individually withstand the loads to which they will be subjected.

The equipment must be installed in a manner that will prevent tipping and sliding while in use. For heavy equipment this usually requires fixing in concrete. Locking devices should be provided for all bolts to ensure that they will not work loose or be removed by hand. Hooks and rings should be durable and all exposed bolts must be covered by a permanent cover that cannot be removed without tools. It is best to countersink or recess bolts.

Practices in respect to these points vary widely from manufacturer to manufacturer. Equipment designed for backyard use is typically bad on most counts. Flimsy pieces of wire may be sold as anchoring devices for swings, support elements may be extremely weak, and bolts are either exposed or capped by plastic or cheap metal covers that fall off in use or may be removed by the children. Manufacturers of carefully designed equipment (usually expensive) either provide heavy-duty protective caps for bolt ends or countersink them into the material. Their equipment is frequently extremely durable (perhaps to a fault). Given such wide variation in durability, the buyer must exercise considerable judgment and caution in making selections.

The potential impact of swinging elements should be within certain safety tolerances. Swing seats currently available may be constructed from rubber (belt-type), wood, plastic, or metal. Weight per unit varies from two or three pounds for the rubber belt-type to over thirty pounds for certain plastic "animal" seats. The belt-type flexible seats are acceptable, the others are not. Wood seats frequently cause severe cuts and mild concussions, heavier seats can result in serious injury or death. There should be sufficient clearance between moving elements and between moving elements and fixed structures to prevent collisions under normal use. Swings that travel in a straight line (two chains and a seat) require less space on each side than do horizontal tire swings (three chains suspended from a swivel) which move in a 360° range.

The velocity of rotating equipment should be limited. This refers to the speed of the outer edge of the equipment. The outer edge should be of smooth, circular design and the base should have no openings accessible to any part of the body. This standard, of course, is directed at such equipment as merry-go-rounds. Speed controllers and improvements in design have led to

(Courtesy BigToys)   (Courtesy Columbia Cascade)

Play equipment should be durable. It should resist tipping and sliding. Exposed ends of bolts should be capped or recessed.

Modern swing seats are made of rubber or other strong, belt material. Manufacturers are also beginning to use old tires in their designs.

The outer edge of rotating equipment should be of circular design and the base should not permit intrusion of body parts.

Commercial slides can be purchased for attachment to handbuilt structures.

a new look for this particular piece of equipment. Yet the more hazardous models are still available. Since rotating equipment is suspect in play value, it is being rejected by more and more playground designers. The merry-go-round is reputed to be extremely hazardous although available reports show that it ranks better than climbing equipment, swings, and slides on frequency of accidents. Proper installation and maintenance is a key consideration in the safe use of rotating equipment.

Slides should be designed in such a manner that speed of descent and landing are within a safe range. Many factors come into play in determining landing speed: type and condition of sliding surface, the incline and length of the slide, and speed of the child upon entry. In addition, the distance from the exit end of the slide to the ground and the type of landing surface are relevant safety considerations. A landing pit filled with sand provides a cushion for rapid or unusual landings and guide rails help ensure that the child will not exit on the way down. The extremely tall, narrow slide connected directly to a ladder is gradually being replaced with lower, broader structures with enclosed platforms bridging the highest zone leading to entry to the slide.

Height of equipment (walkways, landings, decks) should be limited according to the age group or development of the users. In general, there appears to be no sound rationale for constructing play surfaces beyond the height required for child users to walk under them without danger of collision with the understructure. Play surfaces on climbing equipment should be enclosed by railings except for entry and exit areas. In general, ladders leading to platforms should be installed near 90° from the horizontal (straight up and down) and stairways should have a gradual incline of 25 to 35°.

A protective surface should be installed and maintained under and/or around all climbing and moving equipment. The best, most readily available (in most areas) material is sand. A bed 8–10 in. thick is sufficient for most purposes. It should extend across zones where children may fall (e.g., slide exits, around and under swings, around the periphery of merry-go-rounds, around and under climbing structures) and it should be contained by a suitable border (e.g., railroad ties, utility poles). Regular maintenance should ensure absence of foreign materials such as broken glass and the surface (sand) should be replenished or rearranged as needed in heavy-use zones.

Manufacturers, of course, have little or no control over surfacing but they should assume some responsibility in educating consumers

Climbing well above the child's own height serves no useful play function and increases the risk of injury from falls.

about the need for proper surfacing and provide instructions for surfacing with their equipment.

MODERN COMMERCIAL EQUIPMENT

During the past decade a number of manufacturers have modified existing equipment and developed new types of equipment. Several additional companies have been established during this period. The most obvious change is the increasing substitution of wood for metal in manufacturing. This switch has some obvious

A protective surface, sand, tanbark or commercial mat must be installed in all fall zones. Among these surfaces, sand provides the best protection and commercial mats the least protection. (Photos courtesy Columbia Cascade)

advantages, wood is considered more attractive, it is softer and retains a comfortable (to touch) temperature under extreme temperature conditions. However, metal is strong and durable and will continue to be used.

The manufacturers represented in the following description are among a larger group selected by the authors after an extensive review of literature (catalogues, etc.) aimed at identifying those with equipment of higher than average quality. Some manufacturers did not respond to our requests for detailed information. We believe that the equipment the manufacturers finally selected are representative of a "new look" in commercial playground design and manufacture. The philosophy of each manufacturer is taken from printed materials provided to the authors.

CREATIVE PLAYGROUNDS CORPORATION

This company designs and manufactures playground equipment that "promotes creative play and stimulates the imagination and development of gross motor skills." Unlike most other manufacturers of wooden equipment who develop modular designs, Creative Playground Corporation designs each piece of equipment to be used separately for one or more play functions. They design equipment to various scales to accommodate particular age groups. Their stated philosophy or point of view as provided by Charlie Gibson, Secretary of the Corporation, is as follows:*

We at CREATIVE PLAYGROUNDS CORPORATION believe that the out of doors playground is an important and viable learning environment equally important as the indoor classroom.

---

*Creative Playgrounds Corporation. Advertising brochure. Terre Haute, Indiana. Reprinted by permission.

The out of doors learning environment must be planned and budgeted so that each equipment purchase is a wide investment towards a goal of providing the best possible learning environment for young users. Playground equipment is costly so that the greatest care must be taken in each purchase.

All playground equipment is not equal in play value nor is all equipment equal in the skills developed. The more traditional equipment is often the most unwise investment.

Swings, merry-go-rounds, springy ducks and springy horses do little more than entertain the child and the outdoor playground is no more a place merely to entertain than is the indoor classroom. The social and motor skills developed on the playground are as important as, and aid in, the development of skills in the indoor classroom.

A well rounded and integrated outdoor learning environment does NOT just happen. It must be planned for and budgeted.

A well planned learning environment should incorporate quiet areas with a sandbox for digging and forming, a garden area, an area for creative play and an area for wheel-toy activity with adequate storage. Most important of all, an area should be planned with equipment designed for gross motor development. Equipment for balancing, grasping, climbing, sliding, crawling, and strengthening the upper torso are all important ingredients in a well planned learning environment.

The development of gross motor skills is the primary goal, judging from the above statement and an examination of available equipment. The typical layout of equipment is circular, enticing the child to move from piece to piece, each requiring different motor skills, much like an obstacle course. The purchaser, of course, can arrange and rearrange the equipment to satisfy his or her own particular view of play. Like practically all equipment manufacturers, this company does not make available the loose parts needed to supplement their equipment and provide for wide variety in play. This can and should be done by the purchaser.

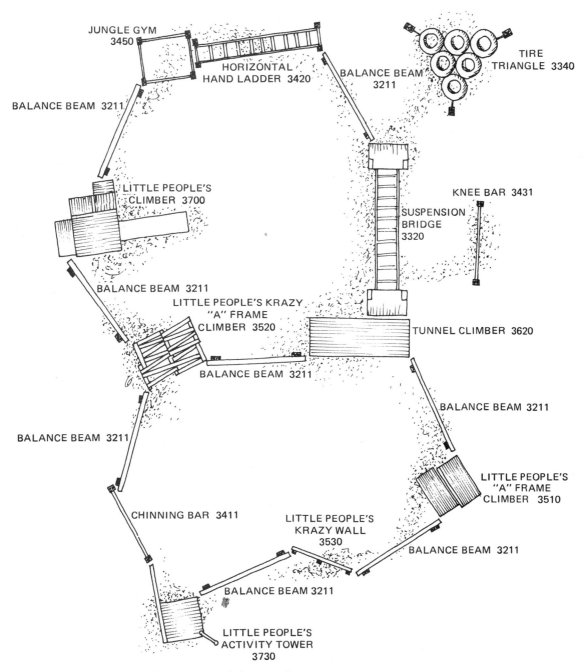

Figure 1 Sample layout of equipment. Courtesy Creative Playgrounds Corporation.

(Courtesy Creative Playgrounds Corporation.)

(Courtesy Creative Playgrounds Corporation.)

(Courtesy Creative Playgrounds Corporation.)

BigToys: Northwest Design Products, Inc.

In 1970 two industrious men came together to develop a flexible, modular system of play equipment. Their intent was to develop relatively inexpensive equipment that could be readily adapted for a variety of sites and play functions. Charles D. Bronson, design manager, provided the following statement of philosophy*

As the idea grew, specific goals were established and a greater understanding of the needs of children became clear. Since safety has always been a primary consideration where children play, and since there is no conclusive information on the subject, we adopted a philosophy of our own. Based on what we have learned from writings on child behavior, talking with educators, therapists, etc., a specific goal has dominated our design efforts. The dominant element is playability.

The more playability a structure has, the safer it is. Structures which lack variety and do not challenge the user, foster misuse and increase the potential for injury. There should be a graduated challenge balanced with a certain degree of risk, built into each structure. As you can imagine this balance is not easy to determine, but each year we learn more and more about how to reach it.

If we were to make a priority list for designing play structures, it would probably be: (1) Playability; (2) Safety and (3) Aesthetics. All three aspects influence the effectiveness of each other, but not to the extent that the order would be changed. Safety would be paramount if it weren't for the fact that it would be severely handicapped without good playability. Aesthetics can have a strong influence on playability, especially fantasy play. We try to avoid theme designs, such as space ships, animals, trains, etc. It is our opinion that the theme approach limits playability.

To summarize, we believe that BigToys play structures fill a definite need, especially for urban children. Also we think the most effective approach is to pro-

*Personal Correspondence from BigToys. Reprinted by permission.

(Courtesy BigToys.)

(Courtesy BigToys.)

vide the most playability for the least cost, and not get involved with the manufacture of frills.

BigToys play structures are made from softwood logs, galvanized steel pipes, and aluminum fittings. They accommodate a number of gross motor skills such as balancing, chinning, crawling, climbing, and sliding. Loose parts for dra-

matic and construction play in relation to the equipment are not distributed by the company. These, of course, are usually available from local sources.

The primary interest appears to be upon the development of structures for the playground rather than for the total play environment. This is a natural emphasis for BigToys manufactured structures. However, it is interesting to note that they are also aware of special and broader play needs. In respect to the needs of handicapped children they state:*

As designers of play structures we have done some research on the needs of handicapped children. We have interviewed educators and therapists, and have observed the children at play under a number of circumstances. We have designed structures for the handicapped and have worked to build structures designed by others.

Basically what we have learned from this is that handicapped children have the same needs as normal children, but with a somewhat lower accomplishment level. They need the vestibular stimulation associated with slides, swings, hanging upside down and rolling over. They need the opportunity to practice hand-eye coordination and balance by climbing and traversing ropes, ladders, nets, tires, logs, etc. They need the upper torso and large muscle development just as school children throughout the United States do. And they need opportunities for dramatic play behind a steering wheel, on a deck, behind a wall, under a shelter, etc.

(Courtesy BigToys.)

---

*Personal correspondence from Charles D. Bronson. Reprinted by permission.

The structures we have proposed for your site address all of these needs. The question remains, however, have we provided them a context appropriate to your handicapped population? We are cognizant of the great variety of mental and physical problems that cause a child to be labeled "Handicapped." Consequently the play structures will be of little or no value to some children who are severely handicapped. But, if the very limited information that we based this proposal on is correct, the structures should serve a "Full range of physically and mentally handicapped, aged 4 to 20 years."

Miracle Recreation Equipment Co. and Jamison, Inc.

Miracle of Grinnell, Iowa and Jamison of Los Angeles, California have merged to make available a very large line of playground equipment in addition to equipment for parks and athletics. They offer improved, traditional metal playground equipment and several varieties of equipment constructed primarily from wood and oriented around themes such as Space, Frontier Land, Imagine City and Story Book Village. Their 1976 catalogue states that "all equipment is built to meet or exceed or surpass Proposed Industry Safety Standards as follows:

- No wood board swing seats; all safety strap seats.

- No high slides without safety canopies at the top.

- No climbers designed with metal under metal. All Miracle/Jamison climbers are "fall free" design.

- No dangerous protrusions, sharp edges, flimsy ladders, open "S" hooks or guard rails.

- No platform equipment more than four feet high without guard rails. All ladders and steps are safety tread."

Like most other major companies Miracle/Jamison provides free professional planning service. A sample plan was provided by Wayne Olson, vice president and general sales manager.

Figure 2 "Wood Mark IV Imagine City Play Area." Courtesy Miracle Recreation Equipment Co.

(Courtesy Miracle Recreation Equipment Co.)   (Courtesy Miracle Recreation Equipment Co.)

(Courtesy Miracle Recreation Equipment Co.)

Columbia Cascade Timber Company

Two manufacturers of wood play equipment, TimberForm and Columbia Cascade Timber merged in 1975 to form Columbia Cascade Timber Company, the largest supplier of wood for play in the world. Their philosophy* is reprinted from materials provided by Ron Green, design director.

TimberForm is a systematic approach to creative outdoor play. Its designs are based upon a philosophy of play which recognizes the child as the ultimate appraiser of the validity of a play facility.

The creative design processes and play analyses which led to TimberForm, developed certain criteria which differed radically from that which is available in most traditional play facilities today. These standards were based upon the child and his relationship to his world.

Play is a child's work. At play, he explores himself and his relationship to the world. In playing, his demands and responses are immediate. He is a continuous animal. His thoughts and physical activities are linear and connected. In the creative play experience, the child quickly outgrows instinct and replaces it with choice and logic. The obvious need then is not just a place to play, but a total play environment to which the child can respond and, in responding, grow into a more total person. The benefits of meaningful play are more than just physical. Play is the training ground for social interaction and from play come the benefits of mutual experience and the shared task.

To fulfill the requirements of the child, facilities must be challenging and functional, flexible and adaptable, and abstract yet natural. Challenge prepares the child for maturity by developing in him a knowledge of his own capabilities. He discovers how high he can go, how long he can balance, the extent of his endurance, and the foolishness of overextending himself. Challenge creates the basic interest for a child at play, and physical challenge is a major

*TimberForm Product Guide. "Our Philosophy." Reprinted by permission.

portion of this interest. Often our inordinate concern for the safety of the child limits the degree of challenge available in the facility.

Safety is a factor in the design of a play facility, but the real perils of the playground have been with us for many years. The swing often becomes a dangerous projectile. Ladders used as approaches to slides force the child to go through unnatural and unsafe maneuvers to assume a sitting position, and, if he should fall, a paved play surface is unforgiving.

So, functional design strives to solve the problems of the playfield while enhancing the play value. There should be no focal point in the area that demands that the children queue up, for it is here that boredom takes its toll. The idea that children should wait in line is foreign to TimberForm systems.

As we have seen, flexible and adaptable play environments answer the needs of the child. In response to these needs for far greater flexibility, we have developed a systems approach to play based on modules. These modular systems allow for the development of total environments keyed to the specific needs of those who will use the facility. The composition is not rigid and inflexible. It is an ever changeable world that develops the child and asks only that he respond in his own way.

The economies of modular play systems are many. Manufactured in factories where workers are experienced and quality as well as controls are markedly higher, these modular prefabricated units offer an innovative methodology of construction novel in play structures. The design of the module provides sufficient weight and horizontal surface to eliminate the need for footings and foundations. The installation process is simple and does not require highly skilled labor.

TimberForm modules offer choice to the designer and landscape architect. By attaching individual modules to each other, the designer can produce an unlimited variety of forms and ideally interject his objectives into the total pattern. The non-professional can secure needed advice from the TimberForm Design Staff or from our many field representatives.

Finally, we believe that abstract forms demand a response from children and that natural activities enhance his physical being. It's our conviction that a play area should be abstract yet natural. By abstract we mean tending away from the realistic or literal, such as rocket ships or dinosaurs. By natural we mean an honest reflection of those activities that one encounters in nature. The child's imagination should span the facility and it should become whatever he imagines it to be. We believe that when you tell a child what a device is meant to be, you have destroyed his initiative and stultified his creative inclinations. We believe it is the child who determines the validity of play equipment.

TimberForm Play Units, Stepping Columns, Clusters, and many of our accessories are constructed of wood. Why wood? As a building material the advantages of wood have long been known. However, as a play apparatus material, wood has often been misused and misunderstood. Because of this, many myths have developed concerning its use.

Wood, used properly, is perhaps the ultimate play yard material. It does not get hot in the summer, nor cold in the winter. Using the right species, smoothly finished (surfaced, eased, chamfered, etc.), splinters or slivers are not a problem. When properly treated, wood is impervious to rot or decay and resists fire. The myths which have developed over the years concerning the use of wood in play areas were generally the result of amateurish attempts to build cheap structures of rough two-by-fours, old railroad ties, or second-hand utility poles.

Our objective has never been the cheapness of wood, (for we use only the highest grades available), but rather the goodness of wood, the warmth of wood, the feel of wood, the ability of wood to gain character with age and, finally, the need for the child to identify with the earth and the products of the earth. At TimberForm we believe in wood.

(Courtesy Columbia Cascade Timber Co.)

(Courtesy Columbia Cascade Timber Co.)

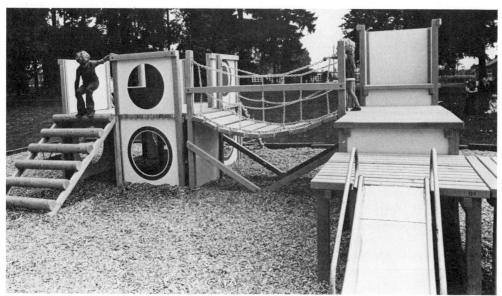

(Courtesy Columbia Cascade Timber Co.)

PROFESSIONAL DESIGNER'S PLAYGROUNDS

As community residents become more aware of the encroachment of humans and their structures upon natural terrain, they select choice areas and seek to protect their delicate ecological balance by careful planning. The more remote areas are sometimes preserved in their primitive form. Other areas, particularly urban ones where space is scarce, are transformed into play and recreation sites. Man-made materials—wood sculpture, steel, and plastic—are woven into the terrain by professional designers, sculptors, and architects who seek to retain some of the natural feel and look of nature while providing for the play and recreation needs of many people. Some are more successful in doing this than are others. In this section we will present samples of the work and philosophy of selected designers.

LTA Limited: Designer, Ronald L. Hartley

In 1973, LTA Limited, Planning Consultant and Landscape Architects of Jackson, Mississippi began the redevelopment of Riverside Park for the Pearl River Basin Development District and the City of Jackson. They were commissioned initially to: (1) evaluate existing facilities, (2) determine immediate recreation needs, and (3) develop general guidelines for a master development plan delineating suggested facilities. Following this preliminary study LTA was commissioned to: (1) redesign vehicular traffic patterns and parking facilities, (2) develop a picnic area with a distinctive atmosphere, (3) develop tot-lot areas for children one to five, (4) develop a playground for children ages six through twelve, and (5) upgrade the existing nature trail. Figure 7.3 shows the relationships between these areas and with the total park facility. Figure 7.4 is an overhead view illustrating location of structures, space relationships, and types of commercial equipment (Columbia Cascade and Miracle/Jamison described earlier) and fabricated structures.

The following description* of the playground provided by Ronald L. Hartley, president of LTA Limited and designer allows the reader insight into the underlying philosophy.

The Adventure Playground, a prime element in the development program, is the result of intensive research into the needs of playground facilities. Determinations made early in the planning criteria and program paved the way for the development of a new and innovative playground offering more than dictatorial use. It was also noted that the playground atmosphere would be important to the overall scheme within this intensive use area due to the interrelationships and the pronounced location on the site respective to views from the nearby interstate highway. Thus aesthetics became one of the prime design criteria.

Our interest is non-dictating play equipment, visual aesthetics, child interest span, maintenance and durability. However, function is the single most general criteria for development.

Design achievement of the playground was made with the use of wood sculpture play equipment and a functional layout thus providing an opportunity for major playground success. The high density concept combined with a linking concept (continual linear play) produced a multi-level sculptured structure offering a wide variety of equipment and costing approximately $80,000. The structure itself challenges the child to be innovative and creative instead of dictating traditional "play" routines. Sand and rounded wood equipment provide built-in safety while the nearby viewing deck adjacent to the promenade easily allows parents to watch their children without inhibiting their play.

The western red cedar observation deck acts as a transitional element between the playground and the picnic area. These features are further related by the

---

*Personal correspondence from Ronald L. Hartley. Reprinted by permission.

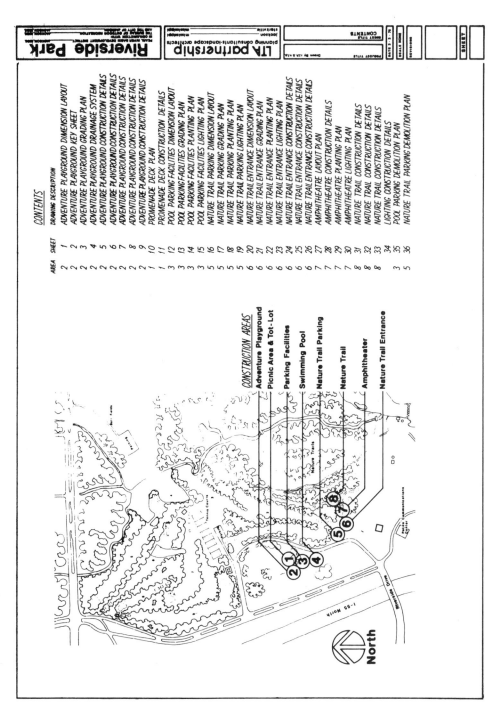

Figure 3 Riverside Park Recreation Area, Jackson, Mississippi. Courtesy of LTA Limited.

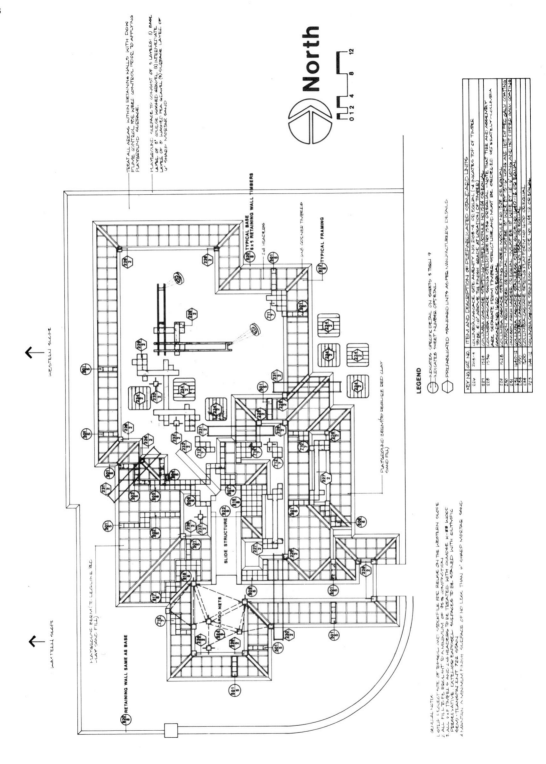

Figure 4 Riverside Park Recreation Area, Jackson, Mississippi. Courtesy of LTA Limited.

Riverside Park Playground in Jackson, Mississippi. Designer, Ronald L. Hartley.

10 foot wide tree lined promenade which separates them.

Conventional tot-lot play equipment has been interspersed throughout the three other locations within the picnic area for convenience to family and friends. Sand beds with cross tie (railroad tie) boundaries contain the tot oriented equipment consisting of 'C' Springs, fiberglass mountains, merry-go-rounds and other fixed creative equipment.

A comfort station is located convenient to all facilities within the intensive use area. Functionally, this was accomplished through the use of walks and actual location.

Design concepts for the two parking lots were based on a need to lower both areas (physically), improve circulation (both vehicular and pedestrian), and improve the aesthetic quality. Also, a partial realignment of the main inter-park road has been suggested along with the cut-off of the existing center access road which originally passed between the swimming pool and the picnic/playground area.

The overall plan therefore will give more design continuity throughout the park, better separation of pedestrians and vehicles than in the original park plan, attempt to hide massive parking areas, estab-

lish a sense of "arrival" for the nature trail, refurbish certain areas of the trail and add new support facilities (i.e., amphitheater, entrance to nature trail, reorganized tot-lot playgrounds and design of a totally new and unconventional adventure playground with observation deck).

Nouguchi Fountain and Plaza Inc., Architects

In 1973 workers at Atlanta's High Museum of Art conceived the idea of providing permanent works of art in a park setting, available for public enjoyment and for use in educational programs for children. During the next two and a half years the museum raised $225,000 for the commission, design, and construction of a playground or sculpture garden to be located on a one-acre site in central Atlanta's Piedmont Park.

The desire to take art to the community led the museum to secure the services of an internationally respected artist, Isamu Noguchi, designer of the successful Children's Land near Tokyo, creator of works of art on exhibit in major museums around the world and the sculp-

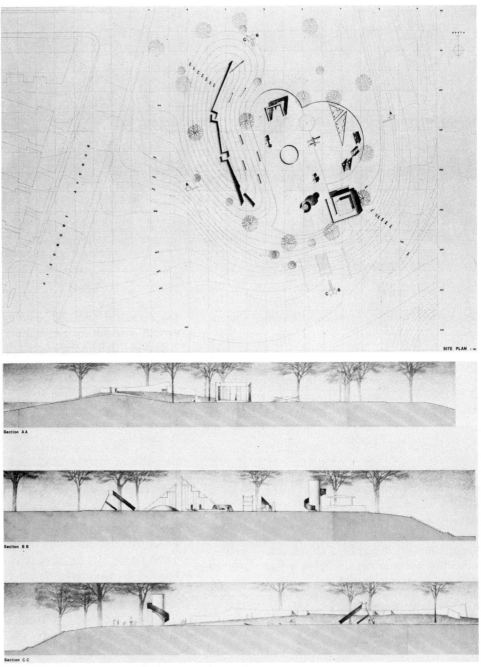

(Courtesy of Isamu Noguchi.)

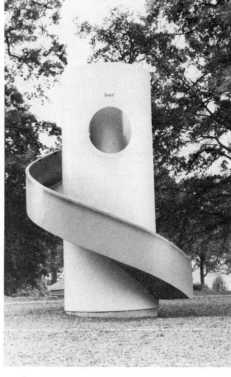

"Sculpture Garden" in Atlanta's Piedmont Park. Designer, Isamu Noguchi.

ture garden at UNESCO in Paris. Noguchi, who believes that art should be a part of everyday life, designed a series of modern abstract pieces of sculpture with play functions called Playscapes for the museum. On May 1, 1976 it was dedicated and given to the City of Atlanta as a bicentennial gift.

Few people recognize "playscapes" as an outstanding work of art. But nobody is insulted. Most visitors are expected to notice it first as an extremely attractive playground for children. Perhaps they will progress from there to an appreciation of the delightfully integrated shapes, forms and colors, and to the recognition that each object is a piece of modern sculpture . . . it is like no other playground you ever saw. A blue slide spirals around a pale blue cylindrical structure. Twin orange triangles support the swings. There are three sets of playcubes in bright blues and greens, and three multi-shaped jungle gyms for climbing, crawling and swinging by hands or feet. In the big circular sandbox, small children build castles, fill and empty pails, or let the soft white stuff spill through their fingers and drift in the wind. There are also a seesaw, a playmound and a triple slide.*

Noguchi sees Playscapes this way:†

I saw it as a complete environment in which children are disassociated with the outside and grown up world and are in the secure dimension of their own environment within which the challenges to play have an interactive and accumulative function. Thus as you will have noted in the playground, there's not one type of slide but a number of slides all of which entice the child to try the other. This also applies to the swings of different lengths and the various other play objects which give a choice of what to do and therefore is not a static thing but a continuous invitation to adventure. The long wall with its surrounding berm which encloses the area and makes it separate from the street traffic and noise is also a frontier of their world and a containment of it. Within this wall also are alternate possibilities of hide and seek and such other adventures as children may devise.

Naud Burnett-Howard Garrett, Inc.
Landscape Architects

Naud Burnett and Howard Garrett have designed several playscapes for the city of University Park, Texas, a suburb of Dallas. They believe that there should be sufficient variety to provide the child with a range of options; active motor play, restful activity, and quiet, solitary play. Reflecting this desire for diversity, they

---

*Lucy Justus. *The Atlanta Journal and Constitution Magazine.* August 22, 1976.

†Personal correspondence from Isamu Noguchi. Reprinted by permission.

Playscapes in University Park, Texas, designed by Naud Burnett. Howard Garrett, Landscape Architects.

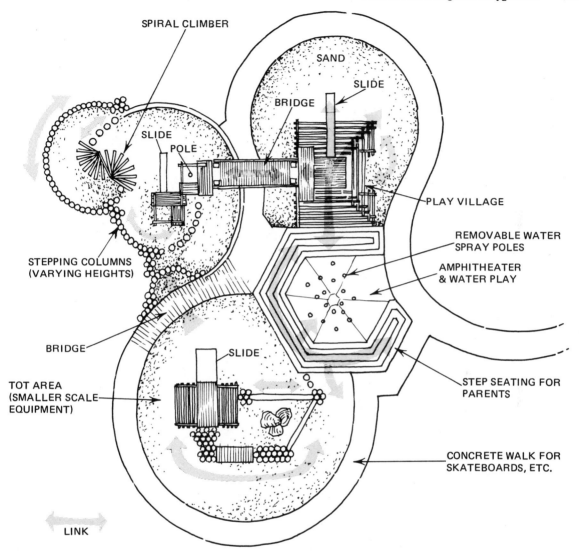

SPIRAL CLIMBER

SAND

SLIDE

BRIDGE

SLIDE

POLE

PLAY VILLAGE

REMOVABLE WATER
SPRAY POLES

AMPHITHEATER
& WATER PLAY

STEPPING COLUMNS
(VARYING HEIGHTS)

BRIDGE

SLIDE

STEP SEATING FOR
PARENTS

TOT AREA
(SMALLER SCALE
EQUIPMENT)

CONCRETE WALK FOR
SKATEBOARDS, ETC.

LINK

Figure 5 Concentrated, linked-play concept. Martin Luther King, Jr. Play Ground. Courtesy of Naud Burnett. Howard Garrett, Inc., Landscape Architects.

use a wide range of commercial and "found" materials including expensive, durable manufactured timber play structures for climbing and such materials as concrete culverts for quiet, sand play.

A central concept in their designs is called linking. This means that play structures are related to one another to encourage continuous movement from activity to activity, using a variety of motor skills. A related view is that the equipment should be concentrated within a relatively small area or zones to give children many options within their immediate play space. These views are illustrated in Figure 7.5.

Ancient Play Garden, Central Park, N.Y. Supervising Agency: N.Y.C. Parks, Recreation & Cultural Affairs Administration. Donors: The Estee and Joseph Lauder Foundation; 85th St. Playground Association. Architects: Richard Dattner & Associates. Engineers—Structural: Goldreich, Page & Thropp. Mechanical: Seymour Berkowitz & Associates.

Water Playground, Central Park, N.Y. Supervising Agencies: N.Y.C. Parks, Recreation & Cultural Affairs Administration; N.Y.C. Transportation Administration; N.Y.C. Transit Authority. Architects: Richard Dattner & Associates. Engineers— Structural: Goldreich, Page & Thropp.

72nd St. Playground, Central Park, N.Y. Supervising Agency: N.Y.C. Parks, Recreation and Cultural Affairs Administration. Donor: Louis and Bessie Adler Foundation. Architects: Richard Dattner & Associates.

Richard Dattner and Associates, Architects

Richard Dattner is well known among playground people for his excellent book, *Design for Play*, but his reputation is more broadly established as a result of his imaginative playscapes. The sampling of his views on play which follow are excerpted from *Design for Play* (New York: Van Nostrand Reinhold Company, 1969) with the permission of the author.

A playground should be like a small-scale replica of the world, with as many as possible of the sensory experiences to be found in the world included in it. Experiences for every sense are needed, for instance: rough and smooth objects to look at and feel; light and heavy things to pick up; water and wet materials as well as dry things; cool materials and materials warmed by the sun; soft and hard surfaces; things that make sounds (running water) or that can be struck, plucked, plinked, etc.; smells of all varieties (flowers, bark, mud); shiny, bright objects and dull, dark ones; things both huge and tiny; high and low places to look at and from; materials of every type, natural, synthetic, thin, thick, and so on. The list is inexhaustible, and the larger the number of items on it that are included, the richer and more varied the environment will be for the child.

A playground . . . should present a series of challenges, ranging from simple things that toddlers can master to ones that challenge older and more experienced children. There should be continuity, so that each child always has the dual experience of having mastered some aspects of his environment while knowing there are other aspects that he may still seek to master.

Choice is quite an important way of controlling one's environment. A playground may provide children with various kinds of choice. A child should be able to decide whether to play alone, with a small group of children, or with a large group. Each of these options implies a distinct kind of space: small, sheltered areas for solitary play, more ample places for small groups, and an open space for group activity.

Children need the freedom to make mistakes, to be clumsy and fall, without an ever-present parent who, with a misguided desire to help the child avoid all disappointment and pain, interferes with the natural process of trial and error by which we all learn. A supervisor often combines the good features of a parent—providing a model and helping children over difficult moments when they undertake more than they can handle—while avoiding excessive concern that is difficult for the parent to control.

Nan Simpson: Play Plans

Nan Simpson is a full-time playground consultant in Dallas, Texas. Figures 6 and 7 are examples of her work.

In May 1977 Nan Simpson was interviewed about her views of playgrounds by April Powers, a student at North Texas State University. A summary of that interview follows.

Nan Simpson aims to design playgrounds that are both "safe and developmental." She attempts to isolate the different ways children use their bodies and incorporates those kinds of movement into the design. A starting point is responding to the question; How many ways can children get on and off a play structure or from one structure to another?

Simpson identifies the main problem of the traditional playground as specific function equipment such as the type slide that requires children to stand in line. Such equipment requires little thinking and promotes anti-social behavior.

Space is not the critical factor that many people assume it to be. Ms. Simpson designs "linked" playgrounds that can allow "200 children to play simultaneously in an area of one hundred feet by fifty feet."

During the next twenty-five years, she would like to see more playgrounds that children could rearrange and modular manufactured equipment that could be rearranged by adults and children working together.

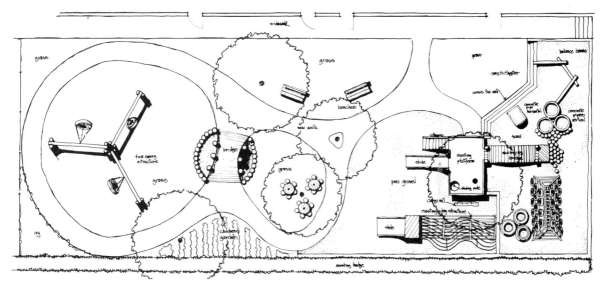

Figure 6 First Presbyterian Church Playground, Fort Smith, Arkansas. Designed by Nan Simpson.

Various agencies could fund research on children's play.

There's so much need for real research in the whole field of children's play.... The biggest problem is, designers who are ... more in love with their design than they are with the function of the thing.... I think that in a way it is unfortunate that it has fallen to sculptors and landscape architects to design playgrounds especially with such a dearth of input from child development and physical education and psychology and other related fields.

Summary and Conclusions

There are no mandatory standards for the manufacture of playground equipment in the United States. Consequently, quality and safety of equipment ranges from slip-shod and hazardous to extremely well-designed and relatively safe. Some manufacturers are constantly working to improve their products and should not be penalized for the omissions and errors of others. While the burden of proper manufacture must rest with the manufacturer, it is the consumer who must ensure that proper installation and periodic maintenance are provided.

Playground manufacturers and playground designers seem to be in relative agreement that play environments should be places for challenging, flexible, creative activities yet safe and aesthetically pleasing. On one of these counts, aesthetic appeal, both groups seem to be successful. Their products are appealing to see, at least to the adult eye. On the remaining two factors, safety and function, a great deal remains to be done.

Many manufacturers and designers are now recommending or providing safer installation of equipment in sand or other resilient areas. But some continue to ignore this need or to construct sand pits in the wrong places. The tendency of some designers to design mammoth, fixed rock and/or concrete structures into their play environments is of particular concern. It makes no sense to speak of flexibility, playability, adaptability, creative challenge or innovative play

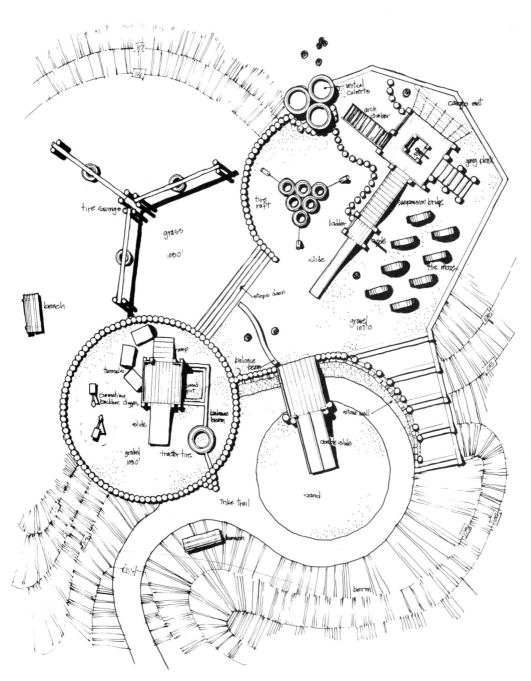

Figure 7 Jewish Community Center Playground,
Dallas, Texas. Designed by Nan Simpson.

when in reality the environment is fixed and hard. Contemporary playgrounds are worlds apart in design and play function from the adventure play environments of Scandanavia and certain other areas of the world. What the Scandanavians already know but what Americans are only beginning to learn is that in building playgrounds, adult intuition and traditional principles of design are out of character with children's play needs. The following chapter on adventure playgrounds will illuminate this statement.

8

THE ADVENTURE PLAYGROUND MOVEMENT*

"My aim was clear and correct—to give children in towns the same chance for creative play as those in the country."

Prof. C. Th. Sorensen†

Prior to World War II, before commercially built playgrounds became widespread, urban children spent much of their time playing in vacant lots and construction sites. The lots were used as garbage dumps by local residents and contained a wide assortment of refuse and junk including the kitchen sink. Children would spend hours constructing forts and clubhouses, and often the constructions would be aided by building materials and tools borrowed from a nearby construction site. Abandoned automobiles became airplanes and submarines, packing crates became castles and palaces. Often a lot would contain rival gangs whose members would delight in laying seige to their opponents' fort with garbage can lid shields and swords made from the slats of orange crates. Caves and tunnels would be dug, and potatoes

would be roasted over bonfires. At dinner time parents would have to drag their children home.

---

*The authors are deeply indebted to the following individuals for their courteous assistance during personal visits to European playgrounds:

Eva Insulander, Swedish Council for Children's Play.
Helga Pedersen and Thomas Foersom, Danish Playground Society.
Jens Sigsgaard, President of the Danish Playground Society and Past President of the International Playground Association.
Bill McCulloch, London Adventure Playground Association.
Mrs. D. R. Bearman, London Handicapped Adventure Playground Association.
†Lady Allen of Hurtwood. *Planning for Play*. Cambridge, Mass.: MIT Press, 1968 (from the Preface).

In an attempt to keep children off the streets, well-intentioned adults began to build neighborhood playgrounds. Unfortunately, in designing the new playgrounds, the play interests of children were ignored. What had once been a vacant lot filled with challenge, excitement, and a wealth of discarded materials became a sterile arena of concrete and steel. In her book *Planning for Play* (1968), the late Lady Allen of Hurtwood outlined the progression of playground development during the past fifty years (pp. 18–19):

I. *The prison period.* These playgrounds resemble prison exercise yards. They consist of a barren expanse of concrete or asphalt surrounded by a high fence. Lady Allen refers to these playgrounds as "an administrator's heaven and a child's hell."

II. *The ironmongery period.* During this period of playground construction, large metal climbing structures, slides, and other pieces of metal equipment were placed on the asphalt play areas. The common activity on this type of playground was climbing to the top of a metal structure and then falling or getting shoved to the pavement below. As noted in Chapter 3, this is the major cause of serious injury on playgrounds today. Unfortunately these playgrounds of concrete and steel have lived up to the claims of their designers and have proven to be indestructible.

III. *The concrete pipe period.* Many playgrounds contain concrete sewer pipes of various sizes and dimensions. Playground builders intended for children to crawl through and on top of the pipes. Sometimes the pipes are covered with dirt to form a mound. What initially seemed like a good idea has proven to be extremely hazardous. One playground in Texas that made elaborate use of concrete pipes was closed shortly after opening due to the number of injuries that occurred daily.

IV. *The novelty period.* At the other end of the continuum are playgrounds that Lady Allen refers to as "over-elaborate, over-clever, too slick, the pride of the architects." These playgrounds often include play sculptures that are nice to look at, but are not very functional and usually hazardous. This type of playground is typically found in the midst of large public housing projects. The novelty of these static playgrounds soon wears off.

Children have ignored these traditional playgrounds in favor of the city streets and vacant lots. Architect Paul Friedberg sums up this phenomenon,

Playgrounds that deny the child; that offer no chance of involvement, participation, or manipulation; that are devoid of choice, complexity, and interaction will be empty of children—a dead ground. The street will be a playground. (1970, p. 27)

ADVENTURE PLAYGROUNDS

How then can a rich, stimulating environment be incorporated into a playground where children ranging from toddlers to teenagers can play safely? One answer lies in adventure playgrounds. In Scandinavia and Britain, educators and playground designers have long recognized the importance of allowing children the freedom to do their own thing. Adventure playgrounds provide children with the opportunity to mold and shape the play environment: to tear it down and to start over again. Here children can create the form and structure of their play rather than having it imposed by an unmalleable environment.

What Is an Adventure Playground?

The London Adventure Playground Association (LAPA) was established in 1962 to promote an understanding of the educational, social, and welfare values of adventure playgrounds and to assist in the development of new ones. The LAPA (Jago, 1971) offers the following description of adventure playgrounds:

An adventure playground can best be described as a place where children are free to do many things that they cannot easily do elsewhere in our crowded urban society. In an adventure playground, which can be any size from one third of an acre to two and a half acres, they can build houses, dens and climbing structures with waste materials, have bonfires, cook in the open, dig holes, garden, or just play with sand, water and clay. The atmosphere is permissive and free, and this is especially attractive to children whose lives are otherwise much limited and restricted by lack of space and opportunity.

Each playground has two full-time leaders in charge who are friends to the children, and help them with what they are trying to do. There is a large hut on each playground and this is well equipped with materials for painting, dressing up and acting, modeling and other forms of indoor play. There is also a record player, table tennis and so on, so that in bad weather and in winter the adventure playground hut becomes a social center for many children who would have nowhere to play except the street.

History

Adventure playgrounds had their beginning in Denmark in 1943. C. Th. Sorensen, a landscape architect who had designed many playgrounds, observed that children seemed to enjoy playing with the scrap materials left on construction sites more than on the finished playgrounds. The children also played with the scrap materials more creatively and for longer periods of time than with the equipment built for them. It was this observation that provided the inspiration for the first junk playground (later copied under the name adventure playground) which was built adjacent to a public housing project in Endrup. John Bertelsen, a nursery school teacher and ex-seaman, was hired as the first play leader. Endrup proved to be a great success. And though it is not now the vibrant place it once was, it served as a model for the adventure playgrounds that followed.

One of those inspired by Endrup was Lady Allen of Hurtwood, an English landscape architect who organized adventure playgrounds in London in spaces left where buildings had been bombed out. Under the guidance of play leaders, children were encouraged to build their own constructions using rubble and other materials provided. Presently there are a large number of adventure playgrounds scattered throughout London. They are supported by neighborhood organizations and provide a wide range of activities for children.

The Growth of the Adventure Playground Movement

The idea of adventure playgrounds was born in Denmark and later exported to England and other countries. Sorensen's brain child was recreated in several areas of Denmark, notably Copenhagen, where a number of "byggelegepladsen" or "building playgrounds" as the Danes prefer to call them are in operation. The best of these are the envy of "play people" everywhere, containing extensive areas for building, gardening, cooking, climbing, and caring for animals in both indoor and outdoor contexts. The Danish play leaders are committed to the notion that recreational areas should be designed for both children and adults in close proximity to their homes.

The Swedish versions of the junk, building, or adventure playground are called, simply, play environments. The Swedes are reputed to have more playgrounds for children per capita than any other country in the world and direct observations do not leave one with much doubt about this. But as in other European countries only a small percentage of these are of a comprehensive nature. The best play environments in Sweden provide a wide array of activities for children and adults while the vast majority are of more limited design, typically a sand area with climbing structures, swings, slide, and a wheeled vehicle area.

In London, dozens of adventure playgrounds are scattered throughout the city. In the main these are truly junk playgrounds, containing an unbelievable array of structures built from scrounged materials. A fence surrounds the area and the ever-present play building containing a play area, the play leader's space, and assorted tools and play materials.

The adventure playground movement was slow to gain a footing in the United States. The American Adventure Playground Association (AAPA) was formed in April 1976 by a group of park and recreation professionals, educators, and commissioners in Southern California. Their major purpose is to promote the concept of adventure playgrounds in the United States through information services. In May 1977 the AAPA identified 16 adventure playgrounds in the United States. This, of course, does not include dozens of playgrounds built or being built by parent and community groups throughout the country (particularly in Pennsylvania, Texas, and Georgia) using scrounged materials but lacking such features as full-time play leaders.

PERSPECTIVES ON ADVENTURE PLAYGROUNDS

The best European playgrounds perhaps represent the "future today" in conceptualizing play environments. The concept of playground, limited in scope, will eventually be replaced by a more vital and comprehensive concept of outdoor environments for people of all ages, combining elements of nature, a wide array of play activities, and involving all family members in specially designed environments within their own immediate neighborhood.

The Play Leader

The key to a successful adventure playground is the play leader. The primary role of the leader is to facilitate a safe, happy play experience for each child while interfering as little as possible. Th.

Sorensen warned against too much supervision and imposed structure for children. Writing in 1947 he stated,

It is my opinion that children ought to be free by themselves to the greatest possible extent. A certain supervision and guidance will of course be necessary, but I am firmly convinced that one ought to be exceedingly careful when interfering in the lives and activities of children. (Allen, p. 55)

The play leader must also be a jack-of-all-trades. At times he or she will be called upon to be a teacher, administrator, carpenter, gardener, veterinarian, social worker, best friend, and substitute parent. In addition to the daily operation of the playground, the leader can serve as a community resource person by putting families in touch with various social services that can have a positive influence on the lives of children.

There are no set professional or educational qualifications for play leaders; however, there are identifiable qualities that a play leader should possess:

Must like children

Should be able to communicate effectively with children of all ages

Accepting of a wide range of individual differences

Support the work of children with a minimum of interference

Be able to thrive in a chaotic environment

Have a good sense of humor

A single set of qualifications, however, will not be appropriate in all settings. For example, an outstanding play leader in an outstanding playground in Copenhagen is an ex-farmer, having special skills in caring for the animals (chickens, goats, pigs, horses) as well as outstanding sensitivity and intuitive skill in working with children. In a ghetto area adventure playground in London a play leader expressed the view that rapport and success might include "smoking, swearing and shoving a bit." This statement is better understood when one views firsthand the social problems generated by poverty. Play structures and play buildings are sometimes burned by "outside groups" and varying degrees of vandalism are a frequent problem. Such problems seem less serious when the alternatives to playgrounds and play leaders—streets, alleys, roof tops, and abnormal influences—are considered.

Interaction with the children is only one of several play leader roles. A substantial amount of time is spent in scrounging materials and in building, repairing, or altering play structures. In London, vehicles are provided for searching out and hauling scrap, abandoned, or gift materials to the play site. The demand for such materials is so great that it is difficult to obtain sufficient quantities for the playgrounds. (In many areas of the United States almost unlimited materials are available to capable scroungers at low cost or no cost.) In London the play leaders spend some time building, particularly while the children are in school. Although there are opportunities for children to check out tools and create for themselves, the bulk of the building activity appears to be assumed by the play leaders. The ratio of adult/child building activity seems to be in proportion to the skill and sensitivity of the play leaders in involving children and the overall quality of the playground. On the worst London playgrounds little of value happens for anyone. On the more advanced ones there appears to be a genuine effort by play leaders to provide rich play experiences for children.

In Stockholm the author observed a group of children assisting a sow in giving birth to pigs. In Copenhagen one group of children fed and brushed the horses, cleaned the stables, and later prepared the horses for riding. On another playground children constructed hutches for their rabbits. And on a third children prepared outdoor fires in the area designed for that purpose and set about to cook their evening meal. All of this with the unobtrusive involvement of play leaders.

In England, Denmark, and Sweden play leadership training is available and a system exists that pays trainees for working in playgrounds. While we are not aware that any such programs exist in the United States many community colleges and universities have training programs on both professional and paraprofessional levels in the areas of child development and early childhood education. This type of training would be helpful for play leaders working with preschool and primary school age children.

The initial capital expense of an adventure playground is much less than that of a commercially built playground, but annual operating expenses are greater. The major portion of the playground budget will be used to pay substantial salaries to leaders. Play leadership is a new concept in the United States, so the salary will have to be determined by looking at similar jobs in other settings.

Playground Safety and Liability

Although adventure playgrounds have experienced great success in Europe during the past 30 years, they have been slow to gain acceptance in the United States. This is due to a combination of factors including objection to their untidy appearance, ignorance concerning the nature of children's play, and fear of injury and liability.

The safety record of adventure playgrounds is excellent. Lady Allen reports that during a 10-year period, with the exception of cuts, scrapes, bruises, nail punctures, and a few fractures, few serious injuries have been reported on British or Scandinavian adventure playgrounds nor have any law suits been filed against them by parents. The Milpitas adventure playground in California has been in operation since 1970 and has a similar safety record. However, public liability coverage is essential in case someone does get injured on the playground. The London Adventure Playground Association recommends that new playgrounds take out public liability coverage, employer's liability, burglary, and fire insurance. If the adventure playground is built on the grounds of a school or public park, it may be covered by existing insurance.

There appears to be an important reason why serious injuries are so rare on European adventure playgrounds. The children have more extensive experiences in climbing, jumping, swinging, balancing, judging, perceiving, and in risk taking than do their American counterparts who typically have only 20 to 30 minutes of playground activity each day on fixed, uninteresting equipment. The author was amazed by the dexterity and skill of London children engaged in a game of tag after dark on an adventure playground consisting of rope tree swings over steep terrain, aerial walkways, and multilevel climbing structures, all involving potential risk for serious injury because of unprotected heights and assorted debris littering the ground.

Characteristics of the Play Environment

The area of the play environment should range from a minimum of one-third acre to about four acres; anything larger would be difficult to supervise properly. Adventure playgrounds vary greatly in size and function. The range includes a small city lot with nothing more than a pile of scrap lumber and a portable cart containing tools, to elaborate playgrounds with a permanent recreation building and areas for gardening, animal care, ball play, as well as a construction area. If a permanent site cannot be secured, a trailer with chemical toilets would serve nicely as a playground office.

Figures 1 and 2 depict a sample adventure playground.* It covers approximately two acres and includes a permanent recreation center. The playground is staffed by two full-time play leaders as well as parent volunteers. The playground offers activities for children ranging from preschoolers to adolescents, and the recreation center is used by a wide range of community groups for meetings. The following is a description of important elements:

Fencing. The entire playground is usually enclosed by a fence. The main objection to adventure playgrounds is their untidy appearance. Therefore, the fence is constructed so that the playground cannot be seen from street level. Portholes, however, may be placed at intervals so that curious passers-by can view the children's activities. An enclosed playground also gives children a sense of being in their own private world. The fence should contain a large gate to allow trucks to enter.

Main Building-Recreation Center. Ideally the main building should contain the play leader's office; lavatories with access from both indoors and outdoors; storage area for play equipment; indoor play area equipped with art supplies, ping pong table, record player, etc.; storage and check out area for construction and gardening tools— this area should have shutters and a counter that opens to the outside so that children do not have to come inside to get their tools. Many Scandinavian buildings contain provisions (feed, etc.) for the care of animals. In Denmark the children pay a small fee for their animal feed but they must assume the responsibility for care of their animal(s).

Construction Area. This is the area in which the children build their club houses, forts, and other

*Appreciation is extended to Andrew P. Cohen for drawing the author's designs.

constructions, dig in the ground, light fires, and cook. A varied terrain makes for a more interesting environment. Large boulders and tree trunks are found on many Scandinavian playgrounds. The play leaders must check that all constructions on the playground are safe, not just when they are erected, but all the time.

Storage Bin. It is advisable to construct simple, open bins for storing scrap materials that the children will use for construction. The bin may be divided into compartments so that the materials may be sorted by size, shape, and weight. The bin should be placed so that deliveries of building materials may be easily made.

Garden Area. A garden area can provide a rich learning experience for children. Since children enjoy caring for their own plants, part of the garden should be divided into small plots. Stepping stones are sometimes placed throughout the garden to avoid trampling plants.

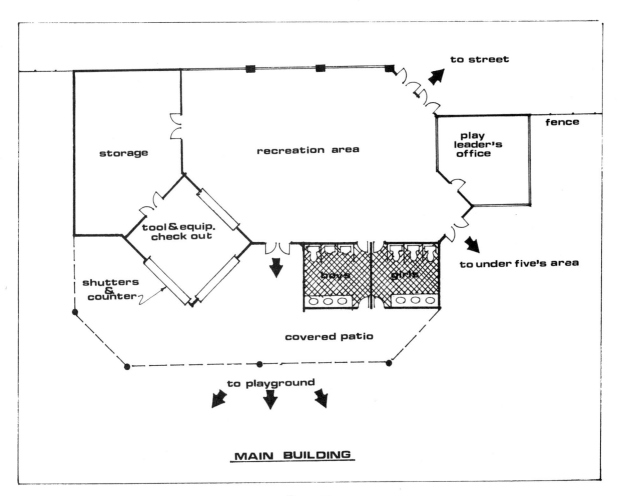

Figure 1

Animal Area. Part of every child's education should include the care of animals. Many playgrounds in Sweden and Denmark have animal houses that contain individual cages for children who do not have room in small apartments to keep their pets. On some playgrounds dozens of rabbit hutches are built and maintained by the children. In addition, pens and stables are provided for goats, chickens, pigs, and horses.

Under Five's Area. A separate area for children five and under should be placed away from the mainstream of the playground. This area should contain provisions for sand and water play, bike path for wheeled toys, large outdoor building blocks, and a playhouse.

Commons Area. This is a flat grassy area that can be used for ball games and games with rules. Scandinavian and British playgrounds are frequently found adjacent to playing grounds where soccer and other competitive games are played.

Fire Pits. Part of the adventure playground experience includes building fires. Therefore, an

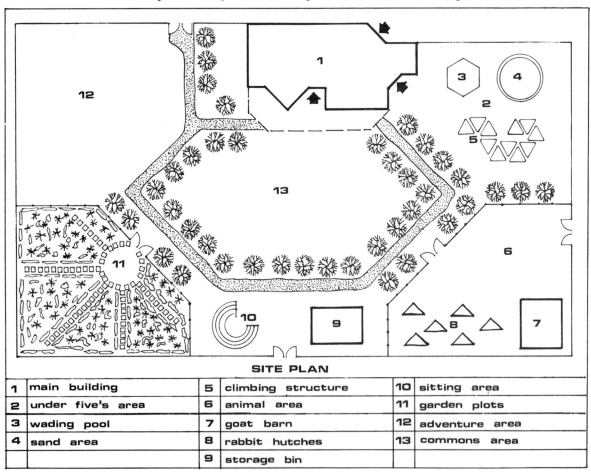

SITE PLAN

1	main building	5	climbing structure	10	sitting area
2	under five's area	6	animal area	11	garden plots
3	wading pool	7	goat barn	12	adventure area
4	sand area	8	rabbit hutches	13	commons area
		9	storage bin		

Figure 2

area for small fires should be provided as well as a large pit for lighting bonfires on special occasions. Grills should also be provided so that children can cook. Many European playgrounds have a large pot over an open fire for making stew. Children bring various ingredients from home to contribute to the pot.

PHOTO ESSAY: EUROPEAN PLAY ENVIRONMENTS

London

Adventure playgrounds abound in the park and vacant lots of London. Two major differences between these and American playgrounds are immediately obvious: (1) they are constructed (primarily by play leaders) almost exclusively from junk materials and, (2) full-time adult play leaders are available. Play leaders construct new challenges for the children while they are in school. The play structures are constantly being modified to ensure the discovery feature. On the most challenging playgrounds children can transverse much of the playground on linked structures and swinging ropes without touching the ground.

Little concern is directed to fall surfaces, protective barriers, or heights, but care is taken to prevent collapse of structures or breaking of swings. Challenge and discovery are the key concepts in creating an adventure playground. As one play leader put it, "challenges help kids learn to take care of themselves."

Stockholm

Sweden has a reputation for providing more playgrounds for children than any other country in the world. Playgrounds are scattered about the huge apartment communities but most are small areas enclosing a sand area, swings and, frequently, one or more commercial climbing structures.

The large playgrounds make extensive use of natural terrain, hills, trees and rocks. This imaginative water play area is woven into the side of a hill in a central play area.

The best of Sweden's playgrounds are more appropriately called play environments. This farmlike atmosphere, located in Stockholm, combines features to meet recreational and leisure needs of all ages. The children's playground is adjacent to a seating area for adults. Coffee, pastries, and other delicacies are available. The barns house animals and games area and the entire area overlooks rolling pasture land and gardens.

Copenhagen

Denmark, the birthplace of the adventure playground, combines the elements of the adventure playgrounds in London and the play environments in Sweden. And on their best playgrounds they do it with style and imagination.

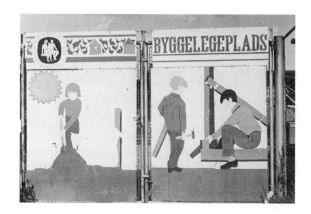

The sign on the gate depicts a *byggelegeplads* or building playground. The range of activities includes building, gardening, and caring for animals in a context designed for all family members.

The playground is laid out much like a small town with main streets and side roads bounding blocks or sections containing rabbit and chicken hutches built by the children themselves with the advice of a play leader.

The main animal area is a miniature farm within a city. Children do most of the cleaning and feeding chores. Veterinarians assist in the health care of animals. ▼

▲ The building area is stocked with scrap lumber. When a new child joins the group, he is assisted in building an animal structure. Old ones are burned in the outdoor cooking fires. Children wear shoes with wooden soles to prevent nail punctures.

▲The Danes are lovers of nature and believe that cities should retain the natural greenery of the country-side. Greenhouses and gardens are maintained by the children. Vegetables grown will eventually end up in their own cooking pots.

Equipment for gardening, building, and animal care is available for use by the children. They buy feed for their personal animals at a fraction of its actual cost. The Danish local and state governments make grants for recreational arrangements intended for both children and adults.

Building outdoor fires for cooking, warmth, or pleasure is common on European playgrounds. Specially designed areas, generally constructed with brick, are set aside for this purpose. The large central pit is frequently circled by smaller pits for individual small cooking fires. The entire area is usually surrounded by benches or logs for group social activities.

A very special type of playground in Copenhagen allows children to learn proper driving skills on a model track complete with traffic lanes, street signs, electric traffic lights, and adult leadership.

CONCLUSION: MAKING A COMMITMENT

In applying Lady Allen's classification scheme for playgrounds to the United States it is obvious that we have yet to emerge from the iron age. In order for adventure playgrounds to flourish in this country, a commitment must be made to provide quality play experiences for children. This commitment includes the active involvement of community members and governmental agencies in planning for play. When new housing developments and schools are planned, funds should be allocated to support recreation programs and full-time play leaders.

Adventure playgrounds provide children with a rich learning environment that cannot be duplicated by a static playground. They learn how to build with tools, to work cooperatively, and to care for plants and animals. When needed, an adult is present to lend a helping hand. Most importantly, children develop competence and confidence in themselves.

Experience in Europe during the past 30 years has shown that, besides the obvious benefits to children, adventure playgrounds exert a positive influence on the larger community. They bring people together, create a sense of community, and serve as a catalyst for other projects. They add to the quality of life.

REFERENCES AND SUGGESTED READINGS

Allen, Lady of Hurtwood. *Adventure Playgrounds for Handicapped Children.* London: James Galt, 1974.

———. *Planning for Play.* Cambridge, Mass.: M.I.T. Press, 1968.

Bengtsson, Arvid. *Adventure Playgrounds.* New York: Praeger, 1974.

———. *The Child's Right to Play.* Sheffield: International Playground Association, 1974.

———. *Environmental Planning for Children's Play.* New York: Praeger, 1970.

Friedberg, Paul M. *Play and Interplay.* New York: Macmillan, 1970.

International Playground Association. *Play and creativity: Planning the environment and training leaders.* Report of the fifth International Conference held in Vienna in September 1972.

———. *Playgrounds: With or without leadership?* Report of the fourth International Conference held in Paris in July 1969.

Jago, L. *Learning through Experience.* London: London Adventure Playground Association, 1971.

Lambert, J. *Adventure Playgrounds.* London: Jonathan Cape, 1974.

A Little about Lots: The Do-It-Yourself Book on Improving Vacant Lots and Neighborhoods. The Parks Council of New York City, 80 Central Park West, New York, New York 10023.

National Playing Fields Association. *What Is an Adventure Playground?* London: The Association, 1976.

Passantino, Erika D. Adventure playground for learning and socialization. *Phi Delta Kappan,* 1975, ———, 329–333.

Rudolph, Nancy. *Workyards: Playgrounds Planned for Adventure.* New York: Teachers College Press, 1974.

Salzer, Michael. A better world for big-city children to play in. *Current Sweden,* 1974, *34,* 5 pp.

Sigsgaard, Jens. The playground in modern Danish housing. Reprint from *Danish Foreign Office Journal,* 1965, *54,* 8 pp.

Utzinger, Robert C. *Some European Nursery Schools and Playgrounds.* Ann Arbor: Architectural Research Laboratory of the University of Michigan, 1970.

Ward, Colin, and Blunden, George. *Safety on Adventure Playgrounds.* London: National Playing Fields Association, 1974.

ORGANIZATIONS

American Adventure Play Association.
P.O. Box 5430, Huntington Beach, California, 92646 (Bill Vance, President).

Danish Playground Society.
Virkefeltet 2,2700, Brønshøj, Copenhagen, Denmark (Helga Pedersen, Director).

Handicapped Adventure Playground Association.
HAPA Office, Fulham Palace, Bishops Avenue, London SW6 6EA, England.

International Playground Association.
Treasurer: Miss M. E. Otter, 12 Cherry Tree Drive, Sheffield S11 9AE, England (American Correspondent, Paul Hogan).

London Adventure Playground Association.
25 Ovington Square, London SW3 1LQ, England.

Playground Clearing House, Inc.
26 Buckwalter Road, Phoenixville, Pennsylvania, 19460 (Paul Hogan, President and American correspondent for the International Playground Association).

Swedish Council for Children's Play.
Socialstyrelsen S-106 30, Stockholm, Sweden (Eva Insulander, Head of Office).

9

PLAY AND HANDICAPPED CHILDREN

"When a child cannot play, we should be as troubled as when he refuses to eat or sleep."*

Educators use a variety of labels, designations, and terms when referring to handicapped children. Terms such as disabled, defective, injured, and impaired are often used interchangeably, but in fact have different connotations. A handicap is the social and personal consequence of an injury or defect that results in impairment or disability. Handicaps may be divided into three broad categories: physical handicaps, communication handicaps, and development and learning handicaps. Table 1 outlines these categories and their social and personal consequences.

Depending upon the nature of their handicap, children may experience difficulty in such skills as: extent of exploration; initiation of ac-

tivities; response and approach to others; attention to people, materials and tasks; acceptance of limits and routines; respect for rights of others; seeing self as able to do and achieve.

Adults who work with handicapped children must understand that there are broad individual differences between children with similar handicaps. Standardized educational fare is no more appropriate for them than for non-handicapped children. Adults must approach children with expectations for growth. Perhaps the single most important principle in working with handicapped children is that they can learn and they want to learn. They are human beings with normal needs for love, praise, attention, success, pleasure, and self-esteem, but, because of the social and personal consequences of their condition, it is more difficult for them to acquire them.

As we have seen in Chapter 1, play is the vehicle by which children develop and demon-

*Hartley, Ruth F., Frank, Lawrence K., and Goldenson, Robert M. *Understanding Children's Play.* New York: Columbia University Press, 1952.

Handicapped children have the same need to play as do nonhandicapped children, but, because of personal, social, and physical barriers, it is more difficult for these needs to be fulfilled.

and social play. When placed on the floor in close proximity to toys, severely retarded children may not move from the position in which they are placed, reach out to examine toys, or imitate the actions of others. The problem is further complicated by the attitudes and actions of people and institutions who care for retarded children. Everyone agrees that retarded children have the same play needs as nonretarded children but retarded children, especially those in training schools, have fewer opportunities to play (Benoit, 1955). This is due to a number of reasons:

- Adults may underestimate the potential of retarded children to develop skills in play

- There has been little thinking and writing on the subject of play and retarded children

- Much of the existing play equipment and materials is questionable for normal children and is unsuitable for the retarded

- Mental retardation is frequently linked with special deficiencies that make play difficult

- An attitude of hopelessness toward teaching play activities to retarded children.

- Ignorance concerning the importance of play in the development of both normal and retarded children

- An overconcern with accident and injury

Once positive attitudes concerning play and retarded children have been developed, parents and care-givers are faced with the task of teaching retarded children how to play. Whereas play, imitation, and exploration occur as a matter of course in normal children, play and other associated behaviors must be systematically planned for and taught to retarded children.

A number of people have studied the play behaviors of mentally retarded children. Some tentative generalizations are available. Social

strate competency in dealing with their environment. If a handicapping condition results in play deprivation, the child's competence in interacting with people and objects will also be lacking.

PLAY AND MENTALLY RETARDED CHILDREN

Mentally retarded children typically lack the skills needed to engage in higher level cognitive

Table 1 Categories of Handicaps and Their Consequences

Category	Specific Handicaps	Social and Personal Consequences

Physical	Crippled
	Birth defects
	Blind and partially sighted
	Neurological disorders
	  Cerebral palsy
	  Epilepsy
	Health impaired
		The child has problems with:
		  Mobility
		  Experiencing the world through all of his senses
		  Mastering his physical and human environments
		  People who are too helpful or too demanding
		  People who do not understand his difficulties in gaining mastery over his world
		  Isolation
		  Diminished energy

Communication	Speech
	Deaf and hard of hearing
	Language disorders of childhood
	Severe language delay
	Multihandicapped
		The child has problems with:
		  Learning or using verbal symbols to think and communicate about his world
		  Isolation
		  Dealing with academic learning which requires the use of verbal symbols

Development and learning	Mental retardation
	Behavior disorders
	Specific learning disabilities
		The child has problems with:
		  Reduced interest in the world
		  Difficulty in relating positively to children and/or adults
		  Developing internal controls
		  Failure to live up to expectations
		  Rejection and isolation

play can be increased by direct teaching, prompting and rehearsing roles, followed by positive reinforcement (Strain, 1975; Paloutgian, Hasagi, Streifel, and Edgar, 1971. Integrating handicapped children into play situations with nonhandicapped or higher-functioning peer models also increases their social play (Morris and Dalker, 1974; Devoney, Guralnick, and Rubin, 1974). Thus, it seems that tools already at our disposal, i.e., direct instruction, modeling, and reinforcement, can be valuable allies in promoting social play among mentally handicapped children. Further, the currently popular concept of mainstreaming or integrating handicapped and non-handicapped children in the classroom should be extended to the outdoor play environment.

Mentally retarded children should be thoroughly evaluated to determine the extent of any motor or sensory deficit and a review of their behaviors should be conducted. This includes analysis of imitation behaviors, tracking and searching skills, language competencies, and social interaction skills. Additional behaviors that have rarely been measured by researchers and clinicians include frequency of action on play materials and toys; diversity of play behaviors, i.e., frequency of novel responses; range of toys or materials acted on; frequency of

Adults must be skillful in supporting and extending the play of handicapped children.

interaction between peers and number of different peers interacted with; affective or aggressive
behavior during play periods (Wehman, 1975,
p. 242).

In working with severely retarded children
who have few skills, it may be more appropriate
to work on a wide range of parallel activities at
a low developmental level, rather than attempting to achieve a high level of sophistication in
one play skill, i.e., block design.

Michelman (1974) constructed a detailed
"Play Agenda"* for the handicapped child that
describes the specifications for designing a play
environment, toys appropriate for various cognitive levels, specifications for play experiences,
and specifications for activities that promote
risk-taking and decision-making abilities.

---

*Adapted from "Play and the Deficit Child" by
Shirley S. Michelman. In *Play as Exploratory Learn-
ing*, edited by Mary Reilly © 1974, pages 194–205.
By permission of the publisher, Sage Publications,
Inc. (Beverly Hills/London).

Specifications for Environment

Play environments for handicapped children should
meet the following criteria:

1. provide a match between the child's abilities, interests, and environmental expectations. Play
   equipment should adjust to more than one purpose, more than one child, and more than one
   developmental level

2. provide substantial sensory-cultural enrichment
   that arouses curiosity and stimulates investigation

3. include play materials and activities that meet the
   requirements of children at different cognitive,
   kinesthetic, and play stages and foster growth
   and learning

   A. At the sensory-motor stage of practice play:

      1) toys that appeal to the senses and muscles:
         soft toys for feeling, squeezing, and throw-
         ing; toys for sand and water play; swings,
         seesaws, slides

      2) toys that challenge growing powers: empty
         containers with removable lids to take off

and put on, cartons or boxes to climb upon or into, building blocks

B. At the symbolic, imaginative play stage:

1) toys that strengthen large muscles: wheeled toys, large balls, large hollow blocks

2) toys for stretching the mind and activating problem solving: puzzles; wooden beads for stringing; aquarium, terrarium

3) toys for make-believe, pretending, and practicing grownup roles: dolls, housekeeping equipment and props, dress-up clothes

4) toys for creating, expressing feelings and ideas, and symbolic formation: crayons; chalk; paint, clay; materials for collage and construction; variety of records and percussion instruments

C. For children who are learning to play games with rules:

1) toys, games, and apparatus for developing skills, teamwork and group participation: bicycle, skates, sports equipment

2) materials for creating, for practicing risk taking and decision making, and for building confidence and self-esteem: art materials, needlework, carpentry tools, model building, camera, musical instruments

3) materials for stretching the mind: measuring instruments; magnifying glass, microscope; binoculars; hobby sets; board games; games of chance; games that develop specific academic skills

4. offer opportunities for success and evoke confidence and self-esteem

5. include models of adults and older children to imitate and learn from

6. be structured by consistency and pervaded by a spirit of playfulness to encourage adaptation

7. be structured by time and space to help children understand these concepts as they build habit structures for dealing with such realities

Specifications for Experiences

1. Play experiences that correspond as closely as possible to the normal stages of healthy children.

2. Sequences of play activities that alternate group experience with periods set aside for solitary play with materials and ideas allow the child to proceed at his own tempo as he practices basic skills and gains understanding of his environment.

3. Art experiences with sensory media and imaginative play activities enhance a child's capacity for adaptive emotional behavior.

4. Play experiences that provide opportunities for repetition, imitation, and problem solving promote learning and help the handicapped child find order and meaning in the environment.

5. Games with rules of graduated difficulty encourage children to practive the discipline of self-restraint and control of immediate impulse as they submit their behavior to a given task.

6. Experiences that evoke the instinct for workmanship and or sense in mastering things for their own sake, such as making sand castles, painting, and model building enable handicapped children to savor intrinsic satisfaction and reward.

7. Motivation stimuli keyed to the child's interests and developmental level as well as enthusiastic adults are devices that get a play experience started.

8. Variables to be aware of in play experience are:

A. the degree and range of required rules and the form and source of personal or impersonal controls exercised over the child

B. the minimum level of ability required to participate in a game

C. the provisions for verbal or nonverbal interactiveness

D. the provision for reward, both intrinsic and extrinsic

9. Individual and group variables to be aware of:

A. the child's readiness, capability, and motivation at the current moment

B. the degree of self-control available to the child at a given time

C. the degree of group cohesion, composition, and mood, influence the course of play development

(Photo by Camilla Jessel)

Some of the most satisfying play equipment is constructed from discarded materials.

D. timing and sequence of play experiences are important variables to control

Specifications for Activities that Promote Risk-Taking and Decision-Making Abilities

1. Art activities that encourage experimentation with numerous solutions to a problem involve children in risk taking and decision making.
2. Table games in which errors and wrong decisions are not irreversible.

3. Activities that allow alternative solutions to problems and adults who refrain from making a child's choices encourage decision making and active learning.
4. Creative activities and imaginative play allow children to revise and alter many previously held wrong decisions about themselves.
5. Activities that are dependent upon group choice help handicapped children learn the dynamics of group decision making.
6. Any play activity or game that provides experiences in success promotes feelings of confidence and competence in handicapped children and builds a framework of security from which children draw courage and flexibility for their daily living.

PLAY AND BLIND CHILDREN

When young children are deprived of sight, the quality of their interaction with the environment is greatly reduced. They have much difficulty orienting to space and time and in separating reality from nonreality. As a result the play behavior of young blind children is greatly reduced and attempts to engage them in play may be difficult. Many are content to be left alone or to engage in repetitive, stereotyped behaviors (Sandler, 1963, 344–345). Play is far less frequently pursued and considerably less important in the blind child's life than in the life of the child with full vision (Rothschild, 1960, p. 330).

However, lack of interest and involvement in the play of blind children need not be an accepted condition of their lives. Blind children are less imaginative in their play than are sighted children (Singer and Streiner, 1966) but special attention to training in fantasy play and imaginative story-telling could improve this condition.

As we have seen in previous chapters, spontaneous play is essential in the intellectual and affective development of the child. Although

Opportunities for risk taking need to be carefully planned and provided.

(Photo by Camilla Jessel)

Activities for vision-impaired and blind children are chosen to provide a wide range of sensory cues.

blind children possess normal intellectual potential, the full potential of a blind child may not be reached due to a lack of spontaneous play and an impoverished fantasy life. Well-meaning professionals may attempt to meet the play needs of blind children by involving them in organized group games and activities. However, these activities cannot be substituted for creative play which develops independently and spontaneously. Parents and educators must become more aware of the importance of play for healthy development and teach blind children how to play so that their full potentialities may be realized.

The following are suggestions for enhancing the play of blind children:

Planning for play. Before the free play period begins, discuss with the children the various play options that are available to them: equipment, materials, toys, games, activities, playmates. Have the children discuss their favorite play activities and what they intend doing during the play period.

Sensory-rich play environment. Design the play environment to include a wide variety of sensory cues to alert and guide the blind child in play, especially through the use of the senses of touch, hearing, and spatial perception. Large play equipment should remain in predictable locations to prevent accidental collisions. Subtle differences in changes of texture and/or slope of the walkway or areas surrounding play equipment would help to orient the child (Morris, 1974). The child could also be trained to sense the slight change in temperature that occurs when walking through a shadow cast by an adjacent or overhead play structure. Tactile maps placed at strategic points would also help to orient the child as would cassette tape recorders with directions. The environment should have a rich variety of textures and materials including sand, gravel, dirt, mud, large rocks; various textures of wood, water, grass, hills; places to crawl into, and through; things to climb, swing, and slide on; plants and animals.

Rehearsal. The teacher should rehearse with the child the use of the various play materials and equipment. For example, the teacher could practice with the child climbing up a slide and sliding down, rolling down a grassy hill, climbing up and down a play structure and so on.

Reinforcement. The teacher should be constantly ready to reinforce appropriate play behavior and accomplishments of the child. Reinforcement should be gradually faded out so that play can become intrinsically rewarding.

Mainstreaming. Blind children should be placed in an integrated setting with sighted children. Children are the ultimate teachers of other children.

Feedback and evaluation. The teacher should evaluate each play period with the children. It is not important that they stick to their original plan. What is important is that the teacher help the children to reflect on what they did and to offer encouragement and praise.

PLAY AND CHILDREN WITH BEHAVIOR DISORDERS

Behavior disorders are "deviation from age-appropriate behavior which significantly inter-feres with (1) the child's own growth and development and/or (2) the lives of others" (Kirk, 1972, p. 389). Children with behavior disorders compose the largest percentage of exceptional children. Children with behavior disorders may be extremely withdrawn or may exhibit severe acting-out behavior. They are children of average intelligence who do not interact effectively with their environment or with other people.

The best indication of positive social interaction of young children is age-appropriate play with other children. One common approach to fostering cooperative social play of children with behavior disorders is the use of behavior modification. A case in point is the work that has been done with autistic children. Instead of playing appropriately with toys or other children, autistic children frequently engage in self-stimulatory behaviors. For example, instead of moving a toy truck appropriately along the ground, the child might turn the truck upside down and spin the wheels for hours at a time. Or, the child might ignore toys and other people and sit in a corner of the room and rhythmically rock back and forth for hours at a time.

The basic procedures in behavior modification are (1) identification and measurement of maladaptive behavior to be extinguished and new adaptive behaviors to be taught, (2) systematic application of punishment to reduce maladaptive behavior and at the same time systematic reinforcement to teach adaptive behavior, (3) gradual fading out of reinforcement to be replaced by intrinsic, naturally occurring rewards. The adult controls both the conditions under which the behavior occurs (physical and social setting) and provides appropriate consequences (punishment, ignoring, reward) immediately following a target behavior. The following are two sample studies that describe the use of behavior modification to increase the appropriate play behavior of autistic children.

Koegel, Firestone, Kramme, and Dunlap (1974) increased the spontaneous play of two autistic children (an eight-year-old boy and a six-year-old girl) by suppressing their self-stimulatory behavior. Each of the children was placed in a playroom containing a variety of toys and play materials. Self-stimulatory responses were punished by one or both of the experimentors sharply saying "No!" and briskly slapping or briefly holding (immobilizing) the part of the child's body with which the response was being performed.

Romanczyk, Diament, Goren, Frunell, and Harris (1975) attempted to increase both the solitary and social play of four autistic children, ages five to seven. During daily half-hour sessions, the children were placed in a 9 × 12 ft cordoned-off area within their classroom. The area contained a variety of toys and play materials. The children were rewarded with food and social reinforcement first for appropriate solitary play with toys and later for appropriate social behavior. Inappropriate behavior was ignored. The appropriate play behavior of the four children increased greatly during the intervention period; however, when the reinforcement was abruptly dropped, the appropriate behavior rapidly declined. In a follow-up study appropriate play behavior was sustained by gradually fading out the reinforcement and then reinforcing on an unpredictable basis.

PLAY THERAPY

Play therapy is a set of techniques used to help children with emotional problems. It is founded on psychoanalytic theory which is concerned with the dynamics of personality and the unconscious feelings of an individual. It is based upon the fact that play is the child's natural medium of self-expression, and, just as in adult therapy where an individual "talks out" his

difficulties, in play therapy the child is provided an opportunity to "play out" feelings and problems (Axline, 1969, p. 9).

There are at least six theoretical approaches to the therapeutic use of play (Schaefer, 1976). The *psychoanalytic approach* to play therapy emphasizes the use of the therapist's interpretation of a child's words and actions to help the child achieve insight into his unconscious conflicts. The therapist seldom directly intervenes or attempts to structure the child's play but rather reflects on the child's words and actions. "I can see that you are very angry Billy." The goal of the *release or cathartic approach* is to work through emotional conflicts by symbolically directing the child's aggression toward the source of conflict. For example, a child may beat on a Bobo doll or symbolically hurt a parent by attacking a doll resembling a parent figure. Axline (1969) stresses the importance of creating *a climate of trust* in which the therapist shows acceptance of the child and trust in the child's ability to "play out" her own problems. The *play group approach* adds the influence of group dynamics to the therapeutic process. The *limit-setting approach* places emphasis on setting clear and enforceable rules regarding a child's behavior in the playroom. For example, if the child is very destructive or physically aggressive toward the therapist or other children, she might be removed from the playroom and not be allowed to return until the next scheduled session. The final approach uses *behavior modification* to extinguish maladaptive behavior and to teach new appropriate ones. Although these techniques represent different theoretical orientations, they are by no means mutually exclusive and may be used in conjunction depending upon the needs of the child.

Based upon the initial interview with the parents and child on the therapist's initial observations of the child, long-term goals will be established. They might include such things as

(Photo by Camilla Jessel)

The play leader must develop a warm, friendly relationship with the child.

a decrease in aggressive, acting-out behavior, an expression of greater self-esteem, a decrease in anger and corresponding positive feelings directed towards a family member. Typically the child spends an hour at a time in the playroom with the therapist. At times the therapist may be nonassertive and observe the child for long periods of time without communicating. At other times she may take a very active role. Therapy may also be conducted with small groups of children. Axline (1969) suggests several basic principles of play therapy:

- The therapist must develop a warm, friendly relationship with the child as soon as possible.
- The therapist accepts the child exactly as she is.
- The therapist establishes a feeling of permissiveness so that the child feels free to express her feelings completely.
- The therapist is alert to recognize the feelings the child is expressing and reflects them back to him

in such a manner that he gains insight into her behavior.

- The therapist demonstrates a strong belief in the child's ability to solve her own problems and provides her an opportunity to do so.
- The therapist does not attempt to direct the child's actions or conversation in any manner (this would not be true in behaviorally oriented therapy).
- Therapy should be viewed as a gradual process and it should not be hurried.
- The therapist establishes only those limitations that are necessary to anchor the therapy to the world of reality and to make the child aware of her responsibility in the relationship.

Play therapy is based on the assumption that everything said or done by the child in the playroom has meaning to the child. However, it is difficult to understand and interpret all of a child's play messages. The task becomes easier when appropriate play materials are provided. For example, a child may enact family scenes by using dolls that represent family members. However, in the absence of dolls, a child may symbolically represent herself and a parent using a big and a little block, causing the therapist to miss the message. The playroom should contain a wide range of materials that lend themselves to self-expression. For example, a child should be able to express anger by punching dolls, or destroying clay figures, as well as by composing poems, writing stories, and painting pictures that depict her anger. Axline (1969, p. 54) suggests the following list of toys and materials:

nursing bottles	didee doll
doll family	large rag doll
doll house with furniture	puppets
	puppet screen
toy soldiers and army equipment	crayons
	clay
toy animals	finger paints
play dough	sand

pictures of people, horses, and other animals	water
	toy guns
empty berry baskets to smash	peg pounding set
	paper dolls
variety of art materials	little cars and airplanes

playhouse materials: table, chairs, cot, doll bed, stove, tin dishes, pans, spoons, doll clothes, clothes line, clothes pins, clothes basket

Parents and Teachers as Therapists

Parents and teachers may gain insights into the feelings of children and help them to work through emotional problems by conducting play sessions in the home or school. Guerney (1976) has established guidelines for parents to use in play therapy. The same guidelines may also apply to teachers with slight practical modifications for use in the school.

- Set aside a specific time and place. In the beginning one-half hour per week is sufficient. Later the length of the sessions can be increased. The time of the session should not be changed from week to week nor should a session be cancelled. It is important that a strict schedule be adhered to so that progress will not be impeded.
- Find a location where there will be no distractions. If the phone rings, let it ring. Make arrangements so that the session will not be interrupted by other adults or children. Play therapy is messy at times so find a room where there will be least concern if things get spoiled or broken.
- Toys should be selected in order to help the child release his aggressions and to represent his feelings (see Ginott, 1960, and Axline, 1969). The toys should be reserved for use in the play session only. The child may not take or use toys out of the session.
- In setting up the first session, it is not necessary to go into a long explanation with the child. You

may simply say you want to spend more time with him. Place the emphasis on *you* wanting to be together, have fun, and improve your relationship, not that you want to help *him*.

- The role of the parent and teacher in a play session is to establish an atmosphere of free play and acceptance for the child. You set the stage by establishing time parameters and the few basic rules, but at the same time make it clear that what the child says and does in the session are totally up to him. The adult must be willing to follow the lead of the child. Therefore, it is important that the parent or teacher engage in:

> No criticism
> No praise, approval, or encouragement
> No questions, leads, or invitations
> No suggestions, advice, or persuasion
> No interruptions or interference
> No information
> No teaching, preaching, or moralizing
> No initiating a new activity

While it is important for the adult not to interfere, it is equally important for the adult to be fully involved with the child by giving complete attention to everything the child says and does. If the adult is asked to join in an activity, he should do so while focusing attention on what the child wants the adult to do following his direction and reflecting on his feelings. Play therapy can be very rewarding for both adult and child. The child is able to play out his feelings and the adult can learn more about his own feelings toward the child. It can strengthen and improve the quality of the relationship outside the therapy session.

PLAY AND PHYSICALLY HANDICAPPED CHILDREN

Children with physical handicaps include those who are crippled, have congenital defects, neurological disorders such as cerebral palsy and epilepsy, or other health impairments. The American Standards Association (1961), lists the following categories of physical impairments:

1. *Nonambulatory disabilities* are those impairments that, regardless of cause, confine individuals to wheelchairs.

2. *Semiambulatory disabilities* are those impairments that cause individuals to walk with difficulty or insecurity; examples include individuals with cardiac and pulmonary ills, those who require the use of braces, crutches, or canes, as well as persons who are arthritics, amputees, or spastics.

3. *Incoordination disabilities* include faulty coordination or palsy due to brain, spinal, or peripheral nerve injuries.

A child with a physical handicap may be of normal or superior intelligence. He may, however, have problems with mastering his physical environment, especially environments that are not designed to accommodate physically handicapped persons. He may have difficulty in dealing with his human environment in that he may encounter people who are too helpful or too demanding, or people who do not understand his physical difficulties. He may also suffer from isolation in that he may be excluded from the play activities enjoyed by nonhandicapped children of his age because of manmade barriers, both physical and personal.

In order to facilitate the play of physically handicapped children, special care must be taken in the design of the play environment. Playgrounds for handicapped children should be super-enriched environments that provide many opportunities for cognitive learning (symbolizing, conceptualizing, problem solving) as well as opportunities for physical learning (vestibular, kinesthetic, proprioceptive, and sensory). The elements of the play environment should be similar to those of creative playgrounds (see Chapter 6): opportunities for sand, mud, and water play; play structures that provide opportunities for exploration; fantasy and gross motor

(Photo by Camilla Jessel)

A primary element in designing playgrounds for handicapped children is accessibility. Equipment is designed with play in mind.

play; digging and gardening; animal care; carpentry; and a wealth of loose parts to stimulate creative play.

The primary consideration in designing a playground for physically handicapped children is one of accessibility. All areas of the playground, plus all play apparatus and structures must be accessible to all children, even children in wheelchairs. The following are suggestions for meeting this goal:*

1. The layout of the playground should allow for continuous circulation. A paved path, at least 36 in. wide to accommodate wheelchairs, should wind throughout the entire playground in an intersecting closed loop design (see Figure 1).

2. Paths should not exceed a slope of 5 percent (a rise of 1 ft over a distance of 20 ft). Best suited to wheelchair travel are walks with slopes of 3 to 4 percent.

3. Ramps one uses to gain access to buildings, play apparatus, hills, bridges, etc, should not exceed a slope of 8.33 percent (a rise of 1 ft over a distance of 12 ft). Best suited for wheelchair travel are ramps with slopes of 6 percent (a rise of 1 ft over a distance of 16.6 ft) (see Figure 2).

4. Sand and water play areas should be raised on one end at least 30 in. high with a 36 in. deep by 30 in. wide indentation to allow children in wheelchairs to enjoy sand play without removal from chair. However, wheelchair-bound children should be encouraged to leave the chair to play in sand, water, play on slide, or roll down hills (see Figure 3).

5. Handrails should be provided on all ramps and play structures (see Figure 4).

6. Stairs should be avoided. If stairs are present they should not be recessed (see Figure 5).

7. Slides must provide access to all types of handicaps (see Figure 6).

*Adapted from "A Playground for all Children: Design Competition, August, 1976," New York City Department of Planning, 76–13. By permission of Victor Marrero, Chairman, New York City Department of City Planning.

1. SLIDES AND CLIMBING AREAS

Access to upper level provides freedom from ladders. Area is flat and can accommodate groups.

Access to slide area is paved walk/ramp.

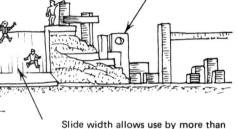

Timber climbing apparatus designed into slope.

Area at base of slide is free-draining and resilient.

Slide width allows use by more than one child at a time.

2. ELEVATED SAND TABLES

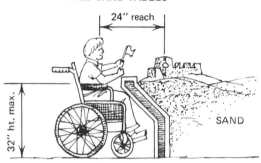

24" reach

32" ht. max.

SAND

Elevated area containing sand or water provides access for those in wheelchairs. Flat area is useful for toy cars, crafts, etc.

3. BASKETBALL HOOPS

7'-0"

Basketball hoops lowered to 7'-0" from standard 10'-0" ht' allow those in wheelchairs and young children to enjoy the game.

4. RAMPED BRIDGE

Provide ramp area at 10% max'. & 3' wide. Handrails are helpful for those on foot.

4" curb at edge is helpful for wheelchairs.

Paved walk allows access to all areas to enable play with other children.

5. ROCKING BRIDGE

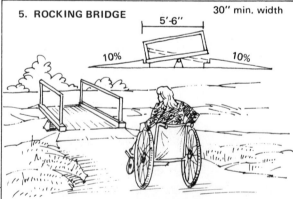

30" min. width

5'-6"

10%   10%

Rocking bridge gives sensation of vertical movement to person in wheelchair. Provide rubber cushions to end edges to minimize impact when end drops and to protect other children's hands if playing at end area.

Figure 1

6. CLIMBING TIMBERS

PAVED WALK

Extending timbers to near walkway allows child with mobility problem to help himself to more central parts to play with others.

7. RAISED SAND AREAS

Area 36" deep, 30" wide, 30" high raised sand area allows person in wheelchair to enjoy use of sand without removal from chair.

Area near wall can be used for toy cars, etc.

CLIMBING TIMBERS

SAND

RAISED SAND AREA

Layout recreation facilities to allow continuous circulation.

Barrier Free Site Design

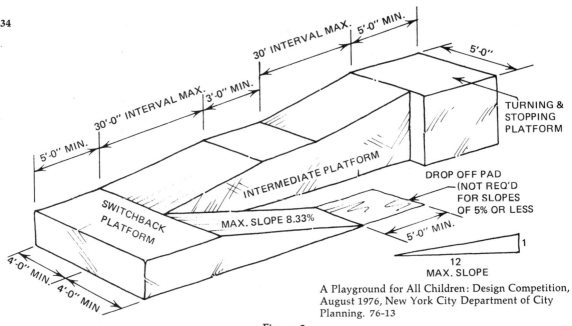

5'-0" MIN.

30' INTERVAL MAX.

5'-0" MIN.

5'-0"

30'-0" INTERVAL MAX.

3'-0" MIN.

5'-0" MIN.

TURNING &
STOPPING
PLATFORM

INTERMEDIATE PLATFORM

SWITCHBACK
PLATFORM

MAX. SLOPE 8.33%

DROP OFF PAD
(NOT REQ'D
FOR SLOPES
OF 5% OR LESS

5'-0" MIN.

4'-0" MIN. / 4'-0" MIN

1

12

MAX. SLOPE

A Playground for All Children: Design Competition,
August 1976, New York City Department of City
Planning. 76-13

Figure 2

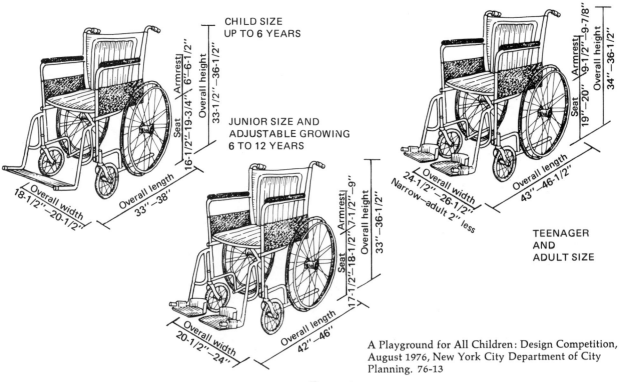

CHILD SIZE
UP TO 6 YEARS

JUNIOR SIZE AND
ADJUSTABLE GROWING
6 TO 12 YEARS

Seat 16-1/2"—19-3/4" | Armrest] 6"—6-1/2"
Overall height 33-1/2"—36-1/2"

Overall width 18-1/2"—20-1/2"
Overall length 33"—38"

Seat 17-1/2"—18-1/2" | Armrest 7-1/2"—9"
Overall height 33"—36-1/2"

Overall width 20-1/2"—24"
Overall length 42"—46"

Seat 19"—20" | Armrest] 9-1/2"—9-7/8"
Overall height 34"—36-1/2"

Overall width 24-1/2"—26-1/2"
Narrow—adult 2" less
Overall length 43"—46-1/2"

TEENAGER
AND
ADULT SIZE

A Playground for All Children: Design Competition,
August 1976, New York City Department of City
Planning. 76-13

Figure 3

HANDRAILS

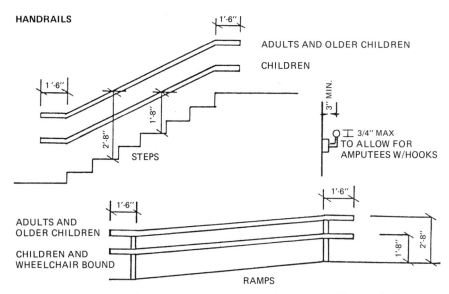

A Playground for All Children: Design Competition, August 1976, New York City
Department of City Planning. 76-13

Figure 4

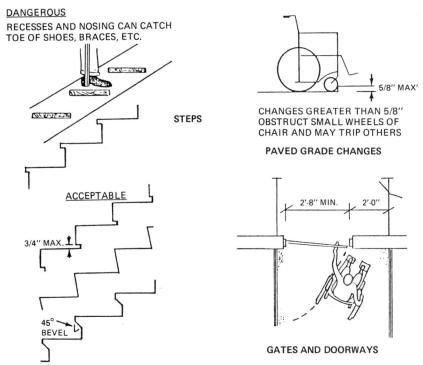

A Playground for All Children: Design Competition, August 1976, New York City
Department of City Planning. 76-13

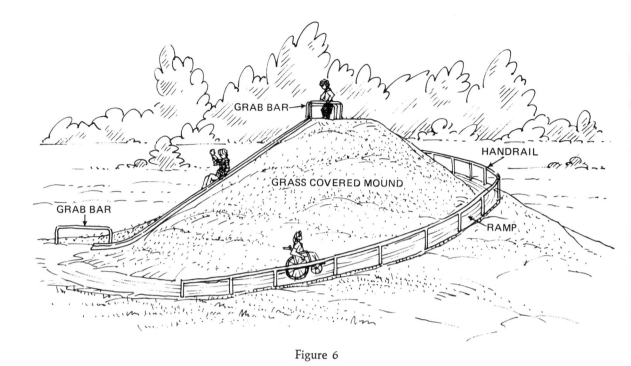

GRAB BAR

HANDRAIL

GRASS COVERED MOUND

GRAB BAR

RAMP

Figure 6

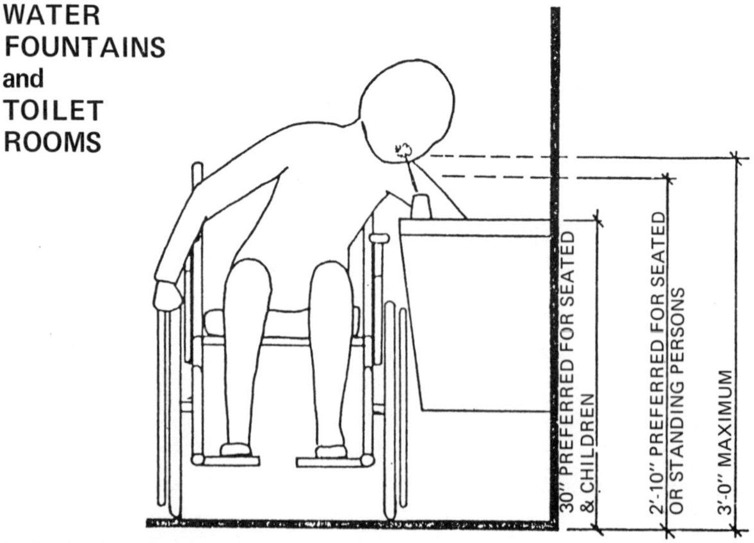

WATER
FOUNTAINS
and
TOILET
ROOMS

30" PREFERRED FOR SEATED & CHILDREN

2'-10" PREFERRED FOR SEATED OR STANDING PERSONS

3'-0" MAXIMUM

Figure 7   North Carolina Building Code

TOILET ROOM PLANS

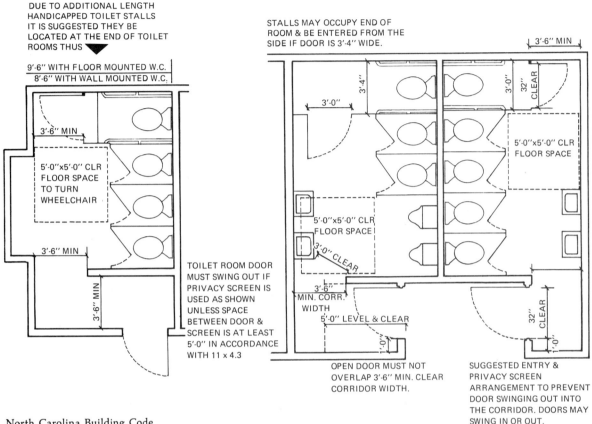

DUE TO ADDITIONAL LENGTH HANDICAPPED TOILET STALLS IT IS SUGGESTED THEY BE LOCATED AT THE END OF TOILET ROOMS THUS ▼

9'-6" WITH FLOOR MOUNTED W.C.
8'-6" WITH WALL MOUNTED W.C.

3'-6" MIN

5'-0"x5'-0" CLR FLOOR SPACE TO TURN WHEELCHAIR

3'-6" MIN

3'-6" MIN

STALLS MAY OCCUPY END OF ROOM & BE ENTERED FROM THE SIDE IF DOOR IS 3'-4" WIDE.

3'-6" MIN

3'-0"

3'-4"

3'-0"

32" CLEAR

5'-0"x5'-0" CLR FLOOR SPACE

5'-0"x5'-0" CLR FLOOR SPACE

3'-0" CLEAR

3'-6" MIN. CORR. WIDTH

5'-0" LEVEL & CLEAR

32" CLEAR

TOILET ROOM DOOR MUST SWING OUT IF PRIVACY SCREEN IS USED AS SHOWN UNLESS SPACE BETWEEN DOOR & SCREEN IS AT LEAST 5'-0" IN ACCORDANCE WITH 11 x 4.3

OPEN DOOR MUST NOT OVERLAP 3'-6" MIN. CLEAR CORRIDOR WIDTH.

SUGGESTED ENTRY & PRIVACY SCREEN ARRANGEMENT TO PREVENT DOOR SWINGING OUT INTO THE CORRIDOR. DOORS MAY SWING IN OR OUT.

North Carolina Building Code

Figure 8

A. No ladders and legs should be used on slides.

B. Slides should be embedded in a grassy mound. Access to the top of the slide should be a ramp or series of ramps.

C. Grab bars should be provided along ramps and tops and bottoms of slides to accommodate the semiambulant.

8. Conventional swings are adequate for most handicapped children. For severely handicapped children, box-type swings can be used.

9. Spray pools could be considered for those who cannot be submerged in water. Spray pools should consist of the following:

A. A jet of water which rises to a height of at least 7 ft and then falls to a paved basin that has sufficient drainage.

B. Benches should be provided in the spray area for those with restricted mobility.

C. A clear area for movement of children in wheelchairs should be provided.

10. Gates and doorways should swing both ways and should be a minimum of 2 ft 8 in. wide (see Figures 3–5).

11. Drinking and toilet facilities should be made accessible to all children (see Figures 7 through 10).

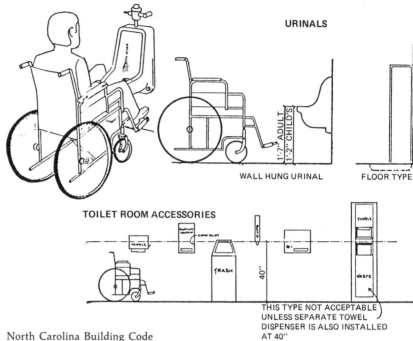

Figure 9   North Carolina Building Code

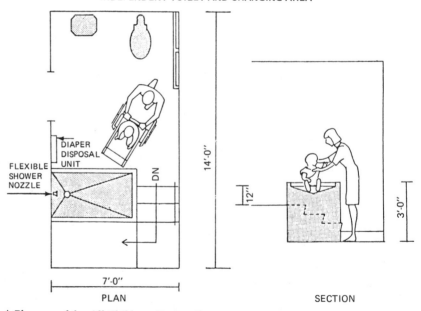

Figure 10   A Playground for All Children: Design Competition, August 1976, New York City Department of City Planning. 76-13

THE ROLE OF PARENTS AND TEACHERS

Parents and teachers have a critical role in fostering the development of play in handicapped children. They must match play environments, experiences, toys, and materials to the needs of children (see Michelman 1974); they must be skilled observers in order to set realistic play goals and to monitor progress; they must be skillful in the use of behavior modification so that they may systematically teach and reinforce play behavior. In addition, adults must know when to intervene and when not to.

Elaborate facilities and expensive equipment are not needed in order for a handicapped child to realize the full therapeutic value of play. Parents and teachers may use common household items to support play. The following are sample equipment and activities:*

Water Play

Equipment: tubs, water-play table, bowls, eggbeaters, cups, sponges, toys that float, brushes, paint roller, waterproof aprons.

Concepts: *Cognitive:* concepts of volume and weight, measurement.
Perceptual-motor: stimulates tactile senses.
Social: cooperative play.

Swimming

Equipment: floating toys, kick boards, inner tubes, sponges, balls.

*These activities are excerpted from the following source: *Early Intervention for Handicapped Children through Programs of Physical Education and Recreation.* Physical Education and Recreation for the Handicapped: Information and Research Utilization Center, 1201 Sixteenth Street, N.W., Washington, D.C. 20036. By permission of the American Alliance for Health, Physical Education and Recreation.

Concepts: *Perceptual-motor:* stimulate tactile senses, facilitates free movement of body parts, body image.
Physical: encourages rhythmic breathing, endurance, muscular development.
Recreation: lifetime leisure activity.

Sand Play

Equipment: sand box or sand pile, shovels, buckets, sieves, spoons, measuring cups, scoops, molds.

Concepts: *Cognitive:* concepts of weight and volume.
Perceptual-motor: tactilely stimulating.
Social: cooperative play.

Rhythm Activities

Equipment: records, rhythm instruments.

Concepts: *Cognitive:* counting.
Perceptual-motor: stimulates auditory and tactile senses, body and muscular control.
Social: cooperation with others, team effort, impulse control.

Painting and Coloring

Equipment: large sheets of paper, large brushes, felt-tip pens, colored chalk, finger paints, aprons.

Concepts: *Cognitive:* color, shape, size.
Perceptual-motor: fine motor control, tactilely stimulating.
Social: sharing materials, work.
Recreation: lifetime leisure activities.

Clay

Equipment: play-dough, clay, brown paper or newspaper, sand, cookie cutters, pots and pans, rolling pin, dull knives.

Concepts: *Cognitive:* shape, size, conservation.
Perceptual-motor: fine motor control, tactilely stimulating, exercise for hands and fingers.

Table 2 The Play History (Takata, 1974)*

1. General Information

   Name: Birthdate: Sex:
   Date: Informant(s):
   Presenting Problem:

2. Previous Play Experiences

   A. Solitary play
   B. Play with others:
      mother   father   sisters   brothers   playmates
      other family members   pets
   C. Play with toys and materials (earliest preference)
   D. Gross physical play
   E. Pretend and make-believe play
   F. Sports and games: group collaboration   group competition
   G. Creative interests: arts   crafts
   H. Hobbies, collections, other leisuretime activities
   I. Recreation/social activities

3. Actual Play Examination

   A. With what does the child play?
      Toys   materials   pets
   B. How does the child play with toys and other materials?
   C. What type of play is avoided or liked least?
   D. With whom does the child play?
      Self   parents   brothers   sisters   peers   others
   E. How does the child play with others?
   F. What body postures does the child use during play?
   G. How long does the child play with objects?   with people?
   H. Where does the child play?
      Home: indoors   outdoors
      Community: parks   school   church   other areas
   I. When does the child play?
      Daily schedule for weekday and weekend

4. Play Description

5. Play Prescription

*Adapted from "Play as a Prescription" by Nancy Takata as reprinted in *Play as Exploratory Learning,* Mary Reilly, ed., © 1974, p. 220, by permission of the publisher, Sage Publications, Inc. (Beverly Hills/ London).

Other Activities

Use any game for young children, such as:

   Peek-a-Boo
   Pat-a-Cake
   Simon Says
   Hide-and-go-Seek
   Hide the Button

   Follow the Leader
   Poor Pussy
   London Bridge
   Mother May I

   Takata (1974) has developed a format for systematically diagnosing the current quality of play of a child and for prescribing appropriate

Water play aids in cognitive, social and physical development.

◄ Children learn such concepts as through, under, between and on top of by playing.

(Photo by Camilla Jessel)

activities and materials to either remediate deficient areas of play or to extend and enhance normally developing play behavior. The Play History is divided into five parts: general information, previous play experiences, actual play experiences, play description, and play prescription (see Table 2). By completing the checklist, a detailed description of the quality and type of a child's play behavior may be obtained. By matching the results with age or stage appropriate toys and activities a play prescription may be generated.

CONTRASTING PLAYGROUNDS FOR HANDICAPPED CHILDREN

The Rehabilitation Playground

Richard Dattner, an internationally renowned landscape architect, has designed a number of playgrounds for handicapped children. His Re-

habilitation Playground was designed and constructed for the New York University Medical Center, Institute for Rehabilitation Medicine. The children's rehabilitation unit is an intensive-care residential facility for children who have serious physical disabilities, including paraplegia, brain damage, and impairment caused by cerebral palsy, muscular dystrophy, wear prosthetic devices and get around only with the help of crutches, wheelchairs, or wheeled beds.

During the design process, Dattner met with the hospital staff to determine what activities are therapeutic and which constitute potential dangers. The staff provided the architect with information pertaining to treatment for various disabilities.

The three goals of physical rehabilitation are to arrest the deterioration of existing abilities; to strengthen skills that are imperfectly developed but capable of further growth; and to provide alternative, compensatory skills to replace those that are irreparably damaged. Thus, a child with a motor problem might be encouraged to walk, to build up his physical power and coordination; for a child who cannot walk facilities that help him move around must be provided. In both cases, as with normal children, the environment should present a series of challenges to be mastered gradually. (Dattner, 1969, p. 110)

(Photos courtesy of William Dattner and Associates, Architects)

Foam mattresses provide extra protection.

This special water play area is designed to allow children to play while sitting in wheelchairs.

Sand play from a sitting position.

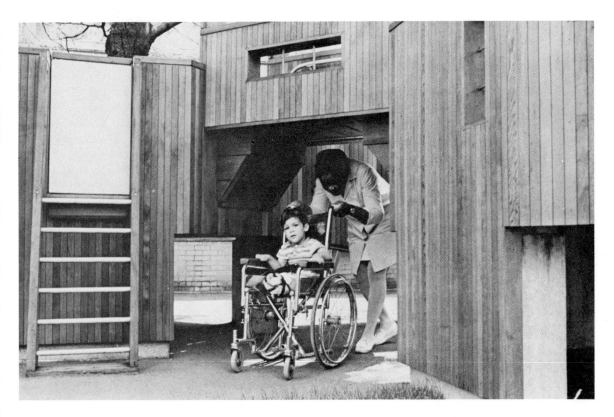

Wheelchair paths wind around and through the play structures.

Climbing ramp.
(Photos courtesy of William Dattner and Associates, Architects)

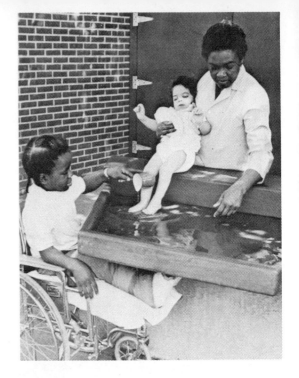

The play environment was designed in close cooperation with the hospital staff and is used as an extension
of their rehabilitation program.

(Photos courtesy of William Dattner and Associates, Architects)

This slide, mounted on a small hill, eliminates the
danger of falling over the side.

Tree pit with periscope

Model of the award winning *A Playground for All Children.*
(Photo courtesy of William Dattner and Associates, Architects)

Dattner and his associates recently won a design competition titled *A Playground for All Children,* sponsored by the New York City Department of Parks and Recreation. The objectives of the competition were to (1) create a public playground that may be enjoyed by all children in the three- to eleven-year age group, regardless of disability, (2) provision of an integrated play experience for disabled and able-bodied children, and (3) development of prototypical playground features that may be used in neighborhood playgrounds throughout the city.

The London Handicapped Adventure Playgrounds

The British have been ingenious in devising adventure playgrounds for handicapped children. The Handicapped Adventure Playground Association (HAPA) was set up in London in 1966 by Lady Allen of Hurtwood. No doubt inspired by the Scandinavians, Lady Allen succeeded in establishing the first HAPA playground, the Chelsea Adventure Playground, in the beautiful gardens of the Rectory, 56 Old Church Street, London SW3 in 1970. Since that time three new playgrounds have opened: one in north London, one in south London, and a fourth, the Fulham Palace Adventure Playground, located in the lovely, secluded garden of the palace, opened in 1976.

These playgrounds have been highly successful. Within a few months of opening, the Chelsea playground was working to capacity, with over 500 children enjoying the facilities each week. Special schools and groups from all over London schedule time slots and transport their children to the playground on a regularly scheduled basis. A waiting list ensures capacity use for the foreseeable future. The photo essay that follows features the first and the most recently established playgrounds, the Chelsea Adventure Playground and the Fulham Palace Adventure Playground.

PHOTO ESSAY: LONDON HANDICAPPED ADVENTURE PLAYGROUNDS

Ideally the playground covers at least an acre and contains trees, shrubs, and grass to contrast with the stark city environment. A high wall or fence is provided for seclusion and security. This broad gate at Chelsea allows access for vehicles.

Inside, the Chelsea playground contains an appealing array of static but modifiable climbing structures, a meandering stream, trees and shrubs, all interspersed or connected with paths and bridges for access by children with many types of handicaps.

A wide variety of specially designed wheeled vehicles are available. These are of durable construction and include both battery-powered and self-propelled vehicles. With ingenuity a form of transportation, usually self-operated, can be provided for each child, regardless of disability.

The staff is constantly experimenting with new forms of transportation. Even this tire swing can be moved laterally along an overhead track.

Many loose parts, cans, buckets,▶ shovels, tires, etc., together with sand, help to stimulate a broad range of dramatic play. The adjacent wheeled vehicle path makes the area accessible.

(Photo by Camilla Jessel)

(Photo by Camilla Jessel)

Water and sand, located in adjacent areas, offer unlimited variety and interest. A recirculating pump

keeps the water fresh. Gradually sloping sides allow ready access by the children.

Perhaps the most amazing feature of London's four adventure playgrounds for the handicapped (HAPA) is the great range of challenges provided and the skill of the children in meeting them. The uninitiated observer could well go away unaware that handicapped children are playing there. There have been no injuries caused by falls from heights.

(Photo by Camilla Jessel)

(Photo by Camilla Jessel)

(Photo by Camilla Jessel)

250

Characteristic of adventure playgrounds, practically all of the equipment on HAPA playgrounds is constructed from scrap or inexpensive materials.

The fire pit, popular on adventure playgrounds throughout Scandinavia and England, is also popular on HAPA playgrounds.

Each HAPA playground has a building for indoor play space, workshop, storage, kitchen, lavatories, cloakroom and office. The play room has exits to the garden with wide doors and ramped approaches. The entire building is specially designed to meet the special needs of the children. Top photo: Chelsea building; Bottom photo: Fulham Palace building.

The play leader is the heart of the program. He/she has a working knowledge of various handicaps; provides for organization, maintenance, supervision and continuous refinement and modification of equipment. In addition the play leader interacts with children at play and deals with "fits, faints, asthmatic attacks, urine bags, calipers, prostheses, hearing aids, bumps and bruises."*

SUMMARY

Handicapped children have the same need to play as do nonhandicapped children: the need to explore, to take risks, to make an impact on the environment, to meet and master challenges, to interact with other children, to have fun. However, because of personal, social, and physical barriers it is much more difficult for a handicapped child to fulfill these needs. Unlike normal children who play naturally and spontaneously, many exceptional children must be systematically taught how to play. Special barrier-free yet challenging playgrounds must be designed for children with physical disabilities.

Adults have a critical role in facilitating the play of exceptional children. Adults must have an appreciation for the role of play in normal development and for the therapeutic power of play. They must be skillful observers of children and be able to prescribe realistic play objectives and activities designed to meet those objectives. Adults must also be skillful in implementing those activities and in supporting and extending the play of handicapped children.

It is not necessary to provide expensive equipment for handicapped children's play. As with normal children, simple, basic materials that can be constructed from scrounged or inexpensive materials are best. It is necessary to expend considerable funds in securing play space, equipment to make children mobile, and, very importantly, to hire skillful, warm adults to support the play of handicapped children.

REFERENCES

American Alliance for Health, Physical Education, and Recreation. *Physical education and recreation for impaired, disabled, and handicapped individuals . . . past, present, and future.* Washington, D.C., 1975.

The American Standards Association Specifications for Making Buildings and Facilities Accessible to and

---

*Handicapped Adventure Playground Association. *Adventure Playgrounds for Handicapped Children.* London: James Galt and Company Limited, 1975, p. 20.

Usable by the Physically Handicapped (Chicago: National Society for Crippled Children and Adults, 1961).

Axline, V. M. Observing children at play. *Teachers College Record*, 1951, *52*, 358–363.

————. *Play Therapy*, New York: Ballantine, 1969.

Barrier Free Site Design, a report conducted by the American Society of Landscape Architects Foundation under a contract with the U.S. Department of Housing and Urban Development, Office of Policy Development and Research, 1975.

Benoit, E. P. The play problems of retarded children: A frank discussion with parents. *American Journal of Mental Deficiency.* 1955, *60* (1), 41–55.

Dattner, R. *Design for Play.* Cambridge: MIT Press, 1969.

Devoney, C., Guralnick, M., and Rubin, H. Integrating handicapped and nonhandicapped preschool children: Effects on social play. *Childhood Education*, 1974, *50* (6), 360–364.

Early Intervention for Handicapped Children: Programs for Physical Education and Recreation. Physical Education and Recreation for the Handicapped: Information and Research Utilization Center, (201 Sixteenth St. N.W., Washington, D.C.)

Ginott, H. G. A rationale for selecting toys in play therapy. *Journal of Consulting Psychology.* 1960, *24* (3), 243–246.

Guerney, L. Play therapy: A training manual for parents. In Schaefer, C. *The Therapeutic Use of Child's Play.* New York: Jason Aronson, Inc., 1976.

Kirk, S. A. *Educating Exceptional Children*. Atlanta: Houghton Mifflin, 1972.

Koegel, R. L., Firestone, P.B., Kramme, K.W., and Dunlap, G. Increasing spontaneous play by suppressing self-stimulation in autistic children. *Journal of Applied Behavior Analysis*, 1974, *7* (4), 521–528.

Michelman, S. The importance of creative play. *The American Journal of Occupational Therapy*, 1971, *25* (6), 285–290.

————. Play and the deficit child. In Reilly, M. (ed.). *Play As Exploratory Learning*, Beverly Hills: Sage Publications, 1974, 117–150.

Moore, T. Realism and fantasy in children's play. *Journal of Child Psychology and Psychiatry*, 1964, *5* (1), 15–36.

Morris, R. H. A play environment for blind children: Design and evaluation. *New Outlook for the Blind*, 1974, *68* (9), 408–414.

Morris, R. J., and Dolker, M. Developing cooperative play in society withdrawn retarded children. *Mental Retardation*, 1974, *12* (6), 24–27.

Nimnicht, G. P., and Brown, E. The toy library: Parents and children learning with toys. *Young Children*, 1972, *28* (2), 110–116.

Paloutzian, R., Hasai, J., Streifel, J., and Edgar, L. Promotion of positive social interaction in severely retarded children. *American Journal of Mental Deficiency*, 1971, *75* (4), 519–524.

Reilly, M. (ed.), *Play As Exploratory Learning.* Beverly Hills: Sage Publications, 1974.

Romanczyk, R. G., Diament, C., Goren, R., Trunell, Harris, S. Increasing isolate and social play in severely disturbed children: Intervention and post-intervention effectiveness. *Journal of Autism and Childhood Schizophrenia*, 1975, *5* (1), 57–69.

Rothschild, J. Play therapy with blind children. *New Outlook for the Blind*, 1960, *54*, 329–333.

Sandler, A. M. Aspects of passivity and ego development in the blind infant. *Psychoanalytic Study of the Child*, 1963, *18*, 343–360.

Schaefer, C. *The Therapeutic Use of Child's Play.* New York: Jason Aronson, Inc., 1976.

Singer, J. L., and Streiner, B. F. Imaginative content in the dreams and fantasy play of blind and sighted children. *Perceptual and Motor Skills*, 1966, *22*, 475–481.

Strain, P. Increasing social play of severely retarded preschoolers with socio-dramatic activities. *Mental Retardation*, 1975, *13* (6), 7–9.

Takata, N. Play as a Prescription. In Reilly, M., (ed.). *Play as Exploratory Learning.* Beverly Hills: Sage Publications, 1974.

Wehman, Paul. Establishing play behaviors in mentally retarded youth. *Rehabilitation Literature*, 1975, *36* (8), 238–246.

SUGGESTED READINGS

Adkins, P. G. *A Priceless Playground for Exceptional Children.* El Paso, Texas: Learning Resources Press, 1973.

Allen, Lady of Hurtwood. *Adventure Playgrounds for Handicapped Children.* London: James Galt and Co., Ltd., 1975.

Barry, M. A. How to play with your partially sighted preschool child: suggestions for early sensory and education activities. *New Outlook for the Blind,* 1973, *67,* (10), 1973.

Black, M., Freeman, B. J., and Montgomery, J. Systematic observation of play behavior in autistic children. *Journal of Autism and Childhood Schizophrenia,* 1975, *5* (4), 363–371.

Bowers, L. *Play Learning Centers for Preschool Handicapped Children: Research and Demonstration Project Report.* College of Education, University of South Florida, Tampa, Florida. (Supported by a grant from the Bureau of Education for the Handicapped, U.S. Office of Education, Washington, D.C. 20202).

Currie, C. Evaluating function of mentally retarded children through the use of toys and play activities. *American Journal of Occupational Therapy,* 1969, *23* (1), 35–42.

Florey, L. An approach to play and play development. *The American Journal of Occupational Therapy.* 1971, *25* (6), 275–280.

Gardner, R. A. Techniques for involving the child with MBD in meaningful psychotherapy. *Journal of Learning Disabilities.* 1975, *8* (5), 16–25.

Gordon, R. *The Design of a Pre-School Therapeutic Playground: An Outdoor Learning Laboratory.* Rehabilitation Monograph No. 47. New York: Institute of Rehabilitation Medicine, New York University Medical Center (400E. 34 Street, 10016).

Gralewicz, A. Play deprivation in multihandicapped children. *The American Journal of Occupational Therapy,* 1973, *27* (2), 70–72.

Handicapped Adventure Playground Association. *Adventure Playgrounds for Handicapped Children.* London: The Association, 1978 (Fulham Palace, Bishops Avenue, London SW6 6EA).

Klein, M. The psychoanalytic play technique. *American Journal of Orthopsychiatry,* 1955, *25* (2), 223–237.

Kliment, S. A. *Into the Mainstream.* The American Institute of Architects, 1975.

Kniest, J. H. The therapeutic value of toys in a training center for handicapped children. *Rehabilitation Literature,* 1962, *23* (1), 2–7, 30.

Lambie, R. How Sweden trains handicapped children. *Journal of Home Economics,* 1975, *67* (5), 13–18.

Leland, H., Walker, J., and Taboada, A. Group play therapy with a group of post-nursery male retardates. *American Journal of Mental Deficiency,* 1959, *63* (5), 848–851.

Lovell, L. M. The Yeovil Opportunity Group: A playgroup for multiply handicapped children. *Physiotherapy,* 1973, *59* (8), 251–253.

McCall, R. Exploratory manipulation and play in the human infant. *SRCD Monograph,* 1974, *39* (2).

Mace, R. I. and Laslett (eds.), *An Illustrated Handbook of the Handicapped Section of the North Carolina State Building Code,* 1973.

Mash, E. J., and Terdal, L. Modification of mother-child interactions: Playing with children. *Mental Retardation,* 1973, *1* (5), 44–49.

Mather, J. *Make the Most of Your Baby.* Arlington, Texas: National Association for Retarded Citizens (P.O. Box 6109, 76011).

Newcomer, B. C., and Morrison, T. L. Play therapy with institutionalized mentally retarded children. *American Journal of Mental Deficiency,* 1974, *78* (6), 727–733.

Ney, P. G., Palvesky, A. E., and Markely, J. Relative effectiveness of operant conditioning and play therapy in childhood schizophrenia. *Journal of Autism and Childhood Schizophrenia,* 1971, *1* (3), 337–349.

Nickerson, E. T. The application of play therapy to a school setting. *Psychology in the Schools,* 1973, *10* (3), 361–365.

Quilitch, H. R., and Risley, T. R. The effects of play materials on social play. *Journal of Applied Behavior Analysis,* 1973, *6* (4), 573–578.

Rafferty, J., Tyler, B., and Tyler, F. Personality assessment from free play observations. *Child Development,* 1960, *31,* 691–702.

Recreation For All. Recreation Planning Section, Office of Planning and Research, Georgia Department of Natural Resources, 1976.

Robinson, A. L. Play: The arena for the acquisition of rules for competent behavior. *The American Journal of Occupational Therapy*, 1971, *31* (4), 241–253.

Rosenberg, B., and Sutton-Smith, B. A revised conception of masculine-feminine differences in play activities. *Journal of Genetic Psychology*, 1960, *96*, 165–170.

Sessoms, H. G. The mentally handicapped child grows at play. *Mental Retardation*, 1965, *3* (4), 12–14.

Sexton, D. Water play for multihandicapped children. *Pointer*, 20 (1), 62–64.

Tait, P. E. Believing without seeing: Teaching the blind child in a "regular" kindergarten. *Childhood Education*, 1974, *50* (5), 285–291.

———. Play and the intellectual development of blind children. *New Outlook for the Blind*. 1972, *66* (10), 361–369.

Takata, N. The play milieu—A preliminary appraisal. *The American Journal of Occupational Therapy*. 1971, *25* (6), 281–284.

Tilton, J., and Ottinger, D. Comparison of the toy play behavior of autistic, retarded, and normal children. *Psychological Reports*, 1964, *15* (3), 967–975.

Turner, C. W., and Goldsmith, D. Effects of toy guns and airplanes on children's antisocial free play behavior. *Journal of Experimental Psychology*, 1976, *21* (2), 303–315.

Wehman, Paul. Selection of play materials for the severely handicapped: A continuing dilemma. *Education and training of the mentally retarded*. 1976, *11* (1), 46–50.

———., and Abramson, M. Three theoretical approaches to play: Applications for exceptional children. *The American Journal of Occupational Therapy*, 1976, *30* (9), 551–559.

Weiner, E. A., and Weiner, B. J. Differentiation of retarded and normal children through free-play analysis. *Multivariate Behavioral Research*, 1974, *9* (2), 245–252.

APPENDIX A

PROPOSED SAFETY STANDARD FOR PUBLIC PLAYGROUND EQUIPMENT
(Condensed and editorial notes added by the authors)

The National Recreation and Park Association* completed a draft, *Proposed Safety Standard for Public Playground Equipment,* on May 1, 1976. The development panel included representatives from consumer, industry, and buyer/installer interests. They met for nine two-day sessions and three one-day sessions over a ten-month period. Task groups comprised of members of the panel focused on particular hazards and reported back to the panel. Over 250 people contributed as corresponding participants. The engineering tests were conducted by the Franklin Institute Research Laboratories.

The proposed standard addressed only heavy-duty institutional type equipment, its installation, and the surfaces upon which the apparatus is installed. It does not deal with lighter-duty, "backyard" equipment, sports equipment, or hand-constructed apparatus, commonly found on discovery or creative playgrounds. No date for implementation of the standard was proposed since "its requirements are not considered to be adequate for promulgation as a federal standard."†

The major intent of the standard is "to reduce unreasonable risk of injury and reduce the severity and frequency of injury associated with public playground equipment under conditions of normal use and reasonably foreseeable misuse."

The following is a condensed version of requirements proposed by the Standard. The general safety requirements do not and probably could not prevent accidents due to abuse and misuse of equipment. Public playgrounds cannot be assumed to be "safe" in the absence of competent adult supervision.

1. *General Safety Requirements*

    A. *Anthropometric Applications* Equipment designed for a specific age group is so labeled and is designed using appropriate anthropometric data (maximum height, gripping contact surface, clearances, step heights, etc.) from *Physical Characteristics of Children as Related to Death and Injury for Consumer Product Design and Use.**

    B. *Use by Handicapped Children* Equipment and parts of equipment modified for use by the handicapped are excluded from requirements of the Standard under certain conditions: modification is necessary for

---

*1601 North Kent Street, Arlington, Virginia 22209
†Personal correspondence from the U.S. Consumer Product Safety Commission

*Ann Arbor, Michigan: The University of Michigan, May, 1975, Highway Safety Research Institute.

use, does not result in a hazard, is isolated from other equipment, is used under supervision, and instructions for use are provided. Editor's note: There may be problems associated with isolation of equipment for the handicapped, particularly in relation to "mainstreaming" ideals.

2. *Materials of Construction*

A. *Durability* Materials will have a demonstrated record of durability or they shall be subjected to appropriate testing and final inspection.

B. *Structural Integrity* After assembly and installation, equipment shall pass static dynamic load testing or be certified by a registered engineer to meet specific requirements (described in the Standard). For example, each suspended element (swing seat, etc.) with the suspending member (rope, chain, etc.) is tested with a load of 300 pounds for each potential child user. Forces are applied to members (platform railings, etc.) receiving lateral forces by tilting the structure on its side and suspending weights from the member according to prescribed specifications.

C. *Stability* The equipment shall withstand tipping over or sliding when installed according to installation instructions.

D. *Hardware* Locking devices (lockwashers, etc.) shall be provided for all bolts. All connecting and covering devices shall be secure, and all hooks, rings, and links shall not open during specified tests.

3. *Sharp Edges, Protrusions, and Crush Points*

A. *Sharp Edges and Points* All sharp edges and points shall be removed, protected, or covered. Covers shall not be removable without the use of tools.

B. *Pinch and Crush Points* There shall be no components moving relative to each other or to fixed components which may cause injury.

C. *Protruding Bolts* Exposed ends of bolts shall not exceed one-half the diameter of the bolt. Recessed and countersunk bolts are exempt.

D. *Suspended Hazards* There shall be no elements less than 1 in. in diameter (wires, ropes, cables, etc.) suspended between components in such manner that they could be contacted by a rapidly moving child (running, riding, etc.).

4. *Moving Impact*

A. *Suspended Elements* No suspended element shall impact in excess of 50 G peak, measured by the Vexiler recorder (details available in the Standard). Editor's note: Although not stated in the Standard, it is expected that swings with heavy board seats and other heavy seats such as those representing animals would fail to meet this requirement.

There shall be at least 18 in. clearance between suspended elements and between suspended elements and stationary elements (measured from the outside edge of the elements). Editor's note: This space would not be sufficient for certain moving equipment such as horizontal tire swings suspended from swivels.

All suspended elements to be used by the hands (trapeze, etc.) shall be above the standing crown-to-sole height of the tallest user.

B. *Rotating Equipment* The peripheral (outer edge) velocity shall not exceed 15 ft. per second (formula for calculation available in the Standard). The shape of the base shall not have a configuration (horizontal plane) that represents potential for impact injury. The base shall be of continuous design with no openings accessible to any part of the body. Editor's note: This rules out many older merry-go-rounds which allow children to stand or run inside the structure.

C. *Slide Exit and Incline* The exit end of slides over 4 ft in height (measured vertically) shall be between 12 and 16 in. from the ground level. The incline of slides over 4 ft high shall average no greater than 30° from the horizontal. All slides over 4 ft high shall have an exit surface at least 15 in. long and parallel to the ground.

5. *Entrapment* ("the impeded withdrawal of a body or body part that has penetrated an opening")

A. *Openings* The equipment shall contain no openings that can trap a user's head.

B. *Angles* Angles forming openings more than 2 ft above the ground must be greater than 55°; or have legs less than 3 in. long; or be inverted.

6. *Falls from Equipment*

A. *High Equipment* Any surface (walkway, landing, deck, etc.) with a direct fall height of more than 12 ft shall be totally enclosed except for necessary entry and exit openings. The outside surface shall not provide for easy climbing opportunities.

B. *Intermediate Level Equipment* Any surface with a direct fall height of 8–12 ft shall have a protective barrier at least 38 in. high, completely surrounding the surface except for necessary entry and exit openings. The outside surface shall not provide for easy climbing opportunities.

C. *Low Level Equipment* Any surface with a direct fall height of 4 to 8 ft shall have guard railings at least 38 in. high com-

pletely surrounding the surface except for necessary entry and exit openings.

D. *Hand-Gripping Surfaces* Hand-gripping surfaces of equipment designed for hanging by the hands shall be between ¾ in. and 1½ in. in diameter.

E. *Side Protection on Slides* Sliding surfaces over 4 ft high shall have protective sides to guide descent. These shall project at least 2½ in. above the sliding surface for the entire length of the slide. "Wave" type slides shall have sides at least 5 in. high.

Flat sliding surfaces over 8 ft high and spiral sliding surfaces shall have guard rails or protective barriers as described in the Standard. Editor's note: There seems to be no reasonable rationale for construction of platforms over 8 ft high for any age group. Preschool and primary requirements should not exceed 5 to 6 ft.

F. *Ladder and Stairway Incline* All ladders and stairways designed to reach heights of 4 ft or more shall meet the following requirements:

1) Ladders with rungs shall have an incline between 75° and 90° from the horizontal.

2) Ladders with steps shall have an incline no greater than 75°.

3) Stairways shall have an incline no greater than 35° and meet construction specifications outlined in the Standard.

G. *Ladder and Stairway Heights* Ladders and stairways leading from ground level to an elevated surface shall not exceed 12 ft in height without a landing or platform that would terminate falls. Ladders or stairways leading to a second platform or surface shall not exceed 8 ft. Editor's note: The Standard sets no limit on height of equipment. It is questionable whether height per se is of any particular value in play.

7. *Surfaces Under Equipment* Editor's note: The Committee did not develop a standard for surfaces under equipment. This variable is a chief factor in accidental deaths and serious injuries on public playgrounds but a requirement on surfacing would not be enforceable.

In respect to falls and surfaces, the Committee deviated from their preoccupation with equipment design to focus on child development. To say that a child was injured or fell does not reveal why he fell. The original cause may have been improperly constructed, installed, or maintained equipment. On the other hand, the fall may have been due to improper judgment of distance, lack of depth perception, miscalculating one's abilities, fatigue, emotional stress, pushing or shoving by other children, or changes in the properties of the equipment (wet from rain, hot from direct sunlight). It is important, then not only to provide resilient ground cover under all climbing or moving equipment but also to properly construct, test and install it. Similarly, it is relevant to understand the social and physical development of child users.

The Standard does require that a statement "Recommendations for Surfacing Materials" be included in all equipment catalogues and installation instructions. Laboratory tests resulted in the assignment of surfacing materials into the following categories:*

EXTREMELY
HAZARDOUS
concrete
asphalt
packed earth

---

*Test data submitted to the National Recreation and Park Association. Appendix C in the *Proposed Standard.*

⅛ in. rubber mat on above surfaces
¹⁄₁₆ in. vinyl cover on above surfaces

CONDITIONALLY
ACCEPTABLE
gym mats (2 in.)
double-thick gym mats
rubber mats (1⅛ in.)
double-thick rubber mats
pea gravel
wood chips

ACCEPTABLE
sand (8–10 in.)

To illustrate the relative effectiveness of these materials, children can suffer serious and permanent injury simply by falling onto "extremely hazardous" surfaces from a standing position. Gym mats and rubber mats are acceptable up to 4 ft and double-thick mats are acceptable up to 8 ft, but they are very expensive and are not manufactured in double thicknesses. High quality pea gravel is acceptable but quality varies greatly. Poor quality results in unacceptable impact levels. Wood chips are acceptable up to 10 ft but they are easily dissipated by wind, water, and wear. In regard to sand, the following statement was made, "The impact absorbing capabilities of the sand tested was excellent. All tests conducted were well below acceptable limits."

8. *Maintenance, Installation and Identification*

A. *Maintenance* The manufacturer shall furnish complete instructions for the maintenance of their equipment and shall include a facsimile of the checklist on the following page.

B. *Installation* The manufacturer shall include with each piece of equipment a set of written instructions and drawings that include the following:

Suggested Playground Equipment Maintenance Safety Checklist

ITEM	LOOK FOR . . .
Structure	Bending, warping, cracking, loosening, breaking, etc.
Surface finish	No protective coating, rust, other corrosion, cracks, splinters, checking harmful preservatives or paints, etc.
Hardware	Missing, bent, broken, loosened, open hooks, etc.
Edges	Sharp points, or edges, protruding bolts, or other protrusions, etc.
Pinch or crush points	Exposed mechanisms, junctures of moving components, etc.
Mechanical devices and other moving parts	Worn bearings, lubrication needed, missing protective covers, etc.
Guard or hand rails	Missing, bent, broken, loosened, etc.
Ladders and steps	Missing rungs or steps, broken, loosened, etc.
Swing seats	Missing, damaged, loosened, sharp corners, etc.
Footings	Exposed, cracked, loose in ground, etc.
Protective surfacing under equipment	Compacted, displaced to ineffective level, doesn't extend to potential impact area, unsanitary, poor drainage, etc.

1) All equipment should be installed in accordance with the enclosed instructions.

2) Concrete footer sizes are suggestions only. Local soil conditions may necessitate significant changes. Check with a local registered engineer.

3) The top of all concrete footers should be a minimum of 4 in. below the subsurface or be covered with a permanent protective surfacing material.

4) Protective surfacing materials should be provided under all equipment. See the equipment manufacturer or refer to Federal Standards for Public Playground Equipment for specific recommendations.

5) No piece of equipment, or composite unit, or other structure should encroach on the use area of another piece of equipment.

6) Equipment designed for use only by the handicapped should be placed in protected areas, removed from normal traffic patterns on the playground, and used only under supervision.

7) Make certain that all hooks are clinched, all bolts tightened or peened and locked, and all bolt caps and tubing end closures inserted as required.

8) Where possible, sliding equipment should be oriented in a northerly direction to avoid build up on the sliding surface resulting from direct rays of the summer sun.

C. *Identification* Each unit shall have a label identifying the manufacturer.

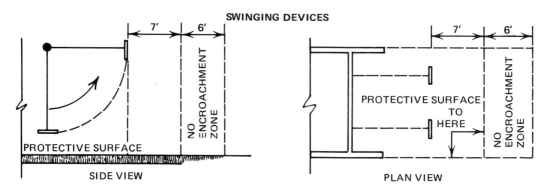

SWINGING DEVICES

SIDE VIEW

PLAN VIEW

PROTECTIVE SURFACE 7' FROM SWING EXTENDED, PLUS 6' NO ENCROACHMENT ZONE

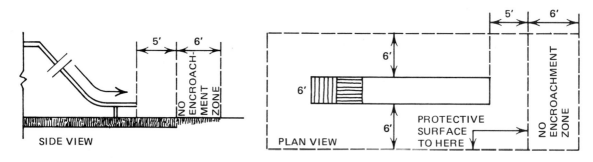

SLIDING DEVICES

SIDE VIEW

PLAN VIEW

TOTAL USE ZONE 11' IN DIRECTION OF MOTION, 6' IN OTHER DIRECTIONS

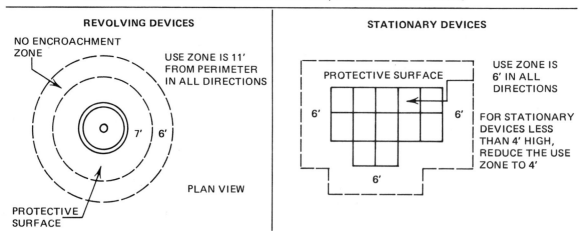

REVOLVING DEVICES

NO ENCROACHMENT ZONE

USE ZONE IS 11' FROM PERIMETER IN ALL DIRECTIONS

PROTECTIVE SURFACE

PLAN VIEW

STATIONARY DEVICES

PROTECTIVE SURFACE

USE ZONE IS 6' IN ALL DIRECTIONS

FOR STATIONARY DEVICES LESS THAN 4' HIGH, REDUCE THE USE ZONE TO 4'

Recommended Minimum Use Zones

Author's Note: Although these dimensions were in the *Proposed Standard*, they are not likely to be implemented. The reader should not assume that they are "acceptable" in the present form.

9. *Referenced Tables and Figures*

A. *Anthropometric Data* Physical measurements, minimum and maximum, are given in the Standard. The original source is *Physical Characteristics of Children as Related to Death and Injury for Consumer Product Design and Use.*

B. *Recommended Minimum Use Zones* Suggested minimum guidelines for protective surfaces and no encroachment zones (area beyond the "impact area" needed for recovery from a fall) are as follows:

Swinging devices should have a protective surface 7 ft wide from the end of the extended swing and an additional no encroachment zone (containing no equipment) for 6 ft beyond.

Slides shall have a protective surface, completely surrounding the structure, 6 ft wide, measured from the outside edge of the equipment. There should be an additional 6-foot no encroachment zone beyond the protective surface at the exit end of the slide.

Revolving devices such as merry-go-rounds should have a 7-foot protective surface in all directions, measured from the outside edge of the equipment. The no encroachment zone should be 6 ft wide in all directions.

Stationary devices (jungle gyms, climbing platforms, arch climbers) over 4 ft high should have a 6-foot protective cover surrounding the equipment. Devices under 4 ft high shall have a 4-foot protective surface. Editor's note: It would appear that certain areas could be safely exempted from this requirement; for example, that side of an enclosed climbing structure having no access, exit, or climbing surfaces. In addition, several pieces of equipment are frequently "linked" to provide continuity and challenge. Such linked equipment should be considered *one* structure in calculating fall and no encroachment zones.

APPENDIX B

PLAYGROUND RATING SYSTEM*

Instructions: Rate each item on a scale from 0-5. High score possible on Section I is 100 points; Section II is 50 points and Section III is 50 points, for a possible grand total of 200 points. Divide the grand total score by 2 to obtain a final rating.

Section I. What does the playground contain?

Rate each item for degree of existence and function on a scale of 0-5 (0 = not existent; 1 = some element(s) exists but not functional; 2 = poor; 3 = average; 4 = good; 5 = all elements exist, excellent function).

_____ 1. A hard-surfaced area with space for games and a network of paths for wheeled toys.

_____ 2. Sand and sand equipment.

_____ 3. Dramatic play structures (play house(s), old car or boat with complementary equipment, such as adjacent sand and water and housekeeping equipment).

_____ 4. Climbing structure(s) (with room for more than one child at a time and with a variety of entries, exits and levels).

_____ 5. Mound(s) of earth for climbing and digging.

_____ 6. Trees and natural areas (including weed areas).

_____ 7. Zoning to provide continuous challenge; linkage of areas, functional physical boundaries, vertical and horizontal treatment.

_____ 8. Water play areas, with fountains, pools and sprinklers.

_____ 9. Construction area with junk materials such as tires, crates, planks, boards, bricks and nails. Tools should be provided and demolition allowed.

_____10. An old vehicle, train, boat, car that has been made safe, but not stripped of its play value. (This item should be changed or relocated after a period of time to renew interest.)

_____11. Equipment for active play: A *slide* with a large platform at the top (best if slide is built into side of a hill); *swings* that can be used safely in a variety of ways (use of old tires as seats); *climbing trees* (mature dead trees that are horizontally positioned); *climbing nets.*

_____12. A large grassy area for organized games.

_____13. Small private spaces at the child's own scale: tunnels, niches, playhouses, hiding places.

_____14. Fences, gates, walls and windows that provide security for young children and are adaptable as opportunities for learning/play.

_____15. Natural areas that attract birds and bugs. A garden and flowers located so that they are protected from play, but with easy access for the child to tend them.

*Joe L. Frost © 1977

265

_____16. Provisions for the housing of pets. Pets available.

_____17. A transitional space from outdoors to indoors. This could be a covered play area immediately adjoining the playroom areas which will protect the children from the sun and rain and extend indoor activities to the outside.

_____18. Adequate protected storage for outdoor play equipment, tools for construction area, and maintenance tools. Storage can be separate, wheel toys stored next to the roadway; sand equipment near or next to the sand enclosure; tools in the workshop area. Or storage can be the lower level of the climbing structure, or separate structures attached to the building or fence. *But storage should aid in pick-up* (that is, make it easy for children to put equipment away at the end of each play period).

_____19. Easy access from outdoor play areas to coats and toilets.

_____20. Places for adults, parents and teachers, to sit within the outdoor play areas. Shade structures with benches can provide for this as well as for seating for children.

Section II.   Is the playground in good repair and relatively safe?

Rate each item for condition and safety on a scale of 0-5 (0 = not existent; 1 = exists but extremely hazardous; 2 = poor; 3 = fair; 4 = good; 5 = excellent condition and relatively safe yet presents *challenge*).

_____ 1. A protective fence next to hazardous areas (streets, etc.).

_____ 2. Eight to ten inches of noncompacted sand (or equivalent) under all climbing and moving equipment, extending through fall zones and secured by retaining wall.

_____ 3. Size of equipment appropriate to age group served.

_____ 4. Area free of litter (e.g., broken glass, rocks).

_____ 5. Moving parts free of defects (e.g., no pinch and crush points, bearings not excessively worn).

_____ 6. Equipment free of sharp edges, protruding elements, broken parts, toxic substances.

_____ 7. Swing seats constructed of soft material (e.g., rubber, canvas).

_____ 8. All safety equipment in good repair (e.g., railings, padded areas, protective covers).

_____ 9. Fixed equipment secure in ground and concrete footings recessed in ground.

_____10. Equipment structurally sound. No bending, warping, breaking, sinking, etc.

Section III.   What should the playground do?

Rate each item for degree and quality on a scale of 0-5 (0 = not existent; 1 = some evidence but virtually nonexistent; 2 = poor; 3 = fair; 4 = good; 5 = excellent). Use the space provided for comments.

_____ 1. Encourages Play:
Inviting, easy access
Open, flowing and relaxed spaces
Clear movement from inside to outside
Appropriate equipment for the age group

_____ 2. Stimulates the Child's Senses:
Change and contrasts in scale, light, texture and color
Flexible equipment
Diverse experiences

_____ 3. Nurtures the Child's Curiosity:

Equipment that the child can change

Materials for experiments and construction

_____ 4. Allows Interaction Between the Child and the Resources:

Systematic storage which defines routines

Semi-enclosed spaces to read, work a puzzle, or be alone

_____ 5. Allows Interaction Between the Child and Other Children:

Variety of spaces

Adequate space to avoid conflicts

Equipment that invites socialization

_____ 6. Allows Interaction Between the Child and Adults:

Easy maintenance

Adequate and convenient storage

Organization of spaces to allow general supervision

Rest areas for adults

_____ 7. Supports the Child's Basic Social and Physical Needs:

Comfortable to the child

Scaled to the child

Free of hazards

_____ 8. Complements the Cognitive Forms of Play Engaged in by the Child:

Functional, exercise, gross-motor, active

Constructive, building, creating

Dramatic, pretending, make believe

Organized games, games with rules

_____ 9. Complements the Social Forms of Play Engaged in by the Child:

Solitary, private, meditative

Parallel, side-by-side

Cooperative interrelationships

_____ 10. Promotes Social and Intellectual Development:

Provides graduated challenge

Integrates indoor/outdoor activities

Involves adults in child's play

Adult-child planning

The play environment is dynamic—continuously changing

INDEX